e-Negotiations

e-Negotiations

Networking and Cross-Cultural Business Transactions

NICHOLAS HARKIOLAKIS
WITH DAPHNE HALKIAS AND SAM ABADIR

Routledge
Taylor & Francis Group

LONDON AND NEW YORK

First published 2012 by Gower Publishing

Published 2016 by Routledge
2 Park Square, Milton Park, Abingdon, Oxon OX14 4RN
711 Third Avenue, New York, NY 10017, USA

First issued in paperback 2017

Routledge is an imprint of the Taylor & Francis Group, an informa business

Gower Applied Business Research
Our programme provides leaders, practitioners, scholars and researchers with thought provoking, cutting edge books that combine conceptual insights, interdisciplinary rigour and practical relevance in key areas of business and management.

British Library Cataloguing in Publication Data
Harkiolakis, Nicholas.
    e-Negotiations : networking and cross-cultural business
    transactions.
    1. Negotiation in business. 2. Negotiation in business--
    Technological innovations. 3. Intercultural communication.
    4. Intercultural communication--Technological innovations.
    5. Electronic commerce.
    I. Title II. Halkias, Daphne. III. Abadir, Sam.
    658.4'052'0285-dc23

Library of Congress Cataloging-in-Publication Data
Harkiolakis, Nicholas.
    E-negotiation : networking and cross-cultural business transactions / by Nicholas Harkiolakis with and Daphne Halkias and Sam Abadir.
    p. cm.
    Includes bibliographical references and index.
    ISBN 978-1-4094-0196-4 (hardback) -- ISBN 978-1-4094-0197-1 (ebook) 1. Negotiation in business. 2. Intercultural communication. 3. Social networking. 4. Electronic commerce. I. Halkias, Daphne. II. Abadir, Sam. III. Title.
    HD58.6.H367 2012
    658.4'05202854678--dc23

                                                                                    2012011051

ISBN 13: 978-1-138-10872-1 (pbk)
ISBN 13: 978-1-4094-0196-4 (hbk)

Contents

List of Figures

About the Authors

Dr Nicholas Harkiolakis holds a PhD degree in Computer Science from the University of Athens (Geoponiko). He is a distinguished academic and researcher whose book and paper publications are in the areas of business information systems, social network mining, artificial intelligence, technology and security issues, disaster recovery, e-commerce, health information technology and entrepreneurship. He is presently Associate Dean of Business, Health and Technology at Abu Dhabi Men's College, Higher Colleges of Technology. In his previous position, Dr Harkiolakis was Technical Coordinator of an EU-funded research project in the area of smart networks. The project involved 15 partners from 7 countries including public, private and academic institutions. He has been involved at the executive level in technology, educational start-ups, consulting and training in the IS/IT area and grant writing in the USA and Europe..

Dr Daphne Halkias is Research Affiliate at the Institute for Social Sciences at Cornell University; Affiliate, Institute of Coaching, McLean Hospital at the Harvard Medical School, Massachusetts, USA; Senior Research Fellow, The Center for Youth and Family Enterprise (CYFE) at the University of Bergamo in Italy; Research Associate at the Center for Comparative Immigration Studies (CCIS), University of California, San Diego, USA; and Editor of *International Journal of Social Entrepreneurship and Innovation*. She is CEO of Executive Coaching Consultants, an international consulting firm and a distinguished academic and researcher with books and paper publications spanning 25 years in organizational behavior, entrepreneurship, cross-cultural management, family business, psychology, migration issues and education. She has been an invited keynote speaker in numerous business and social science forums, including Center for Global and Strategic Management at The Copenhagen Business School and the World Entrepreneurship Summit and Wendel Center for Family Enterprise at INSEAD, France.

Dr Sam Abadir holds a PhD in International Politics from the Centre d'Etudes Diplomatiques et Strategiques, Paris. He is a Fellow at the Judge Business School, University of Cambridge, UK, and on the faculty of the European Centre for Executive Development – CEDEP and INSEAD in France, teaching negotiation skills, international services marketing and safety issues in organizations. His paper publications and book contributions range across the areas of negotiation skills, entrepreneurship, family business, and migration issues. He is President of Executive Coaching Consultants and a distinguished international consultant, facilitator, and speaker in the area of cross-cultural negotiation skills and international service marketing. He is on the Editorial Board of the *International Journal of Social Entrepreneurship and Innovation and African Journal of Business and Economics Resaerch.*

Preface: Social Influence, Information-Sharing Processes and e-Negotiation Skills: Finding Ourselves at the Crossroads of Culture and Technology

Sam Abadir and Daphne Halkias

This book examines how culture is communicated through technology, specifically the use of electronically mediated communication (that is, email, Skype, video conference), to influence negotiator-thinking behaviors during online cross-cultural negotiation. Because of global economics and the pervasive presence of the Internet in every business person's life, the new e-commerce market has taken off from the launch pad. The more e-commerce grows, the more e-negotiation flourishes: because of the certain probability of inter-cultural factors influencing e-negotiations worldwide, understanding e-business strategies and discovering the impact of culture on the parties involved has become increasingly important.

Cultural diversity has become one of the most critical issues in negotiation. The integration of diverse cultures in the decision-making structure to reach an agreement has become an inescapable phenomenon for most organizations as well as negotiators in fields other than business, such as government, diplomacy, the law, and law enforcement. A successful cross-cultural e-negotiation is largely dependent on whether the parties can unravel the puzzle of negotiating patterns originating from a culture other than their own. In a cross-cultural context, negotiation becomes more difficult to yield benefits for all concerned parties. The difficulty is encountered when even seasoned professionals are confronted with different sets of values, attitudes, behaviors, and communication styles. We consider these as the building blocks of understanding and preparing negotiation strategies in cross-cultural scenarios. So, how to avoid setbacks, surprises, and shock so often present by cross-cultural negotiation executives? As this book illustrates, students of e-negotiation skills must also be the students of worldwide cultures and information technology to even begin to formulate winning strategies in dyadic e-negotiations.

As international business consultants and professors who teach negotiation skills to students and professionals alike, we contributed to this book with this primary issue in mind: we wanted to have a book to take into our academic and consulting work that clearly and efficiently brings all these concerns together in a user-friendly pedagogical model. At the same time, if someone does not have the opportunity to learn such skills in an interactive learning setting, this book will be a good place to start and become acquainted with both basic and critical issues e-negotiators will face in cross-cultural settings. We wanted to contribute to a book we could take into our classrooms, workshops, and seminars that simply brings together negotiations skills, technology, and cross-cultural issues in an informative, clear, succinct presentation from which both young and seasoned professionals could benefit.

We believe this book has accomplished this goal. Our hope is that you, the reader, will agree.

Foreword

Negotiation always involves parties or persons with mutual, but differing and probably conflicting, interests, where an agreement to act is important or even necessary. When there are significant cultural differences, finding ways to bridge those differences and resolve the conflicts becomes critical to the goal of negotiating an agreement. Otherwise, even understanding what the issues are will probably escape the players. When the involved parties cannot see each other and may be communicating asynchronously and without the cues that come from visual and/or audible presence, new skills and new strategies will be necessary to achieve a resolution that is beneficial to all.

The new technologies are not only incidental factors to be considered in a negotiation; they transform those processes and require the skills of e-negotiation. Nicholas Harkiolakis and his colleagues explore, analyze, explain, and assess the very complex constituents involved in e-negotiation. If you are involved in business or policy resolutions at a distance, you will be happy to have "E-Negotiation" clearly in mind and ready to hand for frequent reference. If you are an educator seeking aids for your management or policy studies students, you would be lucky to find a more comprehensive introduction that provides them with the particulars of negotiation and the impact of the Internet and related technologies on the knowledge, communications, and other skills of e-negotiation.

This book not only highlights the right idea about the importance of e-negotiation, but it constructs a road map that will help students get to the goal of becoming skillful practitioners.

Thomas M. Rocco, PhD.
Innovation in Higher Education
President Emeritus, Granite State College and Leadership Institute of Seattle

Introduction

1

The prevalence and incidence of business negotiations among people from different countries and cultures has multiplied 20-fold over the last 20 years—according to international trade watchers, even greater increases are expected in the future as emerging economies become key players in world markets. The latest international business analysis reports state that over 50 per cent of an international manager's time is spent negotiating. A typical senior manager in the United States (US) business scene devotes at least a quarter of his/her working day negotiating.

Negotiation processes involve the trade of gains and losses between negotiators' positions. Some of them are planed while others can catch them by surprise. Questions arise, such as: "What are my priorities?," "How far can I go?," "Why does the other side follow a certain strategy?," "Would I be the same if I was them?," "Are they honest and truthful?," "How do they understand commitment?," "Should I start the bidding first?," "Should I be aggressive?," "Should we spend more time getting to know each other?," "Should I walk away?," "Should I make more concessions?" The answers we come up with to these questions will shape our strategy and ultimately lead to the success or failure of negotiations. Strategy and behavior become expressions of each other and establishing one can predict the other.

Traditionally, negotiation processes are considered as a blend of various disciplines ranging from game theory, psychology, political science, communications, law, to sociology, and anthropology. Coming into the field of e-negotiations, what we mostly find is how information technology affects negotiations in the form of communication and negotiation decision support systems. The area has not seen any significant research beyond the communications and technology aspects of it.

In e-negotiations micro-level behavior is most prevalent. Since in most cases there is one person behind the screen or telephone that engages in negotiation, their values directly affect their decisions and the way they interpret messages, handle exceptions, and communicate with others. Cultural values are expected in these situations to influence behavior in ways that cannot be anticipated or predicted by the participants involved in the process.

A major advantage of e-negotiations is the ability to record every detail of the communication process including intentions, outcomes, and information exchanged. This can provide a better understanding of the negotiation process and behavior and allow analysis and evaluation of strategies that would be impossible in face-to-face negotiations. On the other hand, the resulting time lag from the asynchronous communication exchange has been shown to make negotiators pay more attention to the substantive content of messages, and has lessened the emotional stress brought about by conflicting positions. Overall it made it easier to overcome socioeconomic differences.

Another important aspect of e-negotiations is the reduction of communication cues. According to the situation or the adopted strategy, this can act as an advantage or disadvantage. Inability to observe body language, facial expressions, and tone of voice may assist in focusing on the issue at hand, but it can also lead to misinterpretation, frustration, and mistrust. Negative emotions seem to be more influential in online negotiations than in face-to-face situations; but at the same time the faceless world of online communications appears to allow freedom of expression that would otherwise be hindered offline. Research seems to indicate that as individuals become more familiar with the Internet and they use it in their daily communication, they tend to apply the same values as they do with other communication mediums. After all, a world is a "world" whether real or virtual since we function on past experiences that we carry from the physical world.

The loss of visual cues online is of primary importance since it evenly balances characteristics of the offline world like attractiveness, gender, color, and ethnicity. Individuals disadvantaged by geographical location, confinement, threats, mobility, and sight or hearing impairment can now use the Internet to access information and negotiate on equal terms. The virtual environment nevertheless brings its own unique hierarchies and "social" structures. The privileged ones can have fast access with state-of-the-art hardware and software, while the less privileged will be on the other side of the "digital divide." Typing speed and fluency with English can also be a divider in that the fast typists and native speakers can easily keep up in chat rooms and intense communication exchanges.

To convey feelings and emotions online in an attempt to avoid misinterpretation and get our point across, a form of language in terms of symbols and norms have come into use through general acceptance: symbols like 'smileys' can be used to magnify and express feelings of text-based information, while switching from lower case to upper case can be used to emphasize text—an act similar to shouting in the physical world. Time, data, and location tracking along with direct request and translation services can further assist in clarifying the content that is being communicated.

1.1 The Negotiations Framework

A framework suggested in this book will take the negotiator through a spiral of activities that repeat themselves in every cycle while not necessarily preserving their duration each time. These (Figure 1.1) include the stages of *Intelligence, Perception, Strategy,* and *Communication,* which eventually lead to *Deal* or *No Deal.*

It is expected that while initially more time will be spent in intelligence and perception and less in strategy and communication, this will reverse the closer we get to the final outcome. In the beginning, we need to spend more time learning about the issues at hand and understanding our "opponent", while as the process matures and we get more feedback, our understanding grows and

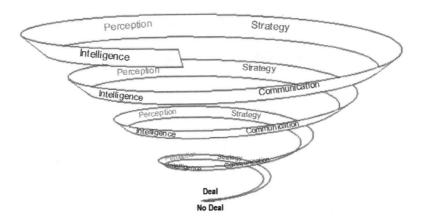

Figure 1.1   Negotiations Spiral Framework

the "opponent's" positions and needs become more obvious. The opposite is true for the strategy and communication phases since the need to move from exploratory positions and offers to a more precise and detailed final position grows in time. At later stages, communication becomes more intense. So while the cycle remains more or less the same in terms of sequence of its phases, the time spent in each phase changes drastically and is directly influenced by the personality, state of mind, and experience of each negotiator.

Negotiation strategies have been identified in the literature ranging from distributing, avoiding, accommodating, integrating, compromising, collaborating, and exploiting, to competing, among others. Naturally, negotiators do not necessarily belong in exact stereotypes, but the general rule is that if the spiral does not progress in the intended fashion then there is something seriously wrong in the negotiation. Competitive negotiators tend to spend more time in the last phases of positioning and communication while cooperative ones spend more time in understanding the opponent and position accordingly.

In our view, though, the suggested spiral will more than cover the process while allowing the individual to employ their own personal style by acting on the time length of each phase. The communication mediums that will be the focus of this book, in reference to the suggested framework, include teleconferencing, videoconferencing, and web-based communication.

It should be taken as a certainty for the future ahead of us that e-negotiations and the technology supporting them will create new and unique advantages and disadvantages. The absence of traditional social cues and their substitution with new forms could lead to more objective evaluations, while also diffusing identity perceptions and lessening self-awareness. The situation will be worse in cross-cultural communications due to lack of nonverbal signs and the effort required for building trust. On the other hand, communicating through the Internet defies logistic boundaries of time, place, and hierarchy, and allows focused considerations of task content and performance.

1.2 The Negotiator

Regarding technology, negotiators, like most people, can be seen as belonging to separate "technology adoption life-cycle" groups, such as:

- innovators and early adopters—including the technology enthusiasts, those that lead and influence new developments and changes;

- mainstream followers—including those that adopt established technology and trends;

- late bloomers—including those that resist change but are forced to adapt in order to survive.

E-negotiations have seen the rise of specific skills that weren't traditionally so influential in negotiations. Since the work of a negotiator is essentially based on language, good typing skills and fluency in writing are extremely important online. Increased bandwidth and fast Internet access can also be an advantage in real-time synchronous communication (chatting, videoconferencing, and so on).

The rise of the Internet posed greater problems to traditional players in negotiation, like governments and public authorities. Coming to grips with technological change is not as straightforward as one would expect for such players primarily due to organizational and professional inertia in dealing with such issues. The amount of information exchanged online is difficult to comprehend and digest especially for older generations of negotiators and diplomats. Suddenly, these groups are faced with a wider audience that is much more involved and influential. Their counterparts can appear with many faces and voices and it becomes difficult even to those familiar with technology to put order to what their senses deliver to their brains.

Traditional negotiators are also challenged in both the information content they were privileged to withhold and the expertise they projected. Nowadays, information flows openly on the Internet and almost anyone can access and consume it, eventually presenting themselves as experts. The involvement of many players can dilute the image of traditional players as field experts. Foreign advisers are expected to be the first victims of the new era. One look at the website of the CIA or those of other government institutions can easily give anyone a good view of world issues and their importance to US policy. One can liken the world of negotiators to a protest where, instead of a leading person having the loudspeaker, there are many with loudspeakers delivering their individual messages.

Despite the changes that have taken place and will continue to take place, negotiators will still need knowledge, judgment, and expertise. All that is needed nowadays is adaptation to the new realities. This is not a matter of choice. It's a survival requirement. Prior to engaging in negotiations online, it is important to consider whether it is "tasks" or people that will be affected by decisions being taken. This is important since tasks are impersonal and can benefit from the structure and permanency of the online medium, while decisions about people need the expressive power of human beings with their verbal and nonverbal cues to fully express and represent a situation. When deciding on the communication mode to negotiate on an issue, it is important to accommodate as much as possible the needs, skills, and communication preferences of all parties and choose the most practical and most efficient option.

Negotiators in this book will be viewed as knowledge systems that are influenced and shaped by different environmental factors as they mature as individuals and professionals. Starting with the basic ingredient of each human being in the form of the DNA each one inherits, we are raised in family environments that operate in societies that are nothing more than microcosms inside nations, regions, and the world at large. Each environmental layer encloses and exerts primary influence on the ones it encloses and to a lesser degree its outside layers. In other words, as we are influenced by the world, we also influence the world at least in our vicinity. To a person this is expressed in the form of education and experience while interacting with others.

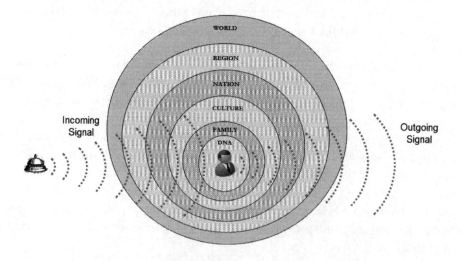

Figure 1.2   The Negotiator's Layers of Influence

Each one of us moves in the world surrounded with these "onion" rings of influence, filtering incoming signals that people and events emit, and modulating the signals we emit. Personality and culture are the primary expressions of this filtering that we do. Negotiators need to be aware of this layering if they are to communicate the right message to the right recipient and make sense of what they receive in return.

1.3 About this Book

Two alternatives were considered when developing the book material. One would have a strong academic emphasis in the print version and supporting material for the professional and lay reader and the other would have more of a hands-on print version and reserve the academic emphasis for the book's website (http://www.e-negotiations.info).

We decided to go with the second approach as print editions are more familiar and personal for a wider audience than their online counterparts. They are also more comfortable to carry and read and can reach general audiences of students and practitioners of various disciplines including professionals and lay readers.

The online section of the book has been developed to function as supplemental course material in addition to expanding the resources presented in the print version. In the online section students and faculty can find:

- chapter objectives;

- sample syllabus;

- case studies for the topics addressed in each section of the book;

- hands-on exercises and projects that can be done in classroom and as homework assignments;

- color book images;

- PowerPoint presentations;

- extended list of online resources for each topic;

- reference publications.

1.4 What this Book Isn't

This book should not be seen as a promoter of e-negotiations over face-to-face negotiations.

We actually take the stand that e-negotiations are an unavoidable "evil" that is here to stay and we all need to be familiar with the new medium and become proficient in its use as negotiators, but not at the expense of face-to-face negotiations.

While the emphasis of this book is on technology's impact on negotiation and as a medium of negotiation, there are certain aspects that will not be addressed and these include the areas of mediation and arbitration. In this respect, the book will only briefly touch on online dispute resolution (ODR) mechanisms in conflict resolution. As a consequence, security, confidentiality, and privacy issues will only be mentioned in a general context and not dealt with specifically or in-depth.

2

Technology in Brief

This chapter will follow a simplified approach to presenting the basic technology elements essential to entering the e-negotiation sphere. In today's world we are usually exposed to simple information technology (IT) concepts from childhood. To better understand the technology solutions adopted nowadays in e-negotiations, this chapter will provide more of an intuitive description of some of the technology elements involved in e-negotiations in terms of their relevance and interdependence. Technology will be presented here in analogy to negotiations as resolutions between goals, physical resources, and money. Although this might sound a little far-fetched, it does accurately depict reality because the evolution of technology is nothing more than meeting needs and communicating actions and intentions. Thinking and behavior that propel negotiation between two parties just don't pop up out of nowhere. There is a need somewhere that we try to satisfy by negotiating options and achieving consensus that in turn is translated into actions that lead to a product which satisfies the initial need.

In our attempt to express and communicate issues, we develop languages that address the specifics of each need. These languages are nothing more than abstractions we adopt as we move into unexplored territory to make our life easier and more productive. They pack meaning into words that, when laid down with the proper syntax, create higher level concepts that can be packed again into words of higher level meaning and the process goes on like that, satisfying our need for higher levels of abstraction. Language, and especially written language, is the most important asset for an e-negotiator and for that reason we will place great importance in this chapter on how computer languages are born and how meaning is communicated through them. While human languages take centuries to develop and address the specifics of each culture, computer languages have taken only years. Of course, they are not as rich as human languages, but they do display similar elements as they serve our purpose to communicate information in efficient and meaningful ways.

From the perspective of communicating information and producing work, technology can be seen as a blend of machines and humans that efficiently communicate with each other to achieve their goals. To be more anthropomorphic, we can imagine technology as an extension of our physical being or a form of add-ons we use to facilitate communication and interact with the physical world of humans and non-humans. In this respect, this chapter focuses more on the efforts we make using technology to convey meaning at various levels (cultures we might say). Hopefully, it will serve as an application of the negotiations context of this book and less of the typical presentation of the topic found in other print and online material.

In this chapter we will also review the challenge in using different languages and terminologies to communicate meaning in the technology setting and hopefully, by analogy, emphasize similar challenges in e-negotiations. Some of the concepts we will present here will help you understand topics covered in subsequent chapters. For example, what is SQL? (Answer: the basis for all query languages that are used in modern search engines like Google).

As e-negotiators we are interested primarily in technology as a communication medium, so our emphasis here will be on communication devices and primarily the services computers provide. As we very well know, computers are nothing more than pieces of electronics (transistors, chips, and so on) that are appropriately organized to process electric signals. It's the way this processing takes place that brings the functionality we value them for. The distance, though, from our human level of communication to the electrical signal level is a huge one in terms of discoveries and scientific progress. Something needs to bridge the gap and that something is nothing other than software. In fact, to be more precise, it is the different layers of software building one on top of the other that allows for efficient organization of actions and processes that eventually enable communication between humans and computers. The basic software from our perspective is the operating system (Windows, Linux, Mac OS, and so on). This usually takes care of the "trivial" tasks like rendering the screen, retrieving keystrokes, tracking our mouse, working our discs, and connecting to other computers, printers and peripheral devices along with serving the requests of the various programs we are using.

2.1 Computers and Networks

A computer can actually be termed "humanoid" on the basis of its structure and workings due to certain similarities it exhibits in its function, such as having a microprocessor in place of a "brain."

In viewing the computer as a processing unit, we can break it down into its main constituents (Figure 2.1), starting with the microprocessor—which is the device (the "brain") that performs the calculations, processes the instructions of the various programs, and controls the devices that are connected to the computer. Its function is supported by the various types of memory it uses to hold the information it needs, such as:

- Read Only Memory (ROM) is where the programs and data necessary for the initial startup of the computer are stored. This is created by the manufacturer and is inaccessible to anyone or anything else. These are high-speed devices with limited capacity for storing data. With an analogy to the human world, ROM is the basic instincts and reactions a baby has when it is born, in, let's say, some part of the brain.

- Read Access Memory (RAM) is where the information of running programs is stored. These devices are microchip types that allow for fast storage and retrieval of relatively small amounts

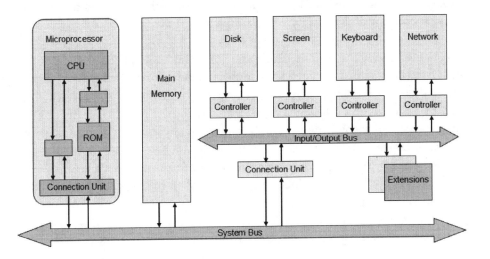

Figure 2.1   Typical Computer Architecture

of information that are state dependent and which are lost when the computer shuts down. These are also high speed devices with limited capacity for storing data. The typical size nowadays is 2GB (which could easily fit about a thousand of this book's data) that we can optionally extend to bigger sizes in terms of capacity. More demanding applications like computer games would need as much as possible. If we were to compare this piece of technology to the human body, RAM is comparable to memory. Our brain can hold a limited amount of information that can be accessed really fast when needed.

- Auxiliary memory, like hard disks for permanent storage of large quantities of information that we can physically carry around separately from the computer. These are mechanical devices (have moving parts) where we trade storage quantity with speed and cost. Our personal auxiliary memory devices come in the form of books, computers and the Internet, among others. Nowadays, electronic devices (without moving parts) like USBs and solid-state hard drives are also used for faster access of data.

The balance of what we use and its size in terms of capacity is always a function of speed and money. Electronic components like ROM and RAM are always faster than mechanical components like hard disks, but they are much more expensive, so what we do is to use limited capacities of the electronics for critical operations and fast processing of portions (or whole) of software and big capacities (hard disks) for large amounts of data that we need to preserve and carry around if necessary.

The computer, of course, cannot be fully functional without its various outside pieces such as the keyboard, mouse, screen, printers, networks, and so on. All these devices are different in terms of the electronics they are built with, requiring a different language (signal groups) to perform their functions. To interface with the computer, manufacturers usually provide the appropriate software, which is called a *driver*. You might have observed that any time you connect a mouse or other device, the computer informs you that an appropriate driver has been installed. When you change operating systems you usually need to reinstall the drivers for the different devices that are connected to your computer. Drivers are like translators that convert messages from your operating system language to the device language and vice versa.

In the same perspective, the operating system is nothing else than a translator between the applications running on your computer and its hardware while the applications you run are nothing more than specialized translators between you and the operating system. Given that the system is mechanical, designed and developed by humans, you can see how simple "translation errors" can result in catastrophic events like computer crashes and program collapses. These errors can be mechanical in nature since devices can be defaulted and become corrupted with age or could be coding errors (human errors) that were made in developing the software.

Communication of the various physical entities is done through communication channels (wires) called *buses*. These are like traffic highways where the electrical signals travel in the lanes, passing messages back and forth. If you open up your computer, you will be able to see some of the them as flat and wide wires that connect various components, while others will be embedded in the electronic devices, like the motherboard, that host the major electronic components of your computer. The more lanes a bus has, the more information we can exchange, so the faster our software performs.

Something that may elude the average person is that the computer knows nothing about what to do and how to do it. Our software needs to tell the machine exactly what to do, where to find the data needed to perform an operation, where to store the result, what command to execute at each step, and pretty much everything other than simple additions. All that information needs to travel through the various buses so you can imagine that the wider they are the more "traffic lanes" they will be able to host and more information will be able to circulate, leading to faster execution of our programs. Although a simple solution would be to use very wide buses, there are technological difficulties that need to be overcome. By analogy to road lanes, imagine what would happen if we don't have traffic lights, traffic police, and driving rules (conventions like who has priority at an intersection). The same applies to the organization of the various buses so we have various arbitration schemes for setting priorities that lead to having different speeds for buses. For instance we use high-speed buses (roads where you can drive a Ferrari) to transfer data from the main memory to the processor while we use low speed buses (bicycle lanes) to transfer data from our hard drive to the main memory. Keeping the previous analogies in mind, a Ferrari is more expensive than a bicycle, so you see that the final design of a computer is a trade-off between speed, size, and cost.

The concept of the buses can be extended to the wireless world where it is more appropriately referred to as bandwidth and has to do with the allowable concurrent accesses we can have on a communication channel. The larger the bandwidth, the more information we can exchange, so the faster we can service requests, which also could mean that more users can interact with the medium.

Having set the main constituents of computer systems, we now need to breathe life into them and this is simply done by developing software that runs everything in an organized and predictable fashion. Software is nothing more than instructions we assembled together to provide guidance from the very simple to the more sophisticated tasks the computer does. Software is developed using various programming languages. When these programming languages are processed, they appropriately convert the command grammar (words and syntax) to proper electrical signals that run the various pieces of computer equipment that produce the desired work.

Two very important pieces of software are the BIOS (Basic Input/Output System) and the operating system. The BIOS comes already installed in the ROM by the manufacturer of a computer and contains the basic code that is needed to "wake up" the various components (disks, keyboard, mouse, display, and so on). From then on it tries to locate in which device the operating system we want to use resides and starts executing it, releasing full control of the computer to it (a process known as *booting up*).

The operating system is the actual "soul" of the computer. This is the piece of software that ensures all the applications we use (office applications, Internet, and so on) run appropriately. To achieve this, it provides certain basic services to the applications that they use to perform more complicated functions. Such basic services could be manipulating files on the disk, displaying information on the screen, retrieving keystrokes and mouse moves, connecting to other computers, and so on. In analogy to our human experience and while BIOS could be considered as the basic "intelligence" embedded in a baby, the operating system is all the basic training, education, and culture that we absorb as we grow to become fully functioning, productive, and creative adults in order to later perform specialized tasks (applications).

Following the description of the basic architecture of a computer, we can move into networking many of them in a communication net that will allow the exchange of information between them. If we view information as something that needs to "travel" from one point to another, we can build an analogy between our communication pathways (roads) as seen in the Google maps picture of

Figure 2.2. What we see there is that we live in buildings (cul-de-sacs in the picture and houses branched off streets) and we move to various other buildings/ locations using pathways, roads, avenues, and highways. In essence, we move from small, low-traffic, low-speed roads to high-traffic, high-speed highways.

There is a direct relationship of how many people and materials need to be transferred, taking into consideration the topology of the terrain. Cul-de-sacs have a star kind of arrangement where all houses are accessing the same roundabout that then connects with a main road that will eventually connect to a highway. Other cul-de-sacs connect to a main road in a similar fashion, creating in this way some sort of a parallel arrangement between them. Reaching our destination is the opposite process, by which we leave the highway at a certain junction, enter a main road, and following a pattern of roads and streets, end up where we want to be (maybe our friend's cul-de-sac and to their house eventually).

If we use the analogy of traveling around to the computer world, we have an accurate representation of computer networks. Figure 2.3 shows a typical arrangement of computers ("homes" in the cul-de-sac analogy) connected through a *star* arrangement (*star* topology in networking lingo) to a central point that is usually the computers (servers) of our Internet provider. That computer then provides access (routing) to a fast Internet highway that will eventually connect to the information superhighways of modern communication networks.

Figure 2.2   Google Earth View of a Highway with Side Roads

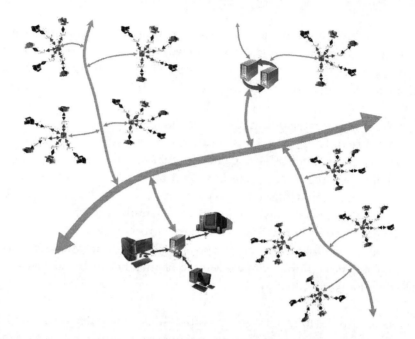

Figure 2.3   Computer Network Topology

The various providers could connect in parallel to the highways or they could connect to a central point (higher level cul-de-sac) that will then link them to a superhighway. In reality, we can have all possible combinations of connections based on the need we want to satisfy. A research or military installation might have a direct access to the superhighway for obvious reasons.

2.2 Internet and Web

There are a variety of buzzwords surrounding technology nowadays and, more specifically, the Internet. The flora and fauna of species that live in the virtual world of modern day Internet communications (Figure 2.4) are enough to confuse even the most trained eye let alone those that are not tech savvy. Those that find themselves needing this virtual world for professional survival can at times find it very difficult to adjust to this new "gadget" that has appeared in their lives. In this section we will try and put some order in the terminology "chaos" (Figure 2.4) that surrounds the Internet as a communication medium without the technical details that could distract a negotiator. A negotiator must grasp the logic behind the workings of the Internet as far as technology is concerned as it is this logic that defines the medium as a human invention device.

There is a cause-and- effect pattern that was followed in the creation of the Internet and the Web. Someone had a need that drove them to create a solution to that need. It all happened with scientists that needed to communicate with other scientists in different locations. That meant not just exchanging messages, but also exchanging documents, data, and whatever else was needed for two persons to collaborate with each other over distances. This appeared as a useful function to the military that needed a communication infrastructure that could function regardless of the damage incurred by the enemy. Thus the Internet was born as a network of computer networks interconnected by communication lines of various compositions and speeds. This was an amazing breakthrough as you could connect various types of machines into a net without a central control point. Every connection/node could search other's connections/nodes and, by a common language, find a way to send a message to its destination.

Having machines connected with each other is one thing, but involving humans in the process is another. You need a tool that serves the role of audio and print to allow them to communicate the language humans understand. Thus the browser was born (Internet Explorer, Firefox, Chrome, and so on). Browsers are nothing more than interfaces/software that understand the language of entities that we call servers, who are the keepers of information in the locations they reside. From that perspective browsers belong to the species called "clients," following the obvious analogy of a client being served. The simplest approach to the Web is nothing more than clients and servers communicating with each other and negotiating the exchange of information.

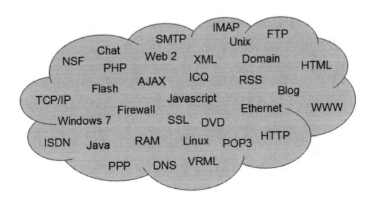

Figure 2.4 Internet Buzzwords

One should always be aware of the distinction between the Internet and the Web. A not so polarized perspective is that everything is Internet while the part of the Internet that refers to the client-server functionality is called the Web.

So now that we've set up the principles upon which the modern communication systems operate, let's move on to more specifics. How can they recognize each other? How does one computer know where another computer is? How do they talk to each other? The answer to all these questions—at least at the conceptual level—is very simple: in exactly the same way we do. Computers have names, they reside in locations that can be identified by addresses (in the computer universe of course), and they speak languages. Having experience from our daily lives, we became a little smarter with computers, so we realized that since they cannot occupy the same physical space (in the computer universe always), their names became their addresses. For example, instead of me using the name Harkiolakis, I use the name *USA. California.SanDiego.6ᵗʰStreet.983number.apartmentA.livingroom.armchair;*

although this might look strange, it does uniquely identify me in our physical universe at the writing of this paragraph.

Luckily for the computers, since they had our wisdom for creation and a fresh start in their life, all we need to identify them explicitly is four numbers each ranging from 0 to 255. Each number identifies my laptop within a finer detail within networks. The first number refers to a global region while the last refers to my laptop within the local network to which I belong. As an example, my laptop at the time of this writing has 109.242.37.190 as its name/address (which can also tell you where I am vacationing at the moment of this writing). In technology terms this is the IP (Internet Protocol) address of my laptop. Using an analogy to the physical world, my laptop lives in the computer/network world in "country" 109, in "city" 242, in "street address" 37, and in "apartment" 190.

To find its way on the Internet, my browser in my laptop relies on DNS (Domain Name Service) servers (sort of a telephone catalog) that keep track of numbers/names and physical locations of everyone in their domain. The domain here refers to the place of the number in the IP addresses. The "telephone catalogs" are not that big since each one holds only 256 numbers, so moving from catalog to catalog to those keeping my laptop location is a very fast process. Each level adds more information to the whereabouts of each computer. There is only one top level catalog with 256 different catalog names/

entries—each one having 256 different catalog names/entries (256x256 total so far), each one having different catalog names/entries (256x256x256 total so far). Having each one of them hold 256 different names, we eventually end up with a total of 256x256x256x256 physically different and distinct addresses. The only thing that remains now that we have unique identifications to complete the communication process is a proper and common language.

2.2.1 WEB COMMUNICATION

From what we have seen so far the Web is built on computers that are connected together electronically. This wiring allows electricity to travel in specific patterns that can be interpreted as codes. Groups of codes represent data (textual or numeric) that carry the messages we want. While this might sound simple enough, going from our level of language understanding to the level of electrical signals, it's one hell of a process and one of the greatest achievements of our civilization. Given our physical and mental limitations in processing such detail, we developed abstractions in the form of communication protocols/ languages that play the intermediary role between our level and the electric signal level.

As one can imagine trust can be an issue when exchanging messages so we had to devise some means to control the security and privacy of our communications. One way to secure communication is by encrypting a message by using another language (French in Figure 2.5) that only we and the receiver understand, then insert/hide our message in an envelope and request safe transfer (by paying extra at the post office). To ensure the receiver is the actual person we want to receive the message, we request that the postman does an identity check of the receiver. Of course, in spite all these measures we can easily understand that the process is far from perfect and that our message can be intercepted, modified, or lost at any point in the delivery chain. For example, other people who understand French can open it and read it, or the people at the post office, or the couriers can easily interfere with it and alter its content if they want to.

By analogy to this description we can understand what happens when messages are exchanged on the Internet. For instance, when we write an email (Figure 2.6) using an email client (Outlook, Gmail, and so on), we add the address of our counterpart; our email client adds our address and packs/ attaches together everything we want to include. Then it uses a special language to communicate/send all this to your SMTP client (your local post

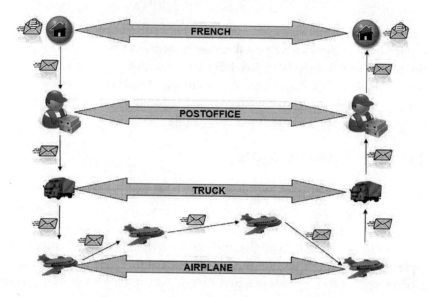

Figure 2.5   Message Exchange in Real World

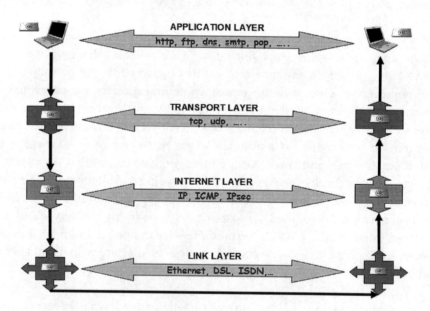

Figure 2.6   Internet Communication Layers/Protocols

office). Our client application and the SMTP server use the SMTP language to understand each other at this stage. Past those layers other intermediaries use other languages to communicate with their preceding and following layers until the packaged message eventually reaches the physical layer (link layer). There our message finally has the form of electrical signals that travel the globe until they reach the mail server of the recipient. When our friend connects to the Internet, his email client will use another language (*pop* protocol) to communicate with its mail server, retrieve our message and display it to our friend in plain text.

A similar process is followed when we want to display a website. We type the address (called URL, from Universal Resource Locator) of the server that holds the information we want. For example, the address http://www.ashgate.com/default.aspx?page=637&calcTitle=1&title_id=10135&edition_id=12896 that points to the publisher page for this book provides complete directions to the exact location where the online page for this book resides at the publisher's website. How does this relate to the four-digit IP addresses that we mentioned before? Well the actual address of the publisher is 83.244.175.202 (also referred to as the IP), but you can imagine how difficult it would be for all of us to remember these numbers in order to move around the web. This is where the DNS servers (the catalogs we mentioned before) come into play.

We use easy to remember names like www.ashgate.com and when we submit them to our browser it accesses a DNS server (telephone catalog) to retrieve the corresponding entry 83.244.175.202 (telephone number), it will then use this number to connect (dial) to the publisher server and submit to it the default.aspx?page=637&calcTitle=1&title_id=10135&edition_id=12896 information that identifies the web page of the book. The server will then return to the browser a text file coded in a structured language called HTML (Hypertext Markup Language). This language that browsers understand includes specific instructions on how to display the information sent by the server, like where to place the title, the colors of the different elements, the pictures, the menus, and the buttons.

All browsers can display the files they receive from servers—simply go to their "options" or "view" menus and select something like "display source". Depending on the page you are viewing, you will notice that the actual information is bracketed among special keywords (*tags* in computer lingo) like <head>, <title>, and <p>, to name a few. If we pay careful attention and if the document is structured properly, we should also notice the corresponding closing tags like </head>, </title>, and </p>. Similar types of tags are used to identify decorated text (bold, underlined, fonts, and so on) and render Word documents on your screen. These are not displayed to avoid confusion and ease the users in concentrating on their work.

HTTP and HTTPS

Ever wonder why you see the "http" symbol on the website addresses on your browser's address bar? Well it is nothing more than a universal indicator of the language browsers use to talk to servers. It's as if we put a label of the language we will use in our communication with someone before we actually start talking. By saying or showing the label "Chinese," for example, one would expect everything that follows to be Chinese ideograms, and so on for other languages. It's a necessity because our browsers are "multilingual" in the communication protocol sense. They usually understand a few languages like HTTP, HTTPS, FTP (for file transfer), SMTP (for sending emails) and pop (for retrieving emails), among others. So given the lack of a better way to indicate which one they speak, they indicate that at the beginning of the address they are connecting to.

While HTTP means Hyper-Text Transfer Protocol, HTTPS is simply HTTP Secure because it provides encryption to the message exchanges for security purposes. This makes your message a little bigger and it takes longer to pack, send and unpack, but at the current speed of computers and networks it hardly makes any difference for typical day-to-day communications. Two of the most common commands included in HTTP and HTTPS are the commands GET, POST, and PUT. What we saw before in the example of accessing the book's web page (page=637&calcTitle=1&title_id=10135&edition_id=12896) was part of the POST command telling the publisher server that we are interested in:

page=637

calcTitle=1

title_id=1035

edition_id=12896

These variables will be passed to software that resides on the server and will be used to identify the file that contains the information about this book.

Wireless protocols

A great deal of communication nowadays is wireless. Naturally, the devices that offer such services need to communicate in their own language, the most popular being WAP. This stands for Wireless Application Protocol and addresses the Application Layer (Figure 2.6). Most uses of WAP involve interactions between the mobile Web and our mobile phone or notebook device. Like the browsers in our computers, WAP is the language used by the browsers on mobile devices to talk to servers and interact with them. Corresponding protocols/syntax exist for the other layers in Figure 2.6, the lowest one being the Wireless Datagram Protocol (WDP).

In reality, our mobiles are connected to the Internet through a *proxy* that is called Gateway. This is simply a representation of a computer that is connected to the Internet and that can additionally send and receive wireless signals. While WAP handles any distance, communication over shorter distances saw Bluetooth as a communication standard become popular. Bluetooth is a technology that allows devices to discover each other using short-length radio wave to communicate (primarily exchange files) securely. So you can use a Bluetooth-enabled mobile to exchange files with your Bluetooth-enabled laptop or another mobile. Something more popular and familiar is the use of the Bluetooth mobile phone headset for hands-free calls.

While Bluetooth was intended as a replacement for cabling and as support for fixed location applications such as controlling your home appliances, an alternative technology that was developed for resident equipment and applications is Wi-Fi IEEE 802.11, or Wi-Fi for short. It uses the same radio frequencies as Bluetooth but with higher power, resulting in faster connections at longer ranges. This type of speed is typically required to connect your laptop wirelessly with the Internet through a wireless router. Wi-Fi is usually used in *hotspots*, areas such as Internet cafés, where Internet access is offered over a wireless network. This service is what you can also get at airports and hotels for free or for a fee.

One important set of technologies worth mentioning here is "Voice over IP" (VoIP) which simply means voice communications over IP networks. Synonyms to that are also terms like IP telephony, Internet telephony and broadband telephony, to name a few. This is a way to perform functions on the Internet like voice communication and facsimile that we used to do with public switched telephone networks (PSTN). The processing steps are conceptually very simple and, in the case of voice, involve the conversion of analog signals produced from our vocal cords and recorded by the microphone in our computers to digital. The addition of appropriate information makes it compatible with the Internet communication protocol (IP) and sending it through the wires and devices that constitute the Internet. Its major advantage is that it is far more cost effective compared to telephone technology.

2.2.2 WEB LANGUAGES

To use the different communication protocols, we humans have developed different languages that target specific needs. These languages need to follow strict syntax since computer software does not possess the analytic capabilities of humans who can filter content and derive meaning even from incomplete messages or approximate representations. For instance, we can remove a certain number of words from a paragraph and still get the meaning or we can see a blurry image and still identify the objects in it. To compensate for that computer deficiency, we enforce strict syntax in the languages we use with them. Even a simple typing error (like missing a comma) can cause a computer program to collapse, dragging with it the whole system and network in the process. The strict syntax, while making learning and using of the various programming languages difficult, ensures to a certain degree safe, reliable, and predictable execution of our software.

Languages are described in documents that different pieces of software, such as the browser, reads and interprets as commands for execution. To make it easy to identify the language each document contains, we usually adopt file extensions like ".html" (for Web documents), ".gif" for a certain type of picture files, and ".pdf" for the Adobe files, to name a few. Regardless of the file extension, we might use another identifier/label like we did with the HTTP in URLs so the first "word" in a document is usually used to indicate the language it is written. It's like we live in a society where every person around us has the same appearance (they are all files), but speaks different languages. How do you communicate in such cases? The simplest way is for all to adopt a common identifier (maybe in English) of each language and by using it as the first word in discussions to indicate the language that will follow. So by saying "Chinese," for example, you indicate then that everything that follows will be in Chinese. To end the Chinese section you might use a keyword like "/ Chinese." The same approach is used to identify the language we use to pass commands to the different software we have developed.

Each language is expressed through commonly agreed upon *tags* (some sort of lingo) that are nothing more than indicators of what is contained and how it should be interpreted. In a Word document, for example, there are great amounts of information that are included, but hidden from user view to ease the display and allow the users to focus on their tasks. This extra information refers to the font we use in different paragraphs, the text decorations like "bold" and "italics", the tabs and paragraph marks, and many others. You can easily reveal some of it by selecting to display *styles* or *formatting* in your documents or try and open a Word document with *WordPad* or *Notepad*. For everyday document writing, we have developed applications like *Word*. When it comes to writing the languages we use for Web communication, we have not really done such a great job simply because production hasn't reached the masses and these languages continue to evolve as our needs and understanding increase.

HTML, XML and WML

At the basic level of a user of the Web we need a humanly understood language to use http. The language we use to build web pages is HTML (Hyper Text Markup Language). As the name indicates, the language is full of markup elements called *tags* that identify different pieces of information along with the way we want these pieces to be displayed by the browser. In the example below, everything between the <! > tags are explanatory comments that the browser ignores, but which help humans to remember what takes place. Tabs are used to provide clarity as to what belongs in each section:

    <html>   <! To indicate this document uses the html language>

    <head>   <! The beginning of a section with brief description of the document. The information included here is not displayed but it can be used by the browser to communicate it with other programs>

      <title>The title of your web page </title>

      <meta name="keyword" content "description"> <! Additional info>

    </head>   <! Indicates the end of the header section>

    <body>   <! To indicate the beginning of the section with the content that will be displayed to the user. From here on a variety of

different commands might appear to satisfy the information and presentation needs of the document>

<h1>A Heading that will be displayed usually as large text</h1>

<p>   <! To indicate the beginning of a paragraph>

The text of a paragraph follows here …

</p>   <! To indicate the end of the paragraph>

<a>   <! To indicate the beginning of a link section>

href="http://www.google.com">Description of the link

</a>   <! To indicate the end of the link section>

<img>   <! To indicate the beginning of an image section. The following describe the location of the image and its display dimensions>

src="ImageNameGoesHere.jpg" width="104" height="142" />

          <! To indicate the end of the image section>

          <! In the following lines we mix various elements to make the same information more presentable>

<p>

Some text of a paragraph.

<a href="http://www.google.com">Description of the link</a>

more text

<img src="ImageNameGoesHere.jpg" width="104" height="142" />

more text

</p>

```
</body>    <! To indicate the end of the display section>

</html>    <! To indicate the end of the language>
```

Having a language to describe the display of information was sufficient enough at the beginning of the Web, but it isn't enough to communicate specific types of information that are application dependent. For example, if we wanted to display the age of a person along with the rest of their details, it is easy enough to do so with html. But what if we want our client application to retrieve this information and do something useful with it, like check if that person is over 18? One way to do it is to write some kind of application that processes the text file the server sends—ignore the html tags and the other information provided in the page and identify the number that refers to the age. And what if the date is also included and happened to be 23 January 2010? It will be extremely difficult to differentiate 23 from 18 since both fall within acceptable age numbers. To solve such issues, the XML (Extensible Markup Language) was developed. XML allows the use of customized tags like <age>, </age> and <day>, </day> that we can use to surround the relevant information in our documents in a way that identifies their content. This way a text <age>18</age> can easily identify the number 18 as the age of a person and the text <day>23</day> can identify the number 23 as the day of the month. You realize of course that all this tagging adds a lot to our original information so our documents are naturally bigger in size than their originals. Bigger documents mean more time to transmit, but it's a disadvantage we can live with given the flexibility and ease of identifying content we gain at the receiver end. Nowadays, also, with the increased transmission speeds and the processing power of computers the whole process goes virtually unnoticed in most cases.

A simple example of an XML document follows below. In essence, it is html structured in a better and stricter way:

```
<! The line below indicates we are using the XML language with the
specific character encoding (could have been Chinese for example>

<?xml version="1.0" encoding="ISO-8859-1"?>

<customer>       <! To indicate the beginning of a root element/entity>

<name>   <! To indicate the beginning of a child entity/property>
```

```
Mickey Mouse     <! The value of the property>

</name>  <! To indicate the end of the child entity/property>

<age>      <! To indicate the beginning of a child entity/property>

60<! The value of the property>

</age>     <! To indicate the end of the child entity/property>

<job>      <! To indicate the beginning of a child entity/property>

Cartoon Character<! The value of the property>

</job>      <! To indicate the end of the child entity/property>

<customer>        <! To indicate the end of a root element/entity>
```

To talk to a mobile we use a specifically designed XML variant—WML (Wireless Markup Language) where different keywords are used to identify the smaller screens of mobile devices. The mobile treats each screen it displays as a "deck of cards." All the information is stored in different cards that are activated appropriately. There are two types of cards, one that displays information and another for user input. In essence, we take the big website pages and break them down into smaller screens for display while preserving continuity and structure.

JavaScript, Applets and Flash

While XML solved the problem of identifying information elements in documents, we still needed a way to process that information at the browser level. For instance, on an online store we might have quantity and item price and we want to calculate the total we will charge the user. This is a simple multiplication of quantity with unit price that we do not know when we design the web page, but we would like to display as the user modifies the quantity variable. What we need is programmatic capabilities embedded in our browsers. JavaScript is the language we use to enable programmatic access to computational objects in our browsers (clients).

If we look at the source of a web page that includes JavaScript, we will see a typical HTML command like <script type="text/javascript> ending later with a </script> that signals to the browser that what is included in between these tags is in the JavaScript language. Typically, within these tags we will see executable code in the form of functions that take as parameters data we fill in forms, or provided directly by our browser (like current time or our IP for example) and perform calculations or make decisions that will lead to us seeing something on the web page (result, animation, another form, and so on). The code that would perform such actions in JavaScript can look like:

```
function total_price(quantity, price, total) {

total = quantity * price;

return total;

}
```

To add more functionality, one needs the full power of computer languages like Java, for example, that are embedded in web pages in the form of *Applets*. These are nothing more than independent programs that run on a window within your browser window. Anything that you can find in the form of a computer program like a game or an office application can be displayed with an Applet. The HMTL keyword that defines them with the associated code can look like:

```
<applet width=300 height=300 code="DrawingShapes.class"> </applet>
```

This line tells the browser to open up a window within its frame window with the dimensions indicated and execute the Java code (bytecode to be more specific) that is found in the file names "DrawingShapes.class" in your computer.

To increase the functionality of browsers, different public and private interest groups developed software that acts as extensions to browsers. These appear in the form of "add-ons" that one installs on the browser and can execute commands written in specific languages. A very popular "add-on" that provides interactivity and animations is Flash. This is a multimedia graphics program specifically for use on the Web. It enables one to create interactive "movies," animation, and graphics by providing a much friendlier and easy-to-learn user interface than a typical programming language like Java (used in developing Applets).

The following HTML code indicates that a program named "shapes,'" that resides in the file "DrawingShapes" in your computer, is written in Flash and will be executed using Flash. If your browser doesn't happen to have the Flash "add-on," it will probably take you to the website from which you can download and install it before continuing with its execution:

```
<object width="550" height="400">

<param name="shapes" value=" DrawingShapes.swf">

<embed src=" DrawingShapes.swf" width="550" height="400">

</embed>

</object>
```

Why so many languages?

You might be wondering why we use so many different languages to do all of the above and not just one. The answer to this question is twofold. Firstly, as the Internet was becoming a reality, it was more like an exploration into the future and as such each exploration phase had to be followed by a productivity phase. While explorations by their own nature are not productive and profitable when "gold" is discovered (in our case interactivity of the user with the web), it had to be followed by investments in streamlining operations and making them efficient.

When things need to be repeated reliably and effectively we need some kind of automation, so in software we create languages that deal with specific areas. It's a kind of abstraction we adopt to convey the meaning of multiple actions with a few words. Just as in real life, different explorers might use different languages until a commonly accepted language dominates the field (like English in negotiations). So languages are created as abstractions that describe something new and allow universal communication. Ultimately, it is a means to get what we want more efficiently (increasing productivity).

Another thing that goes unnoticed here is the misconception that technology creates due to the speed and efficiency by which something happens. We tend to believe that technology treats things differently while in essence the solutions it provides are similar to our daily practices in a faster and more precise way. Figures 2.5 and 2.6 show the magnitude and extent of the analogies we use. It is natural for us to develop practices we can relate with our physical lives as the physical world is our source of stimulation and experience. When we send regular mail we insert our message page in an envelope and we type the address of the recipient and the address of the sender. The envelope provides a level of security and allows us to pack pictures and other documents, or even objects, if we are sending packages, while the address identifies the geographic origin and destination points of the route the message will follow. It is up to the post office then to process our mail, assign it to the appropriate courier that will then pick it up and transfer it to another courier and so on until our message reaches the post office closest to its destination. From there the post office of the receiver will make sure they deliver it appropriately.

At each stage of the journey the different intermediaries use their own language of understanding and rely on simple interfaces to communicate with the layers that precede or follow them. As Figure 2.5 showed, the post office doesn't have to know how the airline will deliver the message. It could be a direct flight or it could be that the letter is transferred through many intermediate stops. Similarly, we don't need to know how the post office will handle our message and although we speak French, in the example, the only thing we need to type in English is the address of our receiver. The different entities involved have different interests and thus use a different language. The airline, for example, isn't interested in which street the receiver lives. It might be interested in which country it lives and who will pick it up at the airport, but other than that it doesn't need to know anything else. The different information needs of the intermediaries involved in the process are what create the need for different languages (lingos in real life).

2.3 Databases

Languages are useful in transmitting and processing information provided by the user and displayed on the screen. But what happens if we need to access stores of data? One way we solve this problem is by organizing our data within folders and subfolders. This is not practical when the number of objects gets to be really big as we might discover when trying to locate the name of an item in crowded folders—especially when we don't remember the exact details (name, size, type, and so on) of the object we are looking for. In such cases we need entities/software that will organize our data and information, store it, and retrieve it in efficient and practical ways. These entities are called databases and they usually consist of an organized collection of data in digital form with appropriate support functions for submission, retrieval, and manipulation of those data whether they are in text, image, or video form. The software that achieves all of this is generally called *database management system,* or DBMS for short. It additionally includes functionality for efficient searching, backup, and maintenance of the database. DBMSs organize data in tables where each row (referred to as a record) represents an entity and each column refers to a characteristic or property of each entity.

To use DBMSs we developed appropriate languages. The most popular language we use is SQL (Structured Query Language) which includes simple commands that are easy to remember and use. SQL contains commands for the creation, deletion, location, and updating of records and their entities along with their organization in presentable formats. The examples that follow are meant to show the simplicity of SQL for basic operations.

The following SQL command creates a table named Clients were we can store customer details, such as name (as a string of 50 characters) and age (as an integer number):

CREATE TABLE Clients (name VARCHAR(50), age INT);

To insert data for a new customer named Donald Duck with age 24 we can use the command:

INSERT INTO Clients (name, age) VALUES ("Donald Duck," 24);

To change some data like age to 36, for example, we can use the command:

UPDATE Clients SET age=36 WHERE name="Donald Duck";

while to completely delete the client information we can use the command:

DELETE FROM Clients WHERE name="Donald Duck";

To search for all clients that are below the age of 40 and display them in alphabetical order we can use the command:

SELECT * FROM Clients WHERE age < 40 ORDER BY name.

For simple databases with a small number of records the above commands will more or less suffice; but what do we do with databases of millions or billions of records where we would normally need hours of processing even with very fast computers? Well, in these cases we apply the same techniques we apply in real life by creating indexes like the alphabetical indexes of dictionaries.

When the databases become too vast for one machine to support them we even break these indexes and the tables into smaller sections that we distribute to different physical locations (distributed database). One example of the progress we have made in this field can be seen in the speed with which Google searches its vast databases that hold most of the information available in the "visible" Web (publicly accessible websites). When you submit a query your request goes to Google's DNS servers that are located around the world. The server will break down your query and send to Google's cluster (collections/ networks of hundreds of thousands of PC-type computers) for concurrent execution. These computers will scan the indexes of huge databases to find the relevant answer to your query entries, assemble the results, and present them to you in something like a quarter of a second. Amazing isn't it?

2.4 Web 2 and Beyond

Something rarely seen in the material world is versioning. It's unlikely that you will ever see a fast-food chain to have a Mega Burger 1.2 and next year coming up with Mega Burger 2.0 as an improved version of the previous product. Versions in software are used to describe minor and major developments. The integer part is reserved for major changes while the decimals are used to indicate minor improvements, usually in the form of eliminating inefficiencies and bugs or the additions of extra features that were promised initially. When we move from Web 2 to Web 3 one would expect to have seen or heard of, say, Web 2.4.

It is customary in the software world to announce something new with the increase of an index. In the beginning we had the Web that we now refer to as Web 1.0. That was the time when the online business world was the territory of a small number of companies and advertisers that had the appropriate tech support to produce content for users to access. Its operational philosophy resembled that of a catalog or that of a lecture where one speaker addresses a big audience. In contrast to that, its later evolution—Web 2.0—is viewed more as a conversation where everyone has the opportunity to speak and share views.

THE DOT-COM BUST

The thing that made Web 2.0 big was simply the implications that the version number 2 brought along. In terms of functionality, we came to the age of participation where a more democratic approach to generating content was adopted. Users were allowed to create content and use it based on their personal preferences and navigation history. Trust became of great significance since it motivated users to invest their time and effort to make significant contributions to websites. Individual content providers began to directly compete with traditional media in the areas of education, entertainment and news.

A great example of how everyone can have a voice and contribute to content is Wikipedia. As the most popular encyclopedia/reference completely generated, edited, and updated by Web users, Wikipedia provides an unprecedented case of active participation of individuals to a common goal. For e-negotiators it can serve as a great channel to getting messages across either by posting on its site or by duplicating the technology in corporate and personal websites in the form of wikis (more on these in subsequent chapters).

Another example is Del.icio.us where users can recommend their favorite sites to others. Other examples include websites like MySpace, Flickr and YouTube where users create the content while sites act as hosts. In the world of business, some of the most successful ventures are entirely based on content created by users. The added value is not just having the collective intelligence of their members, but also in how it is used to make money. Take for example Google. The company does not generate content—it simply organizes what is out there in the form of a catalog that can easily be searched according to users' needs. In doing so it also keeps track of user preferences and tags sites based on their popularity. In essence, the whole business model of Google is based on the simple assumption that whatever is popular now will continue to be popular in a given field. Their catalog is organized by the mere statistical significance of each entry in terms of its accessibility frequency and length of stay of each visitor.

In reality, a more complicated formula is used to rank the popularity of websites with respect to query terms. The secret of success here comes from relevance to each field. Given that fields of inquiry can in many cases be almost as many as the content, one can see the challenge and the feat of what Google does. Another feature of Google that contradicts common practice in terms of human-computer interface is that it offers the simplest possible user interface—a command prompt. There is nothing else there that changes and grasps your attention. Everything has been designed to enforce one purpose. Search as efficient as possible without distractions.

As the world of Web 2.0 and above becomes part of the daily life of negotiators, we need to be aware of its capabilities in order to manage and organize our news feeds, be familiar with the search tools it provides, and gain the insight we need to position ourselves better or at least at the same level as our counterparts. The following chapters aim at empowering e-negotiators to become more knowledgeable and, at the same time, more cutting-edge professionals with the use of the Internet. The same way we need to know how a pencil or a car works (and not its composition), we need to know the basics of Internet to safely surf the information superhighway and use it to our advantage.

WEB 3.0

As humans we are driven by our tendency to bring everything closer to our experience and use it for our benefit and pleasure. The same thing is expected to happen with the Web the more we work with it and use it to conduct business and enhance our social lives and personal development. A more dynamic and closer-to-the-human-experience Web is expected to evolve as times goes by. The new Web is expected to help filter the immense amounts of information produced by Web 2.0 so that people can locate what they are really looking for instead of what others want them to find. This of course poses some billion dollar questions like, "What is the right kind of information?," "Who produces that information?," "Who controls its access?," "How do you retrieve it?," "How do you deliver it?," and "How do you present it?," just to mention a few. These are questions that somebody would expect to be of concern to politics rather than technologies. But this exactly shows the essence of the anticipated Web 3.0—a medium that is so popular and with an expressing power beyond any other technology that forces us to consider its social dimensions and its impact on our personal nature.

In Web 3.0 data is becoming the currency of exchange. The more someone can accumulate and tailor data to users' experiences, the bigger the return on investment. This enhances the personal experience delivered and in return draws the masses to their fulfillment online. Here democracy merges with meritocracy with the final outcome being the bliss of both consumer and producer of information. It's all about engaging a demanding user with multiple personality facets interactively with the applications and services provided by the technology. Customizable user experience will bring higher levels of involvement and participation, making the technology an integral part of everyday personal and professional life.

In technology jargon Web 3.0 is infused with semantic technologies where data are interconnected, interrelated, and annotated. This will allow applications to be customized, become portable and device independent (or system neutral). The goal here is to find the needle in the haystack. In other ways, you are sitting in front of your computer screen, typing your query and, in a flash from the billions of data around the world, a personalized answer will be delivered to your screen, including appropriate pieces from all sources. If one considers the accomplishment, it is like having thousands of encyclopedias with text, picture, and video checked in time frames that your senses could not perceive and presented in the most efficient way for you to perceive and comprehend.

Web 3.0 also belongs to the third decade of Web technologies allowing many to consider the index as an indication of the Web's age. This decade is supposed to finally bring a promise that Web 2.0 failed to deliver: the convergence and integration of all sources and media of information like mobiles, phones, PCs, and appliances. This type of networking will facilitate transparent integration of our personal, social, and professional lives, regardless of the underlying technologies supporting these interactions. What this all means to a negotiator is more or less obvious: better intelligence, at least at the initial stages of negotiation, faster response times, and more empathic communication through a medium that never before existed.

3

Intelligence

Many times in negotiations we wish we could read the other person's mind and tell what they are thinking so we can predict their moves and plan our countermoves. The process of figuring out what someone will do next in a given situation based on their characteristics and personality traits is called profiling. This is of utmost importance in negotiations. By enhancing our predictive power we can anticipate our opponent's moves and counter their offers. Although this sounds like you are manipulating situations and people, real negotiations are not far from doing that.

Profiling (background checking in a more informal way) can be done on people, organizations, and issues. Checking people is more difficult than checking organizations since organizations are required to keep a public profile, while checking issues is the easiest of all primarily because of the abundance of sources one can find on the Internet and the news nowadays.

People have basic traits and personalities (with the exception of abnormal cases) that have been spearheaded by genetic predisposition, family and social environments, education, and personal and professional experiences. These characteristics are the target of profiling as they shape the way one thinks and acts. Deducing someone's genetic predisposition can be done by identifying gender, race, and physical characteristics. Much can be deduced about intellect and personality if one studies academic achievements, hobbies, social behavior, and the way one interacts with their environment and social communities.

The data evaluated when profiling a person online include pictures, videos, and text they developed or others produced about them. Pictures will reveal most of their genetic characteristics and provide snapshots of their interaction with the world. Videos will additionally reveal changes of behavior in social settings. Even looking at a seemingly meaningless video of your subject (attending an event, for example) can offer valuable clues about your subject's psychological and social profile.

Profiling organizations is much easier simply because organizations are legal entities that need to keep public records of their activities, have identifiable internal structures, and need to interact with their environment through rules and procedures that are more or less standard. Having all that information about organizations and combining it with their past and present policies and actions, we can more precisely predict their perspective on negotiation issues. With the advent of the Internet, nowadays it is easier than ever to locate information about organizations, especially large public and private corporations which store a multitude of data on the Internet.

From the information we can locate about an organization, we should be able to speculate about the strategic interests it may have on a negotiation issue. Based on information about their past behavior in similar disputes and negotiations, one can also deduce their tactical style and their probable approach to the issue. Profiling topics on the Internet are extensively covered by a diversity of sources and will provide us with almost every aspect of the negotiation issue we are facing. From simple marital advice to the rationale behind a corporate merger and acquisition, we can nowadays find detailed description of the issue, the politics, and the entities involved and its impact from the standpoint of local society all the way to economic markets around the globe.

3.1 Online Intelligence

The first step in a negotiation process requires the collection of information about the negotiating parties and the negotiation issue. This information will then be processed to determine alternatives that will help them formulate offers and support their argumentation. Familiarization with the subject of negotiation is of utmost importance. All sides will be gathering their own intelligence. Our responsibility is to "guide" our disputants, if possible, to discover only the information and details we want them to. We may choose to block some data and intentionally leak other. We will focus on what technologies exist out there to use technology to our best advantage in an e-negotiation setting. Simple techniques will also be presented for someone to perform basic intelligence online.

3.1.1 SEARCH ENGINES

How does somebody collect information on the Internet? One way to answer this question is to see how others do it. As a case study, we will describe the way search engines like Google locate the information that resides in the web pages around the world. To find content on the Web, search engines use special types of software called *web crawlers* that scan the servers (websites) connected to the Internet for various types of material. Websites can be seen as a collection of files and folders (Figure 9.1 in Chapter 9) within a central folder that the servers consider as the *root* folder of the website. Typically when someone connects to a website the servers that host, the site by convention will look for a file named *index.something* where something could be an extension like *html, htm, shtml, jsp, swf, php,* among others, that indicate the scripting language of its content. Unless the URL you type in asks for a specific file to be displayed (www.e-negotiations.org/somefilename), the *index* file contained in the URL location you type is displayed.

Web crawlers create a list of all files and folders in the root folder of the server and then start classifying and reading them one at a time. If a file contains text, they scan every word and phrase in it and create an index for that file (a dictionary of what is included). This way pairs of indexes with their associated files are created and stored on the search engine databases. If while reading the content they identify links to other pages, the crawlers will make an association of the file and link, store the link in their memory, and follow it after completing the crawling of the website or submit it for another crawler to follow.

Crawlers pay special attention to the name of a file as it normally indicates content along with special keywords called *metadata* that web page designers embed in the html format of web pages. These metadata are not displayed by the browser, but contain classifications/keywords of the content of a web page. If the file is an image, video, or other non-textual format, they usually make a simple association between the filename and the rest of the file attributes like type, size, date created, and so on. If the file is a folder, the crawler will retrieve its contents and follow the same process for this subfolder or alternatively may assign this task to another crawler.

As you can see this process will go on and on as long as there are folders and subfolders and links within the files crawled until the website and its associations are exhausted. If we think of the millions of websites "out there" we can imagine the magnitude and complexity of the task and we can get an idea of the advancement in technology required to achieve such a feat by modern search engines that submit to us results in fractions of a second. Success on providing what we want is based primarily on website popularity in terms of accesses recorded and associated with an index-file pair. When users type queries the search engines try to locate similar terms in their index databases. They retrieve the associated files that contained our terms and display to us their location (link) on the Web with a brief reference to the section in those files that includes our search terms. From then on it's up to us to follow the links that interest us. Of course, this is not an accurate process and that is why we are provided with many "hits" or "near hits," ordered in terms of their selectivity by other users that typed similar queries and in terms of the frequency of appearance of a term in the index. In other words, search engines also keep track of which of their results are popular so they can present them in future searches first. This is part of the "learning" process for search engines.

Doing what search engines do manually is out of the question for us, so what e-negotiators are expected to do is simply use what the search engines provide, evaluate it according to their understanding and knowledge and make the most of it. In many cases we might also use search engines that are searching nothing more than search engines, performing in this way what we call a *metasearch* and providing us with the best of the search engine's work. This might sound a little bit like "cheating," but it's nothing more than what search engines do when they crawl everybody else's websites. "Freedom," as we will see later on, is quite a controversial issue on the web.

Searching

The results of a search can be greatly improved if we know how to structure and submit our queries. When we type a query in Google, for example, like "Where is the e-negotiations book?" you will get (at the time of this writing at least) the following top five hits:

1. "Free **Books** Online **E Negotiations**: Towards Engineering Of ..."

2. "Let Your Dough Ri$e **Negotiations** ..."

3. "Free **Books** Online **Negotiation** Support Systems ..."

4. "**E-Negotiation**"

5.   "Applying the Montreal Taxonomy of the State of the Art
      E-Negotiation …"

The bolded words are corresponding words from the submitted query. If
we were to guess which one refers to this book I would hope that the fourth hit
is the obvious choice. Why though did we get these results? And while the first
and third at least have the word "Book" from our query, how did the second hit
get to be there? Is it a mistake or a smart choice text that the web-page owner
selected to confuse Google's web crawlers to believe it refers to e-negotiations?
Following that link we found that it refers to Chapter 10—Negotiations of the
website for the book *Let Your Dough Ri$e – A Women's Financial Recipe Book
and Other Sage Advice*. What happened here is that when that site was crawled,
a "connection" was made between the first part of the title of the book and
the excerpt of Chapter 10 which is "Negotiations". Bringing the two together,
and given that search engines usually ignore special characters like "$" (as
it is used to indicate prices), the search engine saw "Let Your Dough Ri e
Negotiations" and created an association of "e-negotiations" with the file from
that site. If at the time of this writing, that website was retrieved many times
following similar queries that would raise its popularity and showed it high in
our results. Another reason that caused confusion to the search engine is the
character sign "-" (minus) in the "e-negotiations." It would have been better
to leave that space empty, simply because the search engines also consider its
algebraic meaning of subtraction/exclusion in processing results.

An interesting point that came up with the query is that all the top five hits
refer to PDF documents. This can easily be attributed to the term "book" in our
query that the search engine chose to associate with PDF files. This is not a bad
choice given that most similar materials are in PDF form and that most users
would prefer this format when reading a book.

If the results don't look impressive enough, think that even we occasionally
get confused when we talk to each other, as many times we don't understand
what another person said so we ask for clarification. Since search engines
cannot ask for explanations (yet) they try to compensate for that by asking us
to refine our search within the results they provided. In doing so they also keep
track of their successes to reinforce the relevance of query terms with their
indexes and provide better results the next time a similar query is submitted.

Search engines have their own built-in language that has similarities to the
SQL database query language that we saw in the previous chapter. Some tips

that will enhance your search power on Google include, but are not limited to, those listed in Table 3.1.

Table 3.1   Tips for Forming Queries

Use double quotes to search for exact phrases. If I used "Where is the e-Negotiations Book?," Google will tell me that this didn't match any documents, meaning that this exact phrase has not been found in any document or if it did, it didn't capture the crawler's attention to report it as a significant one. Use double quotes only if you are absolutely certain about a phrase since misspellings or omissions could lead to exclusion of useful hits that could instead appear by using the terms of the phrase only.
Using the plus ('+') or minus ('-') signs in front of words forces the search engine to look for hits that include or exclude those words in the hits. The minus sign is very useful though when you try to refine existing search results and remove unrelated hits.
Common words like "where," "how," "the," "is" are ignored so my original query could have simply been "e negotiations book" and I would still get the same results. If you consider common words important just precede them with the plus sign. Use the keyword **OR** if you want to, include either one of two terms. In my query, if I formed my query as "negotiations OR book" I would get hits that contain either the term "book" or "negotiations."

Use search operators: these are keywords reserved by search engines to refine their searches based on user preferences. Some of the operators that can be quite useful include (look for more on the book website):	
site	This keyword is used to restrict your search results to within one website. If you type in your search box, for example, "site:http://www.e-negotiations.info culture" you will get hits about culture only in the website of the book.
type	To allow for searches of only certain types of file. For example, "type:gif negotiations" will look only for picture files of type gif.
inurl	A lot of times you might remember part of a URL or are looking for URLs dedicated to a certain subject and you guess they would include the name of that subject in their URL address. Typing "inurl:negotiations" will retrieve web pages that their URL includes the term "negotiation." You might be surprised how accurate results you might get many times.
intitle	This keyword is more of an expanded version of *inurl* since a lot more information about the content of a website can be found in the html title tag (see previous chapter) of the web site than the single word descriptions of its URLs.
cache	Remember from the previous chapter that the Web's memory is like the elephant's. It never really forgets. Well, sometimes you might want to use that feature to "sneak" at what was out there at some time in the past. This way you might get a perspective of past positions of a negotiation issue from the point of view of the various stakeholders. Typing "cache:www.e-negotiations.info" will travel you to the past and you will see an older version of that website. These old versions of websites are sometimes real treasure troves because you get to see who was in charge at that time, what were their positions, and, by extrapolating to the current website, you can form a viable hypothesis of what happened in between. An alternative to cache if you know the website URL is to search for it in websites that keep periodic backups of the Internet like http://www.archive.org/.

Use keywords that indicate what you are looking for, like use "define e-negotiations" instead of "e-negotiations" if you are looking for a definition of e-negotiations.

Something that is quite interesting to experiment with is to try the same query from different laptops. When, for example, we tried the same query on another laptop, it produced the following results:

1.   "Free **Books** Online **E Negotiations**: Towards Engineering Of ..."

2.   "**E-Negotiation**"

3.   "Let Your Dough Ri$e **Negotiations** ..."

4.   "The Chartered Institute of Purchasing & Supply-**Books** ..."

5.   "Research"

While, with respect to the original execution, the first result remained the same, our original second became third and our original fourth became second. The rest were completely new hits. Why did this happen? The answer is very simple. Google tries to identify the person using a computer by keeping track of what queries get executed from each computer. *Cookies*, as we will see later on, allow websites (and Google in our case) to keep track of our browsing history and thus the previous searches we made and profile us accordingly.

Of course, if different people surf the net from the same computer (this happens a lot in computer labs) it is difficult to make sense of surfing history as each person has different interests online. You might observe something similar, let's say, when you order for your whole family from amazon.com. If at some time, for example, you order kids' videos from amazon.com, you will see recommendations for more kids' videos regardless that you might now be interested in "e-negotiations".

This is a kind of previous-experience bias that web servers (and search engines) develop and sort of stereotypes us with respect to preferences. We have got to be careful of it especially when searching for something other than what we normally search for as this bias might reduce the success of our searches. Eliminating cookies will correct the issue partially because IP tracking is also another thing web servers do to customize their responses and identify users. This doesn't always work for individual computers as they are usually assigned IPs dynamically, meaning we get a different one each time we connect to the Internet. In addition, we might be connecting using a proxy that is through another computer that presents its IP as our own. This is a typical case of most corporate computers. Easier ways to avoid all these "high-tech" solutions would be to use someone else's computer (nowadays offices and families usually have more than one) or use a different search engine like Microsoft's Bing. For comparison purposes we list the top five results we got from Bing after submitting the query "Where is the e-negotiations book?" at the time of this writing (we cut and pasted the result to preserve the spelling mistake in the first hit and the content of each hit):

- **Neotiations and selling**
  Also, one entire chapter deals with **e-negotiations**. The book would ...

- **RMIT - Sheehy, Mr. Benedict**
  Abstracted: **E-Negotiations**: Fundamental Challenges and Solutions ...

- **Michael Stroebel**
  The CfP for the **e-Negotiations** Workshop 2004 has just been ...

- **Payment Options | Business English Pod:: Learn Business English ...**
  Buy: 1-Year Premium — — — — — — — — — — — e-Books ...

- **The Chartered Institute of Purchasing & Supply - Books - CIPS course ...**
  Study session 19: **E-negotiations**. E-negotiation defined ...

To close the search engines subject it is worth mentioning that a variant of that service is *metasearch* engines (for example, http://www.dogpile.com/ and http://www.surfwax.com/). What these engines do when you submit a query is to submit your query to search engines (like Google and Bing), combine the results they get from them, and display them according to their ranking. Some will also allow you to see snapshots of the websites without visiting the sites. While one should experiment to find their preferred engine, we believe that after selecting one it is better to stick with that choice because we tend to learn the ins and outs of that tool and, despite their difficulties and shortcomings, the familiarity we develop with it over time works in our favor in terms of finding something fast.

3.1.2 SEARCH ENGINE ALTERNATIVES

While search engines might be our first choice of intelligence, we might need to go a little further when we need to dig deeper to find details regarding the opposing party and the issue at hand. Search engines are good at providing relevant information, but they are also prone to providing irrelevant information (false hits) or useless generalizations, forcing us to look at other alternatives.

One good starting point for many might be encyclopedia-type sites (databases), like Wikipedia (http://www.wikipedia.org). This might be a good start especially when searching for subjects and terms (instead of people and corporations) because someone else has already done some research for us. We have to be careful though of the author bias and expertise on the subject since we don't know who exactly wrote the content we are reading. What is very helpful in Wikipedia is the list of resources (notes and references) and external links most entries provide at the bottom of the page. Following those links can provide us with more information from sources we could authenticate much more easily.

Another alternative might be to use online subject directories like Yahoo Directory (http://dir.yahoo.com) and Google Directory (http://directory.google.com/) that contain websites organized in folders and subfolders of various subjects from general (folder) to specific (subfolders). Typing "subject directories" in Google will bring many more websites that provide such services.

The dark or deep Web

Search engines use great technology to do their job, but there are limitations to what they can reach. A lot of the information on the Internet (actually many orders of magnitude of what we see) is stored in databases that are inaccessible to web crawlers. The information we see displayed on our screen when we surf the Internet is many times created on the fly, meaning that the server on the other side that processes our request accesses a database probably by formulating an SQL query based on our request, retrieves the data from the database and processes, organizes, and submits them to our client (probably our browser). If the database in question has millions of records we only get to see whatever the server will allow us to see. The rest is invisible to anyone including the search engines.

In addition to the servers controlling what parts of a database are visible, there are simple things web page designers and owners can do to discourage web crawlers from crawling websites and collecting information not intended for them. Available options include avoiding placing information in text mode and keeping it in image or video format, and inserting special tags (meta tags) that will not display on screen, but cause most search engine crawlers to avoid them.

If the information we are looking for is under a specific category like business, technology, or of a scientific field, one might want to consider looking in specialty databases (dark web) that can be searched by submitting an appropriate form on their websites. Be aware that a lot of them are available through subscription services that we might consider having if we are repetitively interested in a subject. Optionally they allow pay-per-document services. Some such databases can be found at (more links exist on the book's website):

http://search.ebscohost.com/ (almost all subjects)

http://www.emeraldinsight.com/ (business related)

http://www.computer.org/portal/web/csdl (IT and computer science)

http://papers.ssrn.com/sol3/displayabstractsearch.cfm (social sciences)

http://www.bnet.com/ (business source – non-academic)

A good alternative when searching for persons or organizations might be to look in social network sites like http://www.facebook.com/, and http://twitter.com/, and even https://www.blogger.com/ (to name a few). Although search engines also *crawl* these sites, it might be worth actually visiting them and searching by ourselves if we know or guess that a person or organization exists there. This could be a follow up especially when a related reference appears in our preliminary investigation through a search engine.

3.2 Evaluating and Using Results

While retrieving results is the first step in the intelligence process (the identification process), validating what we find is of utmost importance as we will base future decisions and plan our strategies based on what we found and how we perceive our counterparts and our understanding of the negotiation issue. Results need to be evaluated on their authenticity and credibility. While authenticity is the carrier of many "evils," credibility is easier to research and investigate.

Credibility refers primarily to the extent of trust we exhibit on the reliability and trustworthiness of the content we have. We need to know that the level of expertise presented in the information we have is the real one. The best we can do regarding credibility is to apply critical thinking and keep our eyes open for bias or prejudice that website authors could display. This is evident when a website attempts to persuade us instead of informing us. Giveaways of such sites are words that include over-generalizations or simplifications that omit vital details, quotations of experts and famous people (dead or alive), mentions or links to sponsoring organizations, and, in general, anything that looks like an ad disguised as information. In case of doubt try *Googling* (searching) some of the material you have seen on a certain page to see if similar web pages come up. Also look to see if the URL makes sense—especially the top level domain. If the terms in the URL and the content are not related we might want to exercise caution regarding the credibility of the site. A URL like http://www.FindYourDate.com/e-negotiations might not exactly refer to corporate negotiations while a site like http://www.corporateWorld/e-negotiations will most likely be about corporate negotiations.

Another clue to the credibility of a website is the referral website that led us to it. If it was a site we trust that suggested the site we are evaluating, then we have more reasons to trust its content as someone else we trust suggested it (trust by proxy). See if the website has references (links) in support of its claims or follow up material (not on the same site) that we can access and get a better idea of what is going on.

Check the date of the last update of a website to evaluate its currency. A trick that would tell us the last date the website was updated is when we are at the website to copy and paste the following *javascript:alert(document.lastModified)* in the address bar of our browser. As we saw in the previous chapter, we are executing a *javascript* which is nothing more than a program that the browser executes. This should open up a separate window that displays the date of the site's last update. Active sites get updated regularly so we should expect their content to be current, while inactive sites are probably going to reflect views of the past.

3.2.1 AUTHENTICATION

Authenticity in our perspective is the association of the real information provider with the information we have. In other words, we need to know that the person or organization that appears as the information provider really is who they say they are. There are a few ways one can identify the owner of a website which might also directly relate to the author of the content, especially in corporate or personal websites.

Pay attention to "the small letters" ("faded words" would be better in Web lingo) that say *Sponsored Links* as they do not represent search results, but promotional material. Search engines depend on advertisements to make a profit. Advertisers try to promote their sponsors' products and services disguised as search results. To keep a balance (and avoid public outcry for manipulating users), they keep the same format and style as their search results, but display it in a separate section either at the top or right section of the results page. Some, though, might even go further and include them within the regular text paragraphs, creating a really annoying distraction.

As an example of identifying the owner of a website, try copying "e-negotiations" in one of the fields in http://www.whois.net/ (or http://www.dnsstuff.com/) and selecting the ".info" extension. You will then see the details of the person or organization who owns that domain (and pays the money to maintain it). We can do this with the top-level domain of any website we are viewing. Additionally, if we are interested to know where in the world a website resides, we can submit the IP or address of that website to a geolocation service (by searching the Internet you can find many such services). These services will actually locate the geographic location of the server that serves the website in question and most probable location of the author of the content.

This might actually be useful in cases of email exchanges during negotiations. If the email is served by a corporate mail server or a local Internet Service Provider (ISP), we should be able to identify the approximate location of the person we are communicating with by using a site like http://www.ip2location.com/. In emails we can see the originating IP by looking at the full header of the email (usually a right-click on the title of the message should show an option to display the full header). Copy and paste the IP into the appropriate field in the suggested site and you will get the details of that IP, including its geographic location. If our counterpart, though, uses general purpose Web mail addresses like *Gmail, Yahoo!,* or *MSN* the above service will only provide us the location of the mail servers of those services and not the actual location of the sender.

3.2.2 DON'T LOOK ANY FURTHER

As you might have seen in movies and the news, sometimes there are "other ways" of finding information about someone or something. By this, of course, we mean of the not-so-legal approaches at least from the perspective of most rational people. The term that is used nowadays in computer security terminology is *hacking* (in this book we mean the illegal one). It generally refers to applying methods and techniques to access content and affect computers in ways not intended by their owners. Displaying and practicing such knowledge as e-negotiators says some 'scary' things about us and chances are it will create great insecurity on the other side, eventually inhibiting negotiations. Due to the nature of the topic we will avoid technical details simply because by telling you what not to do, we will be telling you how you can do it. Although most of this information could be retrieved by appropriately searching the web, we believe that making an effort to learn shapes character and enforces responsible behavior (we at least hope so). And, since we want to see you successful in your e-negotiations and NOT to blow up your company and your life in the air all at the same time, this "dark" side of Web intelligence will not be pursued in this book.

As with every other human invention, computers suffer from imperfections—some because of human error or ignorance, some because the technology at the time of development had limitations that were overcome later. As we saw in the previous chapter, computers are composed of various units and rely on various types of software to store, retrieve, process, and communicate information. At any one of these stages flaws can be discovered and taken advantage of to damage or gain control of a computer. If one only considers operating systems that reach hundreds of thousands of lines of code, it's easy to see how errors can occur or appear. It's like having an encyclopedia of many volumes where one omits or misplaces a simple word (say instead of "hacking is not ethical" someone accidentally or deliberately removes the word "not") and based on that, someone or the computer acts.

All the various types of ill-intended software belong to the general category of *malware* which is short for *malicious software*. Some of the terms you might hear that belong to this category and affect the various software pieces are:

- *Computer Viruses*—these are programs designed to replicate themselves and spread from computer to computer by attaching themselves to regular software, like Word documents, emails, pictures, and, in general, any type of files users exchange. At a predetermined time the virus might perform some disruptive function in the host computer that could range from displaying a simple message to destroying files in the hard drives. An antivirus program like Norton (http://www.symantec.com/norton/) is probably the best protection against them as these programs update their virus databases as fast as new viruses appear. Another way to protect our systems is to always update our software to its latest version. Software companies fix their product vulnerabilities as soon as they are discovered and immediately release updated versions (or *patches*) of their software. Nowadays one can even find free antivirus (http://www.avast.com) programs to install for personal use.

- *Worms*—are self-replicating programs that spread from computer to computer but, unlike viruses, they don't need to attach themselves to another file in order to be transferred. Worms take advantage of computer network vulnerabilities imposed by operating system deficiencies to act as freeloaders and move from one computer to another. Most of them don't carry a payload that could do further damage to the systems they infiltrate so their primary function is to overload networks by using their bandwidth. That can be a serious problem because their rapid expansion can bring networks to their knees as regular users don't have room to connect to where they want to connect. One popular function of worms after they spread is to attack a Web server by sending continuous messages to it. The server runs out of resources in its attempt to identify and answer each request so the real user request is lost or denied. An attack like this to an e-commerce site (online book store, bank, and so on) can do serious damage to its operations. Typical solutions, until a fix for the operating system is found, is to divert traffic to mirror servers, block the IPs of the computers that send the request, or even counterattack by sending similar worms to the attacking computers. In the case of the individual user, the same solution that we mentioned in the case of viruses should be followed.

- *Trojans*—or *Trojan Horses* (from Greek mythology, of course) to be more precise— is the type of malware that spreads by attaching itself to executable files and comes to life during the installation process of the host as a fully functioning independent entity. Its purpose is to allow some form of control of the host computer by its creator. The most "harmless" type of control would be to interrupt normal operations and display commercial messages (usually referred to as *adware*) while some of the worst could be to hijack credit card numbers and other valuable information that are stored or exchanged. In addition, the host computer can be used to launch attacks or coordinate illegal activities while disguising the real culprit. A good antivirus software should be able to deal with Trojans effectively.

- *Spyware*—is a more passive form of Trojan in the sense that the malware is used to collect information and send it to its owner. This information could be important keystrokes like passwords and credit card numbers. In its more "innocent" form, spyware is used to monitor surfing habits of users, like websites visited, and redirecting browsers to specific sites. Anti-spyware software (most times incorporated in antivirus programs) is the best solution in such cases. Browsers can also identify and prevent spyware so one should always use the latest version of the browser they use or install appropriate add-ons.

Other types of illegal activities you might hear about include:

- *Spoofing*—in our case *Email Spoofing* refers to email activity that disguises the identity of the sender and poses as someone else. An attempt is made in this way to lead you to visit a website or provide privileged information. Typical spoofing activity involves emails where you might be requested to provide personal information like email account passwords, credit card details, and so on. Another popular activity (called *phishing*) is to lead you to a website that looks like your bank's website, for example, where you are supposed to login with your user name and password. In such cases just pay attention to the URL of the pretend site. A URL like https://www.bank0famerica.com/ is not the same as the real URL https://www.bankofamerica.com/, but it can be very misleading especially if someone displays it as https://www.BankOfAmerica.

com/ since the upper case letter "O" in many fonts looks exactly the same as the zero digit. The only way to protect yourself from spoofing is to keep updating the spam terms of your email client and exercise common sense in authenticating emails.

- *Sniffing*—is a hardware intervention technique and it's simply a form of wire-tap to computer networks instead of phone networks. The simplest form of protection against such a threat is encryption. To put you at ease, most network systems nowadays have the ability to identify and trace *sniffing* by employing "switch" technology (search the Internet for more).

All security violations are also considered privacy violations since they access proprietary data without the consent of the owner. While the above are obvious cases of privacy violations, there are cases where these violations are not so obvious and they might be allowed with the data owner's unintentional consent. Think of the times you read the small letters at the bottom of many websites where they list their *Privacy Policies*. A visit to a site like http://www.google.com/intl/en/privacypolicy.html will get you up and running with these practices. The main technology worth mentioning here is *cookies*. These are nothing more than little pieces of data that web servers drop in your computer when you visit their websites. It usually records the time you visited that site and how you spend your time there (products you bought, forms you filled in, web pages you viewed, and how you interacted with the site). Cookies are usually dropped with your permission (intentional or not) through your browser and if you need to modify your browser's behavior, in that respect, it might worth exploring its privacy settings in its Tools/Options menu.

Be cautious when giving personal details online. It might be worthwhile having a "persona" for such purposes only. The easiest way is to create an email account for subscription services like garbage.yournameX@yourFavoriteProvider.com where X could be an increasing number for each account you create. This way you can access the account for the time you need to complete your transactions or receive confirmation emails and delete all of them after some time to reduce spam. Another favorite is to use "disposable email accounts" (http://10minutemail.com/ and http://www.getonemail.com) that delete themselves after a certain amount of time. These types of email addresses and their respective passwords can also be used by group members to keep their communications in one place.

3.3 Counterintelligence

As important as it might be to find out all we know about an issue and our counterparts/disputants, we can also "allow" them to "discover" the proper information about us. This might also include restricting them from finding information we do not want them to access. To achieve this we need to identify vulnerabilities in the systems that hold our information, in addition to ensuring the information available is the appropriate one. Knowing what can go wrong is a first direction in protecting ourselves against what others can find about us that we prefer remains unknown to them and other parties in an e-negotiation.

To protect ourselves and our data we need to use common sense and support our online presence with appropriate technologies. The most important aspect is to manage content carefully. What we say on the Internet has a tendency to stay forever in websites like www.archive.org that keep backups of the visible Web at regular intervals, so past positions and behaviors can be easily accessed especially when in text or image formats. One way to avoid that is to develop content for dynamic access, meaning that it resides in databases and is served to the user through forms they submit. Another way is to be as guarded as possible regarding our professional and personal positions whether on our website or websites where we interact as our "true" selves. If we are active in social networking sites, the golden rule is to exercise caution as to what we reveal about our personal life and professional moves.

Part of a counterintelligence practice is to avoid leaving any traces. As we saw before, there are many ways for someone to keep track of our browsing history. Identification on the web can be avoided by using services like http://proxy.org/ that allow us to surf anonymously. All these services really do is act as proxies for us, meaning anything we send or receive from the Internet passes through them. This way, when we visit a website it will appear to that site that someone from the proxy location is visiting them and they will have no way of telling that it was us. Cleaning up after our tracks is also a good step and can involve simple actions like deleting *cookies* from our browsers to deleting all records of the sites we visited (deleting browsing history). Your browser caches (same as search engines) websites you visited so it can offer them to you faster from your hard drive the next time you visit them. Deleting these track records can be done through the *Command Prompt* that for Windows systems resides in the *Accessories* program folder. Running *Command Prompt* and typing the command "ipconfig/flushdns" will delete all records of the websites you visited.

When confidentiality is essential to protecting sensitive information, use encryption—especially when exchanging emails with critical information. Encryption software (like http://www.comodo.com—free for personal use) usually compresses a message and by using an encryption algorithm transforms the message into an incomprehensive assembly of bytes. The whole process requires that we set up a password that only the real sender and receiver knows. This password will be used to decrypt the message at the receiver's end. What we hope to gain is time to complete our job before those that intercepted our message use various hacking techniques to "break" our message. They would do that by trying different password combinations until they successfully guess our password. Obviously the longer the password and the more variety in terms of characters and digits it contains, the more difficult it will be to break since there will be many more millions of possible combinations that one will need to try before decoding it. The disadvantage though with long passwords is that they are easy to forget. The best approach to remembering a password is to use combinations of upper case and lower case letters with digits. When allowed to do so you can use special symbols that resemble familiar terms. For instance if we needed to use the word "e-negotiations" as the basis of our password, a possible "good" password could be something like "e-ne&0+!@+!0n$."

Technically speaking, the most popular way of protecting a website or our systems is through specialized software and hardware called *firewalls*. The hardware versions of firewalls position themselves literally between our systems and the Internet, screening incoming and outgoing signals based on their properties. They can identify malignant signals or IPs and block them from reaching us or getting out of our system. The software versions (for example, http://personalfirewall.comodo.com/) gain special privileges from the operating system to filter incoming messages and IP addresses based on predefined rules and preferences. Most of this functionality today is performed by routers and antivirus programs.

One last thing we suggest for anyone to do is spy a little bit on yourselves (like trying to break into your own house to see how well your security system performs). Type your name and some of your professional details in a search engine and see what comes up. This is what others will see first when searching for you. Based on that you might decide to modify or update the information you present on the Internet. Given that one is biased about oneself, you might want to consider allowing someone you trust to perform intelligence on you and see what appears before you on the screen.

4

Perception

Perceptions are a critical element in e-negotiations primarily because of the lack of visual social cues found in face-to-face negotiations. Perceptions are based on our subjective judgment. They directly impact the way we communicate, form our strategies, and plan our actions. Our cultural norms and values, whether familial, social, ethnic, tribal, religious, or regional serve as our reference point in conducting negotiations. An analogy that illustrates the issues involved in cross-cultural settings was presented by Ulijn and Campbell (1999) and Ulijn and Kumar (1999) and might help showcase the potential problems. They proposed the iceberg metaphor to explain the complexity of cultural perceptions. There are two layers that an iceberg can be divided into: the explicit, visible top of the iceberg, which represents facts, and the much bigger implicit, invisible body, which represents emotions and unconscious rules.

Social perceptions in negotiations according to social psychology are grounded on three important elements:

- *Perceptions of the bargaining situation.* This category includes feelings and judgments about the negotiation process, like norms, structure, and content, along with communication and information sharing. This perception is highly influenced by prior experience and knowledge of outcomes achieved by other negotiators in similar situations. A social comparison takes place here that, in association with our intuition and subjective feeling of success or failure, helps us identify a situation as advantageous or disadvantageous.

- *Perceptions of the other party.* Here we look to beliefs and impressions of our counterpart and what we can deduce about the way they perceive us. At an individual level we have perceptions about our counterparts based on their behavior (reactions, tactics, strategies), and trait inferences (expertise, cooperativeness, reputation).

While regarding their perception of us, we consider factors like social relationship, trust and, respect as they develop during the negotiation process.

- *Perceptions about ourselves.* This final category is perhaps also the most baffling and challenging. It involves looking inside of us and judging our own traits, performance, and worth from our interactions with others. To achieve this level of self-awareness, we must listen to our internal voice more carefully than ever before. Have we developed the maturity and insight to know our motivations and values as well as judging our own behavior? Issues that affect our self-perceptions are self-efficacy, self-enhancement, and cognitive beliefs about behavior, self-esteem, and preservation of our social status.

Subjective value, whether conscious or unconscious, guides our understanding of a negotiation. This subjectivity is not going to be affected by our negotiation mode—whether we are online or face-to-face. What we will observe though in e-negotiations is a shift in the recourses we use to make our evaluations. Face-to-face negotiations provide the sensory stimuli needed to form a perception since the information is coming at us in a multi-faced format (visual, sound, text, and so on) and from various resource points (face, body, environment, and so on). This might be a good thing as long as we can handle the information richness of the various media in terms of receiving and interpreting it appropriately. In the event that we are inexperienced in coping with such sensory overload, this abundance of information can prohibit our ability to function appropriately, thus reducing our potential for success.

4.1 Theoretical Framework

Perception can be seen as the process of selecting, organizing, and interpreting information about situations in social and physical environments. We are organisms composed of physical and mental entities that function together to shape their environment and ensure our survival. To achieve this goal, we create mental constructs and properties that help us simplify data, create abstract representations, and use analytic and deductive logic to handle the information overflow that we receive from our senses. In essence, we perform an information customization and filtering to suit our needs and capabilities. This comes with both advantages and disadvantages, as from one point of view, it allows processing of great amounts of information, and from another, rejects a lot of it that could be of significant importance. The fact that we managed to survive and build our civilization so far is probably a good indication of the benefits of human thought processing, which apparently we do quite efficiently.

In this book we will take the notion that perception is the transformation of information to knowledge after it's filtered through four generalized layers (Figure 4.1). These layers encase: 1) inherited personality and intelligence (DNA imprinting); 2) environments where we grew and matured and that conditioned us to certain beliefs and values; 3) the society we live in that imposes cultural traits in us; and 4) the world at large with its global economic, social, and political trends. All these layers affect the messages we send and receive. The major activities that penetrate and guide our perspective and being-in-the-world is education and the personal experiences which influence personal style and build intellectual abilities and coping skills throughout our lifetime.

What saves us from the confusion of communicating through these layers is the simple fact that we are all more or less the same in terms of genetic characteristics; our societies generally look alike in terms of familial and social structures and that we all share the same world. It is a certainty that we have a lot (if not most) things in common that would form the foundation upon which we base our communication with others and enhance our ability to cooperate and grow together.

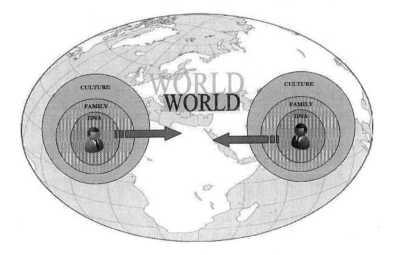

Figure 4.1   Influence Layers during Communications

4.2 Inherited and Developmental Traits

There is the undeniable truth that we all come to life with certain physical features that affect the way we perceive the world and others. Some people can be naturally talented to speak many languages while others can perform fast arithmetic calculations, to name a few of these traits. This also extends to the emotional world where some people show mild temperament, while others tend to lose patience easier and become aggressive in conflicts. The same way it is unlikely to be a professional basketball player with a height of 1 meter, it is unlikely to see negotiators with low IQ or extreme tendencies. While intelligence is genetic (and assuming we all possess enough to become negotiators), we could benefit a lot from self-awareness that could highlight our strengths and weaknesses. Being aware of our personal traits and coming to terms with them it is vital for strategizing about negotiations and selecting the best approach to achieve our goals.

The environment we are raised in and mature as individuals is our first exposure to other human beings. As a result, this environment forms our character and the core of our values and norms. It serves as the mirror that displays our reflection on others. According to the way we are perceived, we form our personality, our principles, and values about ourselves and others. More than any other environment, our closed circle of family and friends impacts and shapes who we are and how we function in society, at least in the early stages of our lives. As children and teenagers we are powerless most of the time to control any of these influences or modify our memories of past experiences, so the most we can hope is to be aware of these influences and come to terms with them. The only difference here with our inherited traits is our ability to rationalize and intellectually adapt those family and early social values that don't serve us well to what we believe can enhance our personalities and ensure success in our adult lives.

Our personal filters help us build our personal and social reality and characterize the way we interact with our environment. These filters are composed by our values, beliefs and interests, needs, goals, and expectations at each instant in time along with our understanding of situations and our communication capabilities. All these, when combined with our cognitive abilities to generalize, hypothesize, and deduct, form our personality and define the way we interact with our environment. Self-awareness is of primary importance in being effective in what we do and negotiations, whether face-to-face or electronic, make no exception to the rule.

4.3 Culture

Culture can be defined as an expression of the common perceptions and experiences among members of a group, a community, or a nation. Organizations can be included in this description as special categories of communities of interests. Through sharing common experiences, groups create their own unique interaction environment, leading to the development of unique sets of values—that is, broad tendencies to prefer a certain state of affairs over others—and practices—that is, visible manifestations to an outside observer such as symbols, heroes and rituals.

If we were to break down culture to some of its constituent elements, we could say it includes language, lifestyle, dress and behavioral code, perceptions of the status and role of gender, and social interaction styles. A general classification of cultures (identified by Lewis, 2005) based on orientation includes:

- *Task-oriented (linear-active)*: highly organized that prefers to do things incrementally. They like structure, follow procedures, and always stick to plans since time dictates schedule for them. They prefer independence to obligation so will only reluctantly accept presents. They rely on logic to resolve conflicts. They value their privacy and don't express emotions. They are punctual. Always separate business and personal. Anglo-Saxons are usually classified in this category.

- *People-oriented (multi-active)*: prefer to establish personal relationships as a foundation for business relationships. They therefore see professional life as an extension of personal life. In this type of culture favors are seen as means of persuasion. They are flexible to changes as time doesn't represent structure for them. Latinos, Mediterraneans, Arabs and Southeast Asians generally fall in this category. They tend to be extroverted, outgoing, and emotional, and tend to consider schedule as a flexible item.

- *Introverted (reactive)*: they tend to act in response to others, so they are also referred to as reactive. They also prefer personal interactions as a foundation for personal relationships. They are concerned with losing face therefore avoid confrontation. This is also extended to the loss of face they might cause to others. Japanese, Chinese, and

Northern Europeans exhibit these characteristics. They tend to be introverted, very respectful of others, with a calm demeanor, along with being punctual.

In negotiations, issues arise when people from different cultures need to communicate and reach an agreement. The problem in these cases is that of perceiving cultural differences as personal differences. Cultural contexts are an essential part of successful negotiations planning. In the case of where, for example, a linear negotiator meets a multi-active one, a change in expectations in terms of punctuality is necessary. The linear negotiator should expect deviations from schedule and time and in most cases should not attribute these to anything other than cultural behavior. On the other hand, if you are from a multi-active culture, an extra effort should be made to be punctual and respect meeting times as this will be conceived positively by your counterparts.

4.3.1 THE DIMENSIONS OF CULTURE

Even as early as half a century ago, research identified general characteristics of cultures that lie along different dimensions. While these can also be reflected in the classifications mentioned before, it is worth presenting them separately. For the purposes of this book we will consider the following five as the more influential in negotiations and e-negotiations:

i. Individualist/collectivist

This refers to the degree to which the common values and beliefs of the community emphasize the needs of the individual instead of the needs of the group. In an individualistic culture there is an emphasis on personal needs and goals, regardless of whether they negotiate for themselves or for the group. The implications for negotiations are that if negotiating with individualists you would expect their personal gains (reputation, personal satisfaction, monetary, and emotional rewards) to also be present irrespective of the negotiation issue. In a collectivist culture the goals of the individuals are aligned with the other members of the group and when negotiating they will consider the impact of their actions on the group and any personal gain will have to lie within the group norms.

ii. Power distance

Is a measure of the perception of and attitude toward authority and power. A characteristic of high power distance cultures is a strong sense of hierarchy with set rules of communications and decision making between different levels of the hierarchy. When negotiating with high power distance cultures you should expect that the negotiator might not be the final decision maker, so there will be time spent in transferring offers and counteroffers up the hierarchy ladder. Also, much emphasis will be placed on structure and social norms as they will try and bring social status into the negotiations before dealing with the actual issue. In lower power distance cultures, although social status differences exist, people are less receptive to the differences and in negotiations, power and social status are considered equal.

iii. Masculinity/femininity

Refers to the importance of masculine characteristics like achievement and material orientation in the culture, versus feminine characteristics like the quality of life of people and relationships between them. You would expect negotiators from masculine cultures to be more *cold* toward human issues and focus on the negotiation issue alone, compared to negotiators from feminine cultures who, apart from the deal, might also be concerned with its impact on people and society.

iv. Time

Describes the degree of structure we impose on our lives in relation to time. In unstructured/polychronic cultures people tend to involve themselves in parallel activities with many more people, while in very structured/monochronic cultures people tend to focus on one activity at a time and involve only people related to this activity. While polychronic cultures may seem chaotic, it is actually that culture's outlook on life that is different. In essence, polychronic cultures live for the present while monochronic cultures live for the future. In literature, polychronic cultures are referred to as having non-linear perception of time while monochronic ones have more of a linear perception of time. In terms of negotiations, monochronic negotiators shouldn't be surprised or offended if their polychronic counterparts concurrently think of irrelevant issues (like their vacation for example) while negotiating.

The perception of time and, as a consequence, the perception of self in time is a key divider of people and cultures. Think of how you personally feel about time. Western societies seem to perceive the passage of time stronger and more intensely than Oriental societies where time is more of an eternal state of change. Based on the finite life expectancy of human beings, the perception that time passes (and thus brings everyone closer to an end) forces people to value their individual identities more and try and exert more control over their lives. This eventually leads them to form more structured life and business practices. On the other hand, when the passage of time is not in focus, people seem to value the present more and that leads them to value their surroundings and look more at their relationships as a frame of reference for their personal identity.

Those that tend to value self more tend to also value their path in time as "unique" and distinct and spend much effort and energy in preserving that path. This makes them more closed to themselves since they don't want to expose themselves to risks that might endanger that path. Others see their path in time as a dim line in space-time that can be altered by various forces and influences including their counterpart negotiators.

v. Context

Communication messages carry a lot of non-explicit information relating to the context of the situation they express. Context is a vital aspect of communications as it enriches our perceptions beyond the literal meaning of a message's text. In high-context cultures the context of a message is interpreted within the context of its transmission as shaped by its environment. This includes the physical environment and the social environment with its power relationships and roles, in addition to the economic and political environment where a negotiation takes place. High-context cultures require more than textual information in order to fully process messages, meaning that social cues like facial expressions and body language play a significant part in forming perceptions. In low-context cultures the content of a textual message carries most of the information required to form an accurate perception.

Another definition of context is "information that surrounds an event." The concept of high versus low context is a way of understanding different cultural orientations. In this view, a high-context culture is one in which people build intimate relationships and as a result social structures and hierarchies are more prevalent. Respect is vital for preserving the social structure and individuals keep their personal feelings largely in check during interpersonal communication. Etiquette dictates a lot of the interactions and, although decorous and understated, can be highly expressive to a keen observer.

On the other side, a low-context culture is one in which people are highly individualized; they form fewer connections with each other (looking rather alienated and fragmented) and in general value their individuality and "freedom" as a birth-given right that can be exercised at any time. Social structures and legal systems are formed in a way that allow and encourage expressions of freedom and entrepreneurship. Logic and rationality are emphasized in low-context cultures at the expense of emotions and feelings that hold a secondary place in decision making. There is a general belief here that an objective and global truth exist and can be reached through reasoning and linear exploration. This is in contrast to high-context cultures, which tend to believe truth will manifest itself through non-linear discovery processes, without any aid from rational inquiry.

The previous classification is the result of research that found that Eastern cultures are high-context and collectivist, with a polychronic time orientation and high power distance, while at the other end are the low-context and individualist Western cultures with their monochronic time orientation and low power distance. Obviously one would expect, and it is indeed true, that the different dimensions are interrelated and influence each other in many respects. Negotiation science is greatly interested in these dimensions as they can provide initial insight into the parties' thought processes and can dictate best approaches to communicating interests and negotiating about issues.

The application of these six dimensions has been frequently studied in the context of conflict management. It has shown that individualist negotiators (for example, American, British, Dutch) are more concerned and focus on individual rights while collectivist negotiators (for example, Colombian, Pakistani, Taiwanese) are more interested in and value relationships more. In addition to these influences, national culture has proven to impact negotiators' style and positions.

4.3.2 CULTURE IN NEGOTIATIONS

In terms of the negotiation process, culture can be seen as practices and values that frequently show up and uniquely characterize one of the parties. Practices mainly refer to organization style such as the degree of centralization of authority, formalization of communication, and depth of organizational hierarchy. Values refer to employee/negotiator preferences in making task execution and coordination decisions. Both categories influence micro-level behavioral patterns in individuals. The presence or absence of culture as a decisive factor in negotiation has been debated frequently and while there might not be sufficient scientific evidence to suggest a direct relationship of culture and outcome, it is a parameter that no one can ignore. Given that traditionally in the past we followed formal etiquette and communication rules in negotiations, it is almost certain that the requirement to understand culture will be an absolute necessity for present day and near future negotiators. Understanding the cultural context in which emotions are displayed is important for knowing how to manage those in moving strategically through the negotiation process.

Real problems in negotiations arise when opposing cultures meet. A low-context negotiator might believe he made his offer explicit in the textual message of his offer while his counterpart high-context negotiator might still be waiting on the non-textual aspects of the message before forming an opinion. In such situations, low-context negotiators should go the extra mile to enhance the communication with additional actions such as making a phone call to introduce themselves and engage in social banter with the other party before addressing any issue.

In the case of intra-cultural negotiation environments, negotiators feel more confident as there are no linguistic or cultural differences to overcome and to an extent they can predict the way the other side thinks and feels. The shared cultural heritage allows members of high power distance cultures (for example, Belgium, France, India, Middle East, Philippines, Venezuela) to experience less conflicts with superiors, and become more susceptible to a superior's intervention in settling conflicts than are the members of low power distance cultures (for example, Austria, Denmark, Israel). Members of low-context cultures (for example, Australia, Germany, Scandinavia, Switzerland, United States) are generally more direct in communicating their needs and intentions than members of high-context cultures (for example, China, Japan, Korea, Vietnam). Monochronic conceptions of time in negotiators (for example, North American, Western Europe) tend to impose more of a sequential processing of issues in a structural way, whereas polychronic conceptions of time (for example, Africa, Asia, Middle East, South America) are more likely to influence negotiators with a parallel processing of issues and frequent interruptions to update the status of their various processing threads. The latter type has low tolerance for turn taking in discussions and can be quite frustrating to other culture types.

4.3.3 EXPRESSIONS OF CULTURE IN INTERNATIONAL BUSINESS NEGOTIATIONS

In international business negotiations, cultural issues are characterized by differences in verbal communication such as language and paralanguage, non-verbal expressions like body language, personal values (mentioned before), and the process by which decisions are made by each individual or group. Some of these forms of expression can be visible and easy to observe and counter like verbal and non-verbal, while others could be more challenging as they are subtle yet quite powerful and influential. It is easy, for example, to notice that two languages are different (like Chinese and Arabic) and counter the difference by learning your counterpart's language or having a translator on hand. Observing non-verbal cues, on the other hand, can be difficult as there are no clear signals to accurately estimate another person's values and style of thinking. On many occasions non-verbal cues can provide more vital information than the actual data that pertain to the negotiation at hand.

The translation issue can be quite significant as the linguistic distance increases between languages. While most of the time parties negotiate in English, it should be understood that people might not be native speakers so they will be limited in expressing their intentions and aspirations of a situation as accurately as they might have intended. Even when English is the native language, the idioms, sounds, and expressions might be different as might be the case between African, American, British, and Indian English speakers. Even within the same country like the UK, you might have problems because of colloquial differences, such as those between English and Scottish speakers. One should always expect that something will be lost in translation.

To counter the language limitations, extra time is usually spent either using additional experts (translators primarily) or going back and forth with additional questions and answers to clarify content. This can be of strategic advantage in some cases when the additional response time allows for more reflection and better decisions. It can also be proven a disadvantage in other cases where it might be interpreted as an evasive move to plot a counterattack or avoid dealing with the issue. Americans are usually in the second category in international negotiations as they are not in general bilingual and they consider that it is the other side that should make the effort and speak their language.

Regardless of language differences, it is generally good practice to consider that language exchanges with counterparts or within each group aim to clarify issues so that the different parties have a common understanding of the issue and each other's intentions.

The primary difficulty of non-verbal cues is that they operate below our consciousness radar. It requires an added effort on our part to be aware of this limitation and consider flexible strategies that can adapt to each circumstance and take advantage of information that gradually becomes available. A typical case is dialog between French and American negotiators. The French tend to be very engaging and interrupt their counterparts frequently, mainly in an attempt to express interest. For an American, though, that is used to taking turns and stating their case, this type of behavior is associated with aggressive and rude behavior and they tend to withdraw. Both sides might end up feeling uncomfortable and they lose the opportunity of a win-win situation. Typical characteristics of selected cultural groups are presented next.

4.3.4 HIGHLIGHTS OF SELECTED CULTURAL GROUPS

A lot of research has been done in classifying cultural groups and identifying some generalized characteristics that seem to appear frequently. While it is helpful to be aware of general trends and idiosyncrasies, we should be extremely careful not to stereotype as each individual is different and it might well be that our counterpart negotiator does not comply with the expected norm. With that in mind, some generally accepted cultural characteristics for some of the main cultural groups in the international business negotiation world are presented here (alphabetically).

- **Africa:** The continent is considered by many the next frontier in business development. In our grouping we will primarily refer to sub-Saharan Africa as the rest of it seems to have its own distinct cultures closer to the Arab or Western societies (for example, South Africa). Africa suffered a lot from colonialism and internal turmoil. These historic traumas have cultivated, among its people, opportunistic attitudes toward business and a tendency to move fast while being suspicious of mistreatments and unfair practices. On African negotiation teams, group solidarity can easily give away to individual interests.

African negotiators exhibit a high level of despondence and misgivings about formal negotiation processes and commitments. Many times critical details might be completely overlooked leading later to problems and clashes. Lack of negotiating experience and the inadequate time dedicated to proper preparation of a team (typically created at last minute notice even without the involvement of appropriate experts) is usually the cause of such behavior. Members of a team also might not know or have worked with each other before, resulting in poor coordination. This factor in combination with the shortage of time to gather, analyze, and process relevant information leads in general to unclear negotiation strategies. In such situations negotiators tend to be more aggressive to compensate for the lack of knowledge and compromising your initial position should be part of a strategy to allow the other side the feeling of achievement and gain. First offers can be rejected for no particular reason.

- **The Arab World:** North Africa and Middle East have gone through many economic, sociological, and political changes over the last centuries that have revolved around geographical and long-standing historical conflict. The independence that most Arab countries gained during the early twentieth century and the discovery and exploitation of oil and gas reserves has created a very dynamic economic environment that is based in traditional Islamic values and a tribal way of government. Although economic and political differences exist between different Arab nations, their common cultural history and religion forges the main character of Arab negotiators.

  Arabs tend to be keen negotiators and bring both emotions and traditions to the negotiation table. Bargaining is a part of their cultural heritage and it's a skill they have honed from childhood. Relationship building is of utmost importance as it could be the main criterion for ensuring a deal. The tribal character is very evident in how Arabs live their daily lives and the preservation of the tribe is paramount. In simple terms, if you are not born an Arab you can never become one. Adopting traditions, religion, and language will still not make you one, so the best chance a negotiator has is to enforce and value personal relations as much as possible while displaying an honest and respectful attitude toward the Muslim way of life.

- **China:** Chinese business negotiation practices can be seen as based on the core values of collectivism, honor, respect, obedience, and harmonious relationships as dictated and influenced by the writings of Confucius and Lao Tzu. China's unique *guo qing* (special national circumstances) adds another layer of complexity to negotiating behavior by shaping the decision-making process politically and setting the tone for doing business with foreigners. China has a long history of foreign interventions that left the Chinese with a feeling of distrust for foreigners. Their tactics are thus shaped to defend themselves and restore their status in the world. Their history of wars, revolutions, and nationalistic emotions instills in them a feeling of uncertainty for the future and drives them to work hard and establish close networks of support to ensure longevity.

  To increase their competitiveness, the Chinese opened their doors to the West, modernized their industry, and allowed foreign investments in technology sectors. Along with these initiatives they learned the management know-how of Western businesses and became familiar with the negotiation practices of the West. In that sense, one should expect to see a convergence of the traditional Chinese negotiation model with that of the Western world, at least in international settings. Despite that type of "modernization," the hard-rooted philosophical aspirations of the Chinese will always be there, so Westerners will do well to respect and value the interpersonal relations they build.

- **Anglophones:** The English language dominates the negotiation world, with the most powerful player being the US (seen separately later). Although common cultural characteristics can be traced in all of the different English-speaking countries, there are significant differences among them that need to be considered when negotiating. As colonies, many of them struggled for their independence from England, leaving them with a general distrust of authority that can be expressed in many ways, ranging from ignoring people who seem powerful, to cynicism. The British can be seen as emotionless at times and speaking in a controlled fashion while using stories to make a point. Australians can seem quite simple with great respect for the average person. Canadians are in general quite direct and one should always be aware that Canada is bilingual and French-Canadians believe they are a separate ethnic group from the Anglo-Canadians. South Africa is a rare blend of quite diverse cultures influenced by their political and ethnic diversity.

It's not a good idea to praise or flatter someone in public as it might be conceived as an attempt to manipulate them into something. Conservative use of humor while appearing authentic and grounded is probably the best communication strategy when negotiating with these cultures. At the same time, teasing and frankness might be considered attempts to establish a relationship and should be welcomed. After an initial introduction, one should expect the communication to follow on a first name basis and with more of an informal and friendly attitude. In that spirit, compromise should be displayed and pursued in reaching an agreement. Giving away needs to be practiced cautiously as giving too much might lead the other party to believe there is something wrong going on and giving too little might seem defensive and disrespectful.

- **France:** The French are generally quite well aware of other cultures due primarily to their colonial years and their preference for traveling abroad and exploring other regions. Having said that, they come with tremendous amounts of national pride, and they have a way of doing things to the point of being perceived as nationalistic and close-minded. A negotiator needs to show respect and consideration for their history and culture and act in all settings as dealing with a great nation. Showing appreciation for their way of life, with the small joys of socializing over a coffee or dinner where you will discuss mainly the world and life (very little about personal life and nothing about business) will help build trusting relationships that will take a negotiator a long way to getting things done.

Speaking French can be an advantage only if you are fluent. No problem there, though, as they can speak and understand English even if it appears they do not. In negotiations they will interrupt their counterpart frequently and become quite inquisitive. This is not to be taken as a sign of disrespect, but rather an attempt to be engaging and cover as much of the issue as possible. Gestures and body language are frequently used to emphasize a point and clarify an issue. Eye contact and close proximity are often interpreted as signs of honesty and sincerity. Logic is an aspect they will respect and value and showing intellect and wit will impress your counterparts. Aiming and expressing your intention to reach a consensus will be greatly valued and is probably the best overall approach to negotiating in France.

- **Germany:** German culture is based on work values and a disciplined approach to business. In general, they are hardworking people that appreciate structure and formal ways of doing business. While initially Germans might appear distant and reserved, when they accept you as a business partner they are quite loyal and supportive of their collaborators. The separation between business and personal life is quite distinct, but trusting business relations can lead to personal relations that can be quite rewarding.

  Communication needs to clearly convey the intended message as they appreciate the direct approach and consider vague statements rude and threatening. They strictly adhere to company policies and rules and a negotiator should be familiar with their practices because it will be unlikely they will break or bend their way of doing things. Punctuality, formality, and preparation are greatly appreciated when conducting business with Germans anywhere in the world as they value time efficiency and effectiveness. Logic will be the prevailing force in negotiations and they will even be willing to make concessions (provided you supply appropriate evidence) if they are absolutely sure this is the last resort to saving a deal.

- **India:** Business practices in India can be quite diverse with Western styles prevailing in the business centers like Mumbai, New Delhi, and Bangalore, and more traditional eastern styles in the remainder of the country. A division might also be observed between government and non-government sectors (especially in the technology area) with the latter being more flexible and active in traditional Western practices. This is primarily due to the international business exposure of certain manufacturing and technology sectors.

The culture is, in general, people-oriented, where lasting and trusting relationships are valued; although to a lesser extent with other East Asian cultures. Generally, people like to know each other more before engaging in business deals. Education is highly valued so higher academic degrees add prestige to a negotiator. Indians have an inherent politeness in their manners and expressions and they greatly value similar behavior. There is a sense of national pride that, in combination with their other personality traits, allows them to be patient and persistent in pursuing their objectives. Behind the polite behavior it's good to assume, in general, that as long as you are viewed as an outsider you are not to be trusted.

The language used in negotiations is English and that makes it easier for international negotiators although the tone of voice and the use of the language might sound confusing at first. Shaking of the head left and right doesn't mean "no" like in most other societies, but rather an agreement with what has been said. Getting a "yes" on the other hand doesn't necessarily mean an agreement with what has been said, but in many cases it's used to indicate that they heard what was said.

- **Japan:** Having been geographically isolated, this island nation has a long tradition and homogeneous culture that, in general, helps make reliable inferences about their business perspective and the way they interact with foreigners. The Japanese are hardworking people who take pride in their values, traditions, and way of life. They don't like to mix with other cultures and it's unlikely they will consider an outsider as their own. Despite that, they have high regard for educated and accomplished professionals from other cultures and treat them with appropriate respect in their interactions with them.

Taking ample time to gain trust, display dependability, and build a strong relationship before closing a deal is a positive strategy and will reward one in both the short and the long term. Strong relationships should be cultivated at all levels of an organization if negotiations are to be conducted on a regular basis as this will help things move faster. If you negotiate from a stronger position you should always help your counterpart save face while in the opposite situation you should express appropriate respect and acknowledge the power difference. Displaying humility will be valued highly even for insignificant cases like being late a few minutes or having things below their expected levels. Japanese live by their own code of conduct and ethics that may sometimes look peculiar to Westerners but it nevertheless needs to be respected and obeyed if significant progress is to be made in negotiations. Doing a small favor can get you much further than almost any other country in the world, while requesting one could easily get you to nothing unless you hold a significant position and they value it as an investment for the future.

- **Russia and Eastern Europe:** The ex-communist bloc lived through decades of political and social isolation that shaped ethnic attitudes—an influence that holds true even today. These nations are the newcomers in the free market economies and one naturally expects them to be less proficient in the required practices than their Western counterparts. Bureaucratic tendencies will be evident almost everywhere and differences in how fair play and good will are considered along with economic values will be intertwined with personal gains and aspirations. Bribing to get things done is not seen as the evil Western societies presented it to be.

  A sense of pride is widespread in these countries and people frequently express strong personalities to the point of stubbornness when entering negotiations. You could easily be perceived as taking unfair advantage of situations and people if your focus is only on business. The slow pace of the communist regimes of the region influenced peoples' lives and while they value personal relationships they like to take their time to develop them. Emphasizing win-win situations might be the best negotiation strategy since you also display an interest in the other side's positions and benefits. This way you come across as less threatening and appear more like a partner instead of an opponent who is attempting to take advantage of them.

- **United States:** When it comes to negotiating, Americans are probably the "loudest" of all negotiators with a "strict" sense of morality and ethics. There are great amounts of arrogance and pride in the American way of doing business and a general expectation that other cultures should adapt to their norms and practices. Their superior economic status makes them quite aggressive and they equally focus on short- and long-term gains. Making deals is like a national hobby and the separation of business from personal life is quite distinct. The country is populated with diverse ethnic groups that tend to preserve their individual cultures while following common business practices under a free market economy.

The United States is by far the most entrepreneurial society and that is reflected in the thirst for business people to succeed and continuously grow. They will work hard to make a deal materialize and they could use almost any means available to them as long as they have the moral and ethical coverage of their civic and patriotic values. A good rule to remember is that they appreciate and place a monetary value in most deals and adapt their argumentation accordingly. Financial success tends to be admired more than other intellectual achievement, especially if a person is self-created.

4.3.5 RELATIONSHIP STYLES

The way of relating to people in different environments is very important for negotiators. Typical relationships include:

- Superior/Subordinate relationship—this relationship differs between cultures, organizations, and people. In cultures with a rigid hierarchical workplace structure, the superiors are never questioned while in others where flatter organizations are preferable, people tend to be treated as equals regardless of their status as superiors or subordinates. For example, in the US it is more common for superiors to treat subordinates as equals and when speaking to each other there is little differential behavior such as eye contact avoidance. The opposite is true in some Asian cultures.

- Gender relationship—the relationship between employees and people of the opposite sex. Each culture treats gender roles differently, so while in some Asian cultures it is permissible to ask a female employee to bring coffee or tea to a male manager, in others (like the US), gender relationships are more equal so such behavior might result in complaints that in extremes can even lead to lawsuits.

- Peer relationship—relationships between co-workers of the same rank. In some cultures (Germans) they remain strictly professional and end at work while in others (like the US) they can extend to personal friendships. In most cultures, though, these relationships are somewhere in between.

4.3.6 MANAGERIAL PERCEPTIONS IN CULTURAL CONTEXTS

The business world revolves around certain values that to a greater or lesser extent exist in every culture and organization. These refer to perceptions about fair play, status, image, self-preservation, objectivity, and formality, to name a few. Misunderstandings usually occur from the different weight each group and individual places on each one of them. Objectivity and merit can be really compromised in certain regions like China and the Arab world were nepotism is important. Ancestry dictates positions in many cases and this impacts negotiations as failure or negative outcomes can be taken quite personally and impact the whole chain of relationships beyond any economic impact.

Cultures that seek consensus like the Japanese would be expected to look at win-win situations, while others like the US have more of an individualistic nature and the winner-gets-it-all attitude is quite persistent (no place for second place). Fast-paced negotiators (US) value time and tend to focus on short-term profits while patient ones (Japanese) take a more careful approach and seek long-term gains. The differences can be explored strategically and become quite advantageous to an aware negotiator, at least at the planning phase of a negotiation.

Time as a variable can be quite influential in international negotiations where, in combination with reactive and proactive tendencies, it can lead to effective strategies. Certain cultures (Russia) tend to look at a deadline as a future event that they need to address as it gets closer, putting more effort toward the end, while others (US) consider it as the end of activity which means someone starts working hard from now and finishes or slows down as the target is approached. In this perspective, Americans will go for an early deal while the Russians will go for a later one. Those who can afford the luxury of time will probably gain the most in such situations.

When faced with a problem, most people will come up with a solution or an action list either by analysis or synthesis. In terms of logic, this is like applying deductive or inductive reasoning. Breaking a problem down into its constituents and studying its individual elements can help reveal the greater picture in a methodological/scientific approach, while studying cases and discovering common elements can help identify what's common and thus persistent in them. We can achieve the first by applying existing knowledge to create a new one while the latter uses generalizations to arrive at first principles. In terms of cultures, this can be seen in complex negotiations where most Westerners will try and analyze an issue by breaking it down into smaller tasks and analyze each one of them (sequential approach) while Asians will try and discuss the issue in general terms and various perspectives and only then come up with a solution (holistic approach). This can be quite confusing in negotiations as the two approaches can't be applied concurrently.

The negotiation perspective of each culture can be an issue if not seen through the idiosyncrasy filter that each nation developed over time. While some cultures (US) approach a negotiation as a single exercise that needs to be solved, others see it as seeking a solution that can potentially be applied to many exercises, either presently or in the future. The way each culture measures success also has to be modified accordingly, as one culture will probably measure progress in terms of issues solved while the other will measure it in terms of issues addressed.

4.3.7 THE POSITIVE SIDE OF CROSS-CULTURAL DIFFERENCES

It is important to realize that the benefits of cultural differences in most cases outweigh the challenges they pose. In today's world, services and products have a global reach and input from different cultures would make them more competitive and lasting.

Cultural diversity, especially in the work place, apart from enriching our knowledge about different practices of other cultures, exposes us to best business practices, alternative problem-solving methods, and different skills. It also creates an atmosphere of mutual respect and appreciation for differences by recognition and understanding of cultural differences.

People from different cultures bring ways of thinking and specific knowledge that add value to businesses if leveraged properly. This is a form of collaborative learning that can improve interactions and increase productivity. Any exposure to other cultures and collaboration with people from those cultures can add a competitive edge to our career as the ability to understand and communicate with other cultures effectively is always considered a valuable skill. Recognizing and understanding cultural differences can minimize friction and conflict between negotiators.

4.4 e-Negotiation Specifics

The widespread use of the Internet affected international negotiations in drastic ways and allowed direct contact between cultures from different parts of the globe. This type of continuous and immediate interaction through a common medium is bound to create in the future a common communication culture that will more than anything improve negotiations between geographically dispersed parties. The use of English as the negotiations language online is a first step in that direction. Presently though, the way technology is used by different cultures and the way online interactions are perceived is still influenced by the beliefs, values, and expectations specific to each region of the world.

When conducting e-negotiations, perception is primarily affected by lack of sensory data and especially the visual stimulus we are so much dependent on. By nature we are creatures that rely heavily on vision since it allows us parallel processing of information. While the acoustic signals are processed one at a time, our visual cortex is designed for processing visual signals from many sources. This is why it is easy to make sense of a picture of a crowd while it is difficult to make sense of it by listening to everyone speaking together.

What we lack in information online, we replace with imagination, especially when it comes to forming perceptions of others. This can range from idealistic images of our counterparts to cold realism with its illusion of objectiveness. All interpretations are based on extrapolations of past experiences and knowledge we acquired in our lives. While this serves as a good first estimate, the inherent generalization of our assumptions might miss the different reality that each situation expresses.

Mutual invisibility in e-negotiations can facilitate adversarial, contentious, and trust-breaking behavior. Denial is stronger when damaging a faceless other, particularly when we feel protected by a shield of anonymity and physical distance. This sense of anonymity and distance can lead negotiators to assumptions that they won't be accountable for the social characteristics of their behavior and as a result they can freely engage in aggressive or trust-breaking behavior.

Classic perceptions of face-to-face interactions tend to be carried online with the most common one being that interactivity translates to interest and enthusiasm while the opposite is a sign of indifference and lack of commitment. This is mainly attributed to the delayed reward associated with the delayed form of asynchronous communication. This can also lead to negative perceptions of trust and can adversely affect future outcomes. At the same time, satisfaction levels and confidence in the quality of one's performance tend to be low compared to face-to-face negotiations.

The principles that dictate real-life interactions are also seen online only in a different and more subtle sense. For instance, while proximity is the primary reason for developing relationships in real life, it is replaced by shared interests online. Since physical presence and proximity is typically not a prerequisite for online relationships, the perceptions of similarity we form while interacting online become important in helping people to decide whether they share interests with their online counterparts.

To counter such trends, it is absolutely necessary to unmask ourselves to the other parties and foster the perception that they know us as persons rather than anonymous and faceless opponents. This will likely lead to more information sharing, confidence on the part of both parties to act professionally, and, most importantly, the build up of trust. Attempting to establish a working relationship and building trust will help assess sincerity and is often considered necessary to reach an efficient and satisfying agreement.

The e-business boom and the globalized nature of business nowadays have raised the popularity of e-negotiation as a means of conducting business and making deals. The practice allows for a fast and more cost-effective alternative to traditional face-to-face negotiations. Understanding how national culture affects negotiation behavior under these circumstances is becoming more and more critical for businesses and negotiators. Research over the past decade has shown that a negotiator's behavior and tactics are affected by their counterpart's cultural background.

Some of the findings of research include:

- Eastern and Western negotiators have unique perceptions of the negotiation process;

- Negotiation behavior is influenced by cultural background for both Eastern and Western negotiators;

- Negotiations between Easterners and Westerners tend to include fewer instances of private interactions and procedural behavior while focusing more on the task and engaging in persuasive behavior;

- Compared with their Eastern equivalents, who are more adaptable to their environment, a Western negotiator's cross-cultural negotiation behavior is more consistent with their intra-cultural behavior: they are less likely to significantly alter their tactical and behavioral approach.

When the most typical signs of culture like facial expressions, mannerisms, and the physical distance people try to keep from each other are removed, as they are in e-negotiations, it becomes challenging to identify expressions of culture that could help one gain understanding of the other party. Adjusting our responses and behavior according to our counterpart's culture, as we could in face-to-face negotiations, cannot be based on visual cues and we have to rely on the scripts of the written language. The situation gets worse in cases where the negotiation language is not the native language of negotiators (a Chinese person negotiating in English) and cultural aspects that could normally be observed in writings are missed or distorted in the negotiation language. Cultural differences also exist in the way negotiators prepare for negotiations and the outcomes they consider successful. These, combined with the negotiator's personality, experience, and the situational constraints that might exist, can strongly influence initial expectations and dictate the strategy they will adopt and follow. These parameters have a direct impact and will eventually influence the end result of negotiations.

Listed below are variables of the cross-cultural e-negotiation process that influence perception and the e-negotiator's performance, assessment of the process, and the final outcome.

- *Situational constraints* refer to the circumstances of the negotiations and the constraints imposed on the process. They include the specifics of the negotiation issue, organization within which the negotiation is conducted, and means and technologies of communication.

- *Negotiation atmosphere* and *process* have been thoroughly studied and found to play an important role in negotiations. The concept of "atmosphere" includes variables describing the personal attitudes of the negotiators during the process.

- *Negotiation strategy* reflects the negotiator's concern for their own outcome and their concern for the other party's outcome.

- *Contending strategy* means negotiators are concerned mainly with their own and less with the other party's outcomes. Such negotiators tend to have high aspiration levels and make fewer concessions. The process is competitive, leading to "win-lose" agreements.

- *Problem-solving strategy* is used by a negotiator's consideration of the other side's outcomes and their perception of the other party's outcomes as being instrumental for their own outcomes in leading to an agreement. These negotiators consider the negotiation as a way of solving a common problem to the satisfaction of both sides.

- *Yielding* and *inactive strategies* incorporate low concern for own outcomes and are therefore of less interest in this context.

- *Attractiveness* describes the personal "chemistry" between the negotiators. Both negotiation strategy and attractiveness can be observed during the bargaining process.

- *Results* and *post-negotiation assessments* are task-related and satisfaction-related outcomes. The former are objective outcomes defining the achieved compromise and possibly the compromise utility levels. The satisfaction-related assessment is a subjective evaluation of the negotiation, the results, and the negotiator's and the counterpart's performance. If negotiators from different countries obtain different results, it is not because they are from different countries, but because they have different expectations and behave differently during negotiations. These differences should be captured by variables describing the negotiation process or atmosphere.

People tend to only look at national culture when they go into international negotiations, but there is the issue of the individuals they will have to face since they will carry their own gender, race, educational, and religious culture. All of these aspects can be considered cross-cultural and can impact the way negotiators behave. E-negotiators cannot underestimate the role of culture as just having a national theme. As negotiators, we need to try and have a more holistic perspective of what culture embraces than just an ethnic or national dimension. Considering the wide range of dimensions that define culture, e-negotiators can better understand how the other person thinks and communicates, and can negotiate and persuade that person better.

Considering intercultural issues like differences with homogenous groups is also a component that needs consideration. Ideally, one should consider every negotiation as a cross-cultural exercise that, in addition to the way people interact with each other, adds an important and influential dimension in which rituals have a major impact. Training or coaching can help e-negotiators avoid some of the pitfalls of faulty assumptions, inter-culturally and intra-culturally. Before the start of the e-negotiation process, consider consulting with someone from the "culture" of the other side in the negotiations. Get an understanding of what normally goes on within that ethnic, religious, social, and gender group. Talk to someone who is or has lived through a bi-national experience— someone who has lived in the country with which you are about to enter an e-negotiation process. And if you need to, get a translator who can better capture the cultural nuances and language idioms used by your counterpart on the other side of your electronic communication.

5

Strategy

The strategy phase in our framework is the planning stage where the analysis of all the different issues involved translates into an action plan. While each negotiation case has its own characteristics and is defined by the circumstances that surround it, the core elements of negotiation analysis are more or less always the same. This enables the study of the subject and the formation of universal strategies to address it.

Analysis will become more useful as the negotiation process progresses and its variables change. Even post-negotiation analysis is valuable in providing clues and lessons that could guide successful negotiations in the future. Variables that need to be clearly defined include the parties involved with their interests, beliefs, and power status, along with the value that will be created and the way it will be distributed. With respect to e-negotiations, the situation regarding strategic choices and the way we approach a negotiation does not change. What changes is the way we communicate and implement our positions, as we will cover in the next chapter.

The aim of this chapter is to present strategies and their outcomes in relation to the many factors surrounding negotiations. Traditionally, attempts to understand different aspects of negotiations have used many perspectives, such as game theory, psychology, political science, communication, labor relations, law, sociology, and anthropology. With the advent of electronic communication and e-commerce, technology became an active player in negotiations. Information technology affects negotiations by providing the communication mediums and all the supporting structures for conducting negotiations, and in all respects is the enabler of e-negotiations.

E-negotiations offer certain strategic advantages that do not exist in face-to-face negotiations, like the opportunity for in-depth intelligence and analysis before initiating the actual communication. They also allow for more reflection during the process as time in most cases is not of direct influence. These aspects of present day negotiations, combined with the fact that negotiation behavior can often be deduced by the strategy used, offer great opportunities for solutions that can be quite rewarding and lasting.

5.1 The Negotiation Environment

Each negotiation takes place in an environment formed by the different parties, their interests, the power dynamics between them, and the barriers imposed, such as ethical considerations. Identifying the parties in a negotiation might seem self-evident, but often it is not. Influential players might be involved that are not visible at the negotiation table and their presence can redefine the whole endeavor. With the exception of videoconferencing, this is probably the norm in e-negotiations due to the absence of visible cues. With this in mind, it's best to shape a productive environment that will provide creative solutions instead of simply reacting to whatever deals happen to arise.

Many times, also, interests are not self-evident. Although financial/ monetary gains might be easy to identify, there might be other opportunities of increased utility like long-term capital appreciation that might be worth exploring. Keeping an open mind frame and structuring your approach appropriately, a deal might open up more opportunities to increase earnings. Failure to see behind the façade of a counterpart and reveal their true interests might reflect lack of insight and unwillingness to think outside the box. It could also be a by-product of the negotiator's fear of being exploited if they reveal their interests, so they might prefer to close up and lose opportunities to maximize the potential value of a deal. This can even reach the extreme of dropping off the negotiations and losing the deal.

Physical and psychological barriers often arise in negotiations. Identifying them and the means to overcome them is a key element of forming a negotiation strategy. One such barrier is strategic behavior that can be expressed when negotiators overplay their hand. This might lead the other party to frustration and force them to walk away from a deal that could have benefited all. The same dynamic can be observed when there are value-creating opportunities. If the two parties hold a defensive position, it may be hard for either one of them to concede. If they are too friendly, they may forfeit mutual gains. If they concede too early, they might lose benefits.

Formulating a strategy is always situation dependent and one must weigh the benefits and risks of each tactic being considered. Drawing a firm line on what is acceptable may increase the chances of getting a fair deal, but involves the risk that your demand will exceed the other party's maximum offer. It's all about creating and claiming value. As we will see later on, another factor that influences negotiations is emotions. Perceived power and status can also influence negotiations. A sense of loss of control will always be there especially when the stakes are high. This might lead us to regard the other party as opponents that are standing in our way to something we need and deserve. As a result, our attitudes might be defensive and we might lose sight of the substantive objectives. We usually become aware of these issues as we mature and grow as negotiators. Self-awareness is probably the best assistance we can get in structuring and managing emotionally controlled negotiations.

Sometimes we might also face institutional barriers that, although more obvious than personal barriers, greatly influence negotiations. It might be organizational politics at play and certain parties within the organization might have personal benefits from the outcome of a particular deal. Overcoming organizational barriers might require drafting new policies, seeking management support, and lobbying on the part of the negotiator. One should be inquisitive enough to know the limits set and imposed by the organization and achieve maximum value within the restrictions set, without compromising personal integrity. While survival might be at stake in such situations, it might help to see restrictions (for want of better alternatives) as opportunities for breakthrough and radical transformation that will elevate an organization instead of repressing its growth.

5.1.1 THE TIME VARIABLE

Traditionally, negotiations took place in a geographical location at some point in time. Both location and time can influence the negotiation outcome. From the perspective of this book, "place" is the e-negotiations environment as mediated by technology and will be discussed in detail in the next chapter. Time is the prime architectural feature of negotiations, whether it is seen as the instance at which the negotiations take place or as the duration of the process. Time can be a great source of power if expressed in terms of deadlines and ultimatums provided there is enough substance to support such strategies.

Setting deadlines can force people to reach agreements or retaliations that could escalate to wars. Whether reactions are expressed or not, people usually don't take well to this type of threat, particularly if there are many things at stake, like reputation, control, and status. Eventually, these tactics lead to misunderstandings because the dialog is limited to threat exchange and as a result the parties stop being creative and exploring alternatives that could bring agreement.

The timing of a negotiation might be perceived differently by each party. Whether the reasons for that are real or perceived, negotiations might be stalled or not even concluded simply because of factors we are unable to perceive. This doesn't necessarily mean that negotiations need to be abandoned or postponed. Instead it might be that a different approach needs to be adopted, like maybe an ongoing dialog without pushing for immediate agreement.

5.2 Problem-solving and Decision-making Styles

Negotiation behavior is often described in terms of different strategies. The negotiation process involves a series of state changes resulting from the selection of strategies and movements, referred to as the "negotiation dance." The negotiation outcomes include the final agreement and how satisfied or confident the negotiators are with the result and with their own performance.

Negotiation strategies are formulated based on negotiators' perspectives and objectives. The participating members need to evaluate their interests and those of their opponents to gain a realistic perspective of the situation they are in and the issues they need to address. According to the emphasis they place, strategies can be proposed. One such strategy is the *contending strategy* where the negotiators are primarily concerned with their own gains and to a lesser extent with those of their counterparts. These negotiators in general tend to have high aspiration levels and tend to make fewer concessions. They also tend to make a competitive stance toward the negotiation process, leading to "win-lose" agreements. Another strategy is the *problem-solving* strategy where the negotiators see both parties as trying to solve a common problem. In such cases, negotiators consider the other side's positions and perceptions as variables of the same equation and try to find solutions that satisfy most of the objectives.

The way each individual thinks and formulates their strategy is always unique and, as we saw in the previous chapter, is shaped by a combination of inherited and developmental traits that have been formulated under the influence of their past and present environments. This is evident, for example, when one compares an individual's way of approaching negotiations, planning a strategy, and making decisions with that of team-based decision making. Extremes like teams with strong and authoritarian leaders that dominate decision making in negotiations can be observed. This might be the case of Western negotiating teams while the opposite might be true for Oriental teams. US leaders, for example, tend to make decisions on their own and accept all responsibility for the outcome of a negotiation while Japanese leaders will try and ensure team consensus before committing to a deal. The first approach can be quite fast and risky as it is based on one person's perspective and experience while the second takes longer, but is more rational from the point of view of reflecting on the perspectives of more and diverse experts. This understanding, combined with knowledge of the stereotypes of each culture, can help negotiators adapt their strategy to reflect the underlying priorities and attitudes of their counterparts. The US leaders, for example, consider it quite natural to change their mind and follow another strategy to counter obstacles (in fact it's considered to reflect flexibility), while the Japanese will consider it shameful to change their mind once a decision is made.

Two cognitive approaches to decision making are generally observed in negotiations. One is a deductive approach where a top-down process is followed and the negotiators present the maximum benefits if all the conditions are accepted by the other side, and the other is the inductive approach where negotiators present the minimum allowed value that can further be increased if additional conditions are met. In simple terms, the first approach is where you present and promote the greater picture from the beginning while in the latter approach you present the most conservative gains first and expand to greater payoffs later.

The purpose of negotiators is primarily converging interests and this can be ultimately seen in cases of conflict management. The early perspective on conflict management through negotiations was defined by two orientations: cooperation and competition. In a cooperative orientation, a negotiator is concerned about his self-benefit, but also the benefit of others, whereas a competitive orientation only involves self-benefit. Cooperative negotiators feel friendlier to the negotiation process and more satisfied with the outcome of their negotiation process while competitive ones push more by proposing more offers while providing fewer messages. This can also be an indication that the negotiator is less in control. These two orientations play a particularly important role in negotiations in that they provide the basis for the best approaches to use.

An interesting question is whether a negotiator has only one orientation or a mixture of two or more. Some consider negotiators to be either cooperative or competitive, whereas others believe that negotiators can exhibit a mixture of these two orientations. This led to a dual-concerns model being proposed, in which five strategies—*distributing, avoiding, accommodating, integrating,* and *compromising*—are proposed, based on the degree of concern about one's own outcome and that of others. Another four proposed strategies—*exploiter, competitor, yielder,* and *cooperator*—are based on whether the orientation of oneself and the expected counterpart's orientation are competitive or cooperative.

5.2.1 BATNAS AND ZOPAS

The limits or allowances of the parties in negotiations is important and is usually expressed through their BATNA (Best Alternative To Negotiated Agreement). Many times this is also viewed as the bargaining power of negotiators. Although this can be misleading because it isolates the negotiation from the rest of the organizational and business environment, it could be considered as a power form at the beginning of an analysis.

The concept of BATNA poses challenges that often make its application difficult. BATNAs should be seen more as preferred courses of action to be followed if no other sources of information exist that could lead to better alternatives. It is not a bottom line and it should always carry a value with it. So effectively, one should look at a BATNA as some sort of benchmark that we use to compare alternatives. Other factors, tangible or intangible, could be, in effect, like time pressure, relationships, risk tolerance and insights about the other side. By contrast, a rigid BATNA can be dangerous in that it can be seen as the goal of the negotiation thus discouraging the negotiator to look for better alternatives that could bring more. Also it tends to narrow the negotiator's view to look at the deal only in terms of money and ignore other aspects that could add more value and lead to more creative solutions.

Assessing both party options involves both science and art. While science, as we will see later, lies in specifying all plausible alternatives and rating them according to their value, art lies in imagining creative alternatives and weighing their relative value. No matter what our personal traits might be (optimistic or pessimistic), one should always consider the perceived BATNAs of both parties if we are to deduce whether an agreement is possible and how much room for bargaining is available.

In reality, any efforts to identify BATNAs will lead to a bargaining range that is called the "zone of possible agreement," or ZOPA for short. Any price within this range will leave a gain to both parties and would lead to a deal. Unfortunately, in real life neither party can be sure of the other party's perceived BATNA and ZOPA, otherwise they would split the difference and close the deal. Additionally, we rarely have single-issue negotiations, so precise calculations of the previous variables are difficult to make. Although general market conditions may provide some clues, one should take into account the behavior of the other party as it evolves through the negotiation process. The pattern of offers and concessions along with the level of interest in making the deal should be considered, regardless of how subjective this might be.

BATNAs can be used as a defensive mechanism as much as an offensive one. A negotiation strategy might be to exert force by attacking the other party's BATNA. In this case, instead of making an offer attractive, we can make it look bad for the other side by refusing it or putting it down. Although this can be a dangerous and uncertain approach, it is not unusual in negotiations. Lawsuits are primarily based on this approach to bring people to the negotiating table. When using BATNAs defensively, you need to make sure the other party is convinced you are really prepared to walk away if your BATNA is jeopardized. When there is leverage holding your ground, then displaying an "infinite" stubbornness can sometimes get the desired result. Displaying persistence and perseverance can send the message across that you can wait forever to get what you want—a luxury the other side might not be able to afford.

Key negotiation lessons include:

- It is possible to reach agreements that create gains for both parties;

- Gains do not have to be evenly divided;

- Introducing alternatives and new variables is part of the negotiation process.

Negotiations shouldn't be viewed as either win-win situations or as gains against the other party. It is best if they are viewed as creating and claiming value since then the focus is on the pie and not on the people that will eat it. Creating value usually requires innovative approaches to problem solving that can come from brainstorming and the right atmosphere to nurture it. This should be carefully displayed as such disclosure may be exploited, particularly if it is about one's needs or the lack of good alternatives. By establishing the right problem-solving atmosphere, parties can identify all the variables and parameters involved and affected in order to develop proposals that maximize profit. An interesting point to remember is that differences can sometimes add more value than commonalities. They usually lead to exploring more options and ending with better solutions.

5.2.2 INTERESTS STRATEGY

Positions are the visible parts of negotiations while interests are their hidden aspects. Focusing on interests might be quite a successful strategy if one is clear about the interests of both parties, and in many cases might work as a catalyst for success. This approach assumes that parties are cooperators in solving a common problem instead of competitors looking for wins and losses. This is more motivational as everyone is focusing on solutions that result in gains, so implementing the negotiation is the aim of everyone involved.

Sharing interests is of primary importance as they will become common ground for argumentation and concessions. In this process, the interests are assigned weights based on their importance and become variables of the problem. Finding a solution is like solving an equation whose variables are the interests and their importance are the constraints on those variables. Since both sides are going to work toward finding a solution, the actual conflict is in establishing and accepting the level of significance of the various interests. An important point to make here is that although this is a synergetic strategy, in order for it to succeed, parties need to allow for flexibilities in their interests to make the problem solvable and keep a deal on track. In addition, allowances that could in the future provide gains should be considered as long-term objectives that might be quite appealing and beneficial.

5.2.3 EMOTIONS IN NEGOTIATION STRATEGIES

Emotions can be considered as relatively short-lived expressions that we use to respond to events and situations in our environment that make an impact on our senses and perception. Using positive and negative emotions in negotiations can drastically influence their outcome. This can be achieved by interpersonal means where one negotiator influences the other; and intrapersonal means where our emotions impact our behavior. Interpersonally positive emotions allow the buildup of trust as one person confesses to another by displaying appropriate emotions while also promoting a receptive atmosphere for creative solutions to surface and result in win-win situations. On the other hand, displaying negative emotions, especially at the beginning of negotiations, can limit the opportunity for beneficial solutions for all parties involved and decrease the chances of success. In addition, this can severely damage relationships, resulting in an unwillingness to participate further in the negotiation process.

When displaying emotions, we trigger complementary or reciprocal emotions in our counterparts, establishing in this way a kind of social communication that supplements language. Displaying anger, for example, might trigger a *fight or flight* response in another person. Which one will prevail has to do with the way the other person perceives the situation and the skills and experience they have in dealing with similar situations. From the strategy point of view, one has to be quite sure what gets triggered in order to influence appropriately and in a controlled way. Looking at another example, being cheerful in some cases can induce happiness and sympathy, while in others it can be seen as a lack of seriousness and lack of appreciation for the subject and process.

Another concern with displaying emotions is that it positions us with respect to our outlook on a situation. This can serve as an incentive or a deterrent that invites the other party to express certain behavior. For example, displaying negative emotions like anger can be a strategy to add value to our position, especially when the other party is negotiating from a weaker position. In many cases, it's safe to assume that emotional states can affect and even predict negotiation outcomes, so an appropriate emotional strategy can influence information processing and help manipulate the situation to achieve the strategic objectives set by negotiators.

The goal of emotional strategies is always to increase the overall satisfaction of one of the parties, measured as the sum of the value of a deal plus the emotional charge associated with the process. If we place this in the form of a mathematical formula it would look like:

Total Value = Objective Value + Emotional Value

Presuming the objective value has been clearly defined, the emotional value is quite subjective, and includes elements of satisfaction level and perceived deception. Satisfaction might include commitment due to time pressure, conflict avoidance, and the negotiation process. A lot of times there are many issues on the negotiation table that pressure a negotiator to accept a deal in order to address remaining issues. Some other times, conflict-averse negotiator personalities can lead them to accept inferior deals and in other cases still, a timely and properly scheduled process might positively predispose someone to attend and accept a deal.

Another concept worth mentioning here is perceived deception. This is a predominant strategy in card games like *poker* and can be seen many times in negotiations. It includes bluffing, lying with a purpose to mislead, and partial acceptance of a deal. Historically, humans have been involved in give-and-take situations, especially in commercial settings where in many cases unethical or unlawful behavior has been displayed. In some cultures this can even be considered part of their tradition, so one should always consider the possibility of deceptive behavior, especially in first-time instances where not a lot of information is available on the parties involved. This is a major concern in online negotiations where our skills in assessing a person are at a disadvantage due to the lack of visible ques.

E-negotiations might seem unsuitable for emotional strategies primarily due to their asynchronous nature (except videoconferencing of course) and lack of visible ques, but can nevertheless be used for emotional strategies, although to a limited extent. These might include expressions of politeness, informal requests, praises, flattery, threats, purposeful time delays, and restrained communication, to name a few. These can be intentional or unintentional such as in the case of spelling mistakes and insufficient use of language. Proper exploitation of the advantages offered by online negotiation will definitely lead to better communication and eventually more satisfying deals (see next chapter).

5.2.4 APPRECIATIVE MOVES

For many negotiators, building a relationship with opposing parties is of primary importance. A great part of building relations, especially when negotiations are in effect, is to display appreciation. This type of tactical move helps break defensive and offensive cycles, that can cause one side to resist or raise obstacles because that leads them to become cornered and isolated.

Appreciative moves explicitly build trust and encourage the other side to participate in the process. Not only do these reduce the adversarial atmosphere, they also hold the promise for productive future cooperation. It is a sign of respect for the other person that will only contribute positively to changing their perception and feelings about the process.

Open communication is very important for overcoming differences and appreciative moves remove personal discord and allow different points of view to surface and become a true measure of the differences. It also allows opportunities for additional information to come to the surface and affords the other side more time to rethink the proposal and adjust their offerings. Frequently, it becomes apparent that the issue at hand might be a symptom and not the cause of the differences. A deeper understanding on behalf of both parties will then lead to the root of the problem and the actual issue that needs to be resolved.

5.3 Power Schemes

In many negotiations, the issues at hand are well understood and the participants have more or less an understanding of their negotiating power. It is more or less evident who holds a more powerful position and who the real players are. This knowledge predisposes someone to certain attitudes and behavior that can influence the outcome of a negotiation in either positive or negative directions.

5.3.1 NEGOTIATING FROM BELOW

There are times when we are faced with negotiations (especially informal ones) where the other party has no real need to negotiate. These types of situations are common in workplaces where we have to negotiate with superiors that have no gain from the issue we are raising. Since there might be no apparent advantage in negotiating for the other parties, they tend to avoid responding to messages, postpone meetings or, if they do take place, the subject gets diluted and doesn't get addressed; or even worse, ideas and suggestions get ignored or overruled, and demands dismissed.

This type of behavior is a natural part of the negotiation process and the issue will only be addressed if there is something desirable for the other party to gain. The primary objective in such cases is to foster the perception (create the "illusion" if you have to) that there are mutual gains from the negotiation. Emphasis should be given to provide the right incentives that will emphasize the proposed value to the other person and if these don't work then alliances should be sought that could exert additional pressure for the other party to actively participate in the negotiation.

5.3.2 NEGOTIATING FROM ABOVE

Regardless of how high up a negotiator is in an organization, it is not always desirable to enforce solutions especially to subordinates by the sheer force of their positions. By working behind the scenes, such negotiators can build support for their positions and ensure consensus before a formal process begins. This will create momentum behind an agenda by bringing others in line with the proposed deal. Growing support will also isolate opposition to the deal and create a groupthink environment in support of the proposed plan. It is easier and more efficient to create the impression that participants are contributors to an idea instead of enforcing it. In addition, it relieves the negotiator/supervisor from using their position to dictate terms thus allowing the wider adoption of a deal.

5.3.3 NEGOTIATING UNDER THE SUPERVISOR'S EYE

Negotiators are rarely on their own when working on a deal: they are usually part of or representatives of organizations with some kind of hierarchical structure. This implies that they are accountable to someone in the organization that acts as a supervisor or evaluator. This in itself is enough to create some kind of performance anxiety that negotiators should be aware of. Organizational politics might be very influential whether the negotiator is aware of it or not. Many times there is a bigger "game" being played and the negotiation that's taking place might just be a strategic move with completely different objectives than the negotiation itself. It might be that the negotiation is just an intimidation tool for something else that the management is working on that might not even involve the party we are negotiating with. This makes it extremely difficult for the negotiator unless they have inside knowledge of what is going on.

In case we don't know or cannot imagine the game being played, but we suspect something might be going on, the best approach is to just act as professional as possible without sacrificing personal connections that we might have committed to the process. Feeling like a pawn can be very uncomfortable and a threat to someone's personality, but the truth of the matter is that businesses rarely act in good faith and good intention. We shouldn't forget that the very essence of competition in the business world is survival of the "fittest" and elimination of the "weakest." Executives need to back up their vision of a negotiation with actions that have an impact at the negotiating table.

5.4 Strategic Process and Guidelines

While process moves do not directly concern the negotiation issue, they directly affect the way these issues will be heard and perceived and thus influence outcome. Some general tips for handling the negotiation process are summarized here.

I. PREPARE THE AGENDA

Negotiations actually begin from the moment any one of the parties starts manipulating the process, long before the various parties come together physically or online. For example, organizing the agenda and the way people will be heard and ideas presented can exert strong influence and affect the receptivity of the proposal we want to promote.

Although manipulating the agenda to one's benefit might sound Machiavellian, it is a standard practice in the world of business (and politics of course) and negotiators should master the skill early enough in their career. Negotiators can engineer the agenda so as to frame the subsequent discussion to support their proposal before positions become fixed in the opponent's mind.

II. PRE-NEGOTIATIONS PHASE

A good step in the direction of subliminally influencing the negotiation is to plan seed ideas early. Sometimes parties might ignore certain comments, or even people, for whatever the reason might be. Being ignored doesn't have to be a relationship of our low participation or strength of negotiating. It could also be that your opponents were caught off-guard and their behavior is just a defence mechanism. Negotiators, like most people anyway, tend to reduce their attention span whenever something looks or sounds familiar.

Warm up the atmosphere, but don't overdo it. You want the negotiation issue to be the main discussion issue and nothing else. When you sense that the other side is drifting, that could only mean they are not so interested or they know exactly what they want and they are not willing to bargain. In such a case, it's best to state your position as early as possible and consider the negotiations closed at that point. You can get back later to close the communication by which time it is most likely that you will get an appropriate reaction. Any efforts in between to address the issue directly will only be perceived as your intention to compromise.

If an offer (even an extreme one) is made very early in the process, it is usually a good sign that the other party intends to leave with a deal, so they want to have enough time to bargain. It's also an indication of multi-objective negotiations, meaning they will bring more to the negotiating table. In such cases, one traditionally starts with open-ended questions and statements and proceeds with closed ones toward the end to narrow the deal and clarify gains.

III. STATE YOUR PROPOSAL CLEARLY

Frequently communicate agreement to whatever level it has been achieved as this defines the intersection of interests and allows for a clear realization of the differences. In addition, emphasizing agreement becomes the basis for creative problem solving.

Allow ample time for your opponents to process and comprehend the material you presented to them. Not everyone makes decisions quickly or progresses at the same speed, and sometimes people need time and help to see beyond their initial ideas or biases. Given time to analyze the issues, they may eventually modify their position and be more receptive to your proposals. As long as there is ongoing communication and the other party isn't forced or brought to a pre-emptive conclusion, there is always a chance the opposing party's resistance will fade and a beneficial settlement will be achieved.

IV. CHANGE IN PERSPECTIVE

Many times negotiators get trapped in their own views and this might be the greater barrier to overcome in a negotiation. The reason for this is that it's more comfortable and less time- and energy-consuming to become enamored with our opinions than make the effort to see the issue from a different perspective. Our own viewpoint might be the road block to a successful resolution since we become stuck with the notion that we are right and the other side is wrong. The human brain is an expert at building rationales and supporting arguments for any stand we might want to take. To avoid this detrimental situation, it is imperative that we keep an open mind frame and allow ourselves the belief that more efficient solutions might be possible. The same assumptions should also be made for the other party since we can only speculate on what the other party's agenda might be.

V. HELP YOUR OPPONENT SAVE FACE?

Image is important to any professional and for negotiators counts as much as the particulars of an agreement. It captures the perceptions others have about us and the qualities we want them to see in us. This can be a positive or a negative influencing factor in negotiations and can be part of our strategy at the negotiating table. If you are dealing with a career negotiator then their image is of great importance to them and it will affect the way they negotiate. If they don't hold a position of power then you can anticipate fierce competition since, to them, "losing" the negotiation might impact their image and subsequently their professional progression. In such a case, it's good if you take the extra effort to help them save face as much as possible since that will be a good investment for the future. It is always better to have allies than foes and the investment you make in preserving the opponent's "face" might reward you in the future. This can be of great importance in cross-cultural negotiations, especially with some Asian countries (like Japan and China) where saving face is a social characteristic and valued immensely.

If your counterparts hold a position of power then you should be extremely careful and plan your moves very carefully because it is unlikely they will make serious concessions unless the alternatives you present are really attractive. In case the positions seem of equal power, it helps to consider the worst case scenario, that is, that the other side has the upper hand.

Experienced negotiators and superiors are not the only ones that value face. Subordinates and team members are also affected by it. Team members are affected by the "weakest" link in the team so it becomes important to preserve a "team" face of high value because it will be reflected in all. Subordinates also benefit from feeling respected since they can be more forthcoming to reporting problems and providing creative solutions.

VI. WALKING AWAY FROM THE DEAL

Many times negotiators believe that their success hinges on their ability to close deals and that failing to close a deal will be considered a personal failure that will also damage the organization they represent. Although a significant amount of time and money might have already been dedicated to a negotiation, closing a bad deal might be much worse than having no deal at all. The best thing in such a case might be to go back to the drawing table regardless of how well prepared the negotiator and his organization was to make the deal. If a lot of work and effort has been dedicated to a negotiation and nothing came out of it, it might give the impression that there is nothing more to be done. This kind of thinking often puts a negotiator in a box and throws the process into a cycle of concessions that allows the other side to control the process and lead the deal.

To get out of the box one should always keep in mind all alternatives available to them. Negotiation results can be greatly improved by keeping BATNA in mind and always evaluate each proposal against that alternative. If the negotiated agreement is better than your BATNA, consider closing the deal unless you believe there is more to get without risking the existing deal. If the agreement is worse than your BATNA, set the ground for potential comeback, ensure minimum damage to any relationships you might have with the opposing party, and walk away. The BATNA approach has a big influence on negotiation strategies. It is no longer an issue of producing agreement, but rather a decision-making process that leads to making good or bad decisions. From that perspective, rejecting a deal because it falls below the acceptable BATNA is a good decision.

If there is a case where no obvious alternative to a deal exists, the negotiators and the organizations they represent need to think about creating one. Walking into a negotiation without a BATNA is negotiating from a position of weakness. Companies should ensure BATNA evaluations become an explicit step in the negotiation process, requiring, for example, that negotiators discuss with their managers how each alternative compares to their BATNA, otherwise they risk making the assumption that BATNAs are lines they cannot cross.

VII. CLOSING THE NEGOTIATION

Strategizing for the closure of a negotiation is as important as the initiation process because it is a safeguarding of everything that took place and the deal that was reached during the process. Many deals collapse at the end because negotiators were too focused on the other stages and badly prepared for the closing stage. It's worth remembering that a deal is valid only when official acceptances are exchanged. The most important aspect of a closure to remember is that it is all about trust and reassuring confidence.

Some tips to help the closing stage include:

- Don't show anxiety because it might be perceived that you are hiding something in which case your counterpart might ask for more time to re-examine the deal;

- Don't look desperate because your counterpart might think there is more to get from you;

- Don't pressure your counterpart as they might express resistance unless you know they have no other option but to accept your offer;

- Make sure you address outstanding issues;

- Reaffirm the agreement and its individual points;

- Try to have the agreement in writing; this adds clarity and rigidity to what has been agreed.

5.5 Formal Methods of Decision Analysis

Rules of thumb, intuition and experience might not be enough for someone to comprehend the multiple dimensions of negotiations today, making the use of any techniques that theory can provide imperative for reaching successful outcomes. Decision analysis methods provide the theoretical background for quantitative support of negotiators and decision makers. The purpose of formal decision analysis is to select decisions from a set of possible options, especially in the case where uncertainties regarding the future exist. These uncertainties are usually expressed in terms of the probabilities of the various outcomes and our goal will be to optimize the resulting return or payoff in terms of some decision criterion.

Specialists in developing models usually focus on formalizing a problem and working analytically to develop mathematical models to describe it. Models allow understanding of a situation in terms of the variables affecting it and add predictive capabilities and visualization of outcomes. Developing a model is reaching a balance between reality and representation. Too analytical models tend to be difficult to understand and apply in negotiations, while too simplistic ones will be viewed as a waste of time for stating the obvious. The model that provides insight and can handle the most probable alternatives is what creates solutions and adds value to a negotiator.

The basic principle upon which models for decision analysis are built is that of a system. In the systems perspective, everything can be determined from its parts and their interaction with the environment. In terms of modeling, that means that models are assumed to be closed in that they inherently include or represent every possible solution that may exist. Although this might sound quite rigid and far from reality where situations change dynamically due to uncertainties in their parameters, for certain cases they become good approximations of reality.

For our purposes here we will consider two types of models: deterministic ones, where the value of a decision is completely judged by the outcome; and probabilistic ones where, in addition to outcomes, we have an amount of risk to consider for each decision. The two models are directly related to past and future experience, as in the first case we know exactly what happened, while in the latter we have to guess with some degree of uncertainty. The concept of probability is very important in real life situations since there is no such thing as complete knowledge of events, issues, and people involved. Of major concern in decision analysis, and something we should always be aware of, is the degree of reliability of our estimation and the probability distributions we use to represent situations, along with the fact that emotions can be involved in risky decisions.

Decision analysis is based on combining decision alternatives with possible future events in pictorial representations that make analysis and location of optimum solutions easy to identify and view. From the plethora of models applied in research and real life situations, we will present here simplified forms of three of the most popular and frequently used models. Payoff table analysis, decision trees and game theory have been extensively studied and used in negotiations and can be quite practical for situations with few alternatives and states of nature. A final method we will present as an alternative to the normative methods mentioned before is simulations.

5.5.1 PAYOFF TABLE ANALYSIS

Payoff tables represent situations as matrices of rows and columns. They are ideal when we are facing finite sets of discrete decision alternatives whose outcome is a function of a single future event. The rows of the matrix correspond to decision alternatives while the columns correspond to possible mutually exclusive future events (states of nature). They presume free choice of decision alternative and no control of future state. Figure 5.1 represents the payoff table (see book website) of an investment scenario. The numerical cells represent the payoffs (monetary gains or losses) of the decision alternatives (investment options in rows) with the states of nature (market trend in columns).

In cases where there is no knowledge of the probabilities of the states of nature, subjective criteria will influence the decision process. Decision-maker personalities can range from pessimistic to conservative to optimistic, influencing the strategy of approaching the decision problem and selecting an option. A pessimistic decision-maker usually expects the worst possible result no matter what decision is made, while an optimistic one feels that luck is always shining and whatever decision is made, the best possible outcome will occur. Somewhere in the middle, we find the conservative decision-maker that ensures a guaranteed minimum payoff regardless of which state of nature occurs. The reward is always a function of risk, so great rewards come with higher risk and one needs to balance what they need with what they can afford.

| PAYOFF TABLE | States of Nature | | | | |
Decision Alternatives	Large Rise	Small Rise	No Change	Small Fall	Large Fall
Gold	-100	100	200	300	0
Corporate Bonds	250	200	150	-100	-150
Growth Stock	500	250	100	-200	-600
C/D Account	60	60	60	60	60
Government Bonds	200	150	150	-200	-150

Figure 5.1   Payoff Table of an Investment Scenario

If some knowledge of the probabilities of the various states of nature exists, payoff table analysis can assure optimal decision in the long run because it takes into consideration every possible state of nature. The main drawback of payoff tables is that they attract attention to gains and neglect the decision-maker's attitude toward loss. A very useful technique to enhance the analysis is to combine it with Bayesian analysis and utility theory (see book website). Bayesian analysis uses sample information to aid decision making by fine tuning probability estimates while utility theory allows for utility values that reflect the decision-maker's perspective for each possible outcome.

5.5.2 DECISION TREES

A decision tree (Figure 5.2) is a sequential representation of all possible events involved in a scenario. It uses combinations of decision and states nodes to represent decision alternatives and their outcomes. Decision nodes (represented by square shapes) are the available alternatives to a decision-maker at each stage of a decision, while states of nature (represented by circles) are the possible natural events that can happen following a decision. The latter is expressed in terms of probabilities for each possible outcome.

Traversing the tree we get to leaves that represent the expected payoffs of each branch. The tree of Figure 5.2 represents a situation (see book website) where a decision needs to be made to purchase land. Dark shaded leaves represent profit branches while the rest represent losses. A critical path can be found based on the degree of risk we want to take.

The formalism of decision trees is very powerful in situations with clear objectives and predetermined states of nature. The disadvantage of using them stems from our inability to assign realistic probabilities for future events. In addition, the more complicated a situation, the more branches we need to represent it realistically, making detection of the optimum path difficult.

5.5.3 GAME THEORY

Many negotiation situations are *zero-sum* transactions, meaning that whatever one party gains, the other loses. Such cases are ideal for applying game theory to determine the optimal decision. The payoffs here are based on the actions taken by competing individuals who are seeking to maximize their return. From that perspective, decision theory can be viewed as a special case of game theory in which we play against nature.

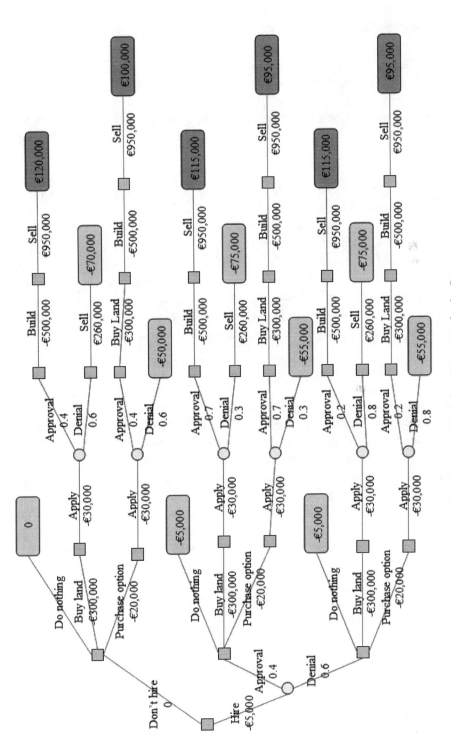

Figure 5.2   Decision Tree Analysis Case

Parameters taken into consideration when applying game theory include:

- Number of players—we can have situations with two players, like in a game of chess or many players like in a game of poker;

- Total return—it can be a zero sum game like poker among friends and non-zero sum game like poker in a casino where the "house" takes a cut;

- Player turns—it could be sequential where each player takes a turn that affects the states of nature like *monopoly* or simultaneous where each state of nature is defined after all players declare their moves like in *paper-rock-scissors*.

Figure 5.3 shows the situation where two supermarkets compete in certain food categories. The table shows the gains of one against the other based on what promotion strategy each one chooses. The objective here is to find the best strategy that will ensure gains in the long run and across many categories.

5.5.4 SIMULATIONS

Simulations are nothing more than artificial imitations of reality (in our case with the use of computers). They are descriptive techniques that negotiators use to conduct experiments when a problem is too complex to be treated with normative methods, like the ones presented before, and also lacks an analytic representation that would allow numerical optimization approaches. Simulations require a proper definition of the problem, the development of a suitable model, the validation of the model, and finally the design of the experiment. By running the simulation many times (performing lots of trials), we will be able to see prevalent patterns that lead to optimal behavior.

		AB's Emphasis			
		Meat	Produce	Groceries	Bakery
MP's Emphasis	Meat	2	2	-8	6
	Produce	-2	0	6	-4
	Grocery	2	-7	1	-3

Figure 5.3   Gains of Competing Strategies

In practice, there are different types of simulations:

- Probabilistic simulations—can be applied for discrete or continuous probability distributions;

- Time-dependent and time-independent;

- Object-oriented simulations—different entities are represented with properties and behaviors;

- Visual simulations.

A critical part of simulation experiments is the implementation of a realistic random event generator. Randomness is quite difficult to achieve artificially even when events are equally likely. In practice, we use software that uses algorithms to produce what we call *pseudorandom* events/numbers. For most purposes, pseudorandom values are good enough because they are virtually indistinguishable from truly random numbers.

The main advantages of using simulations include:

- The theory is fairly straightforward;

- A great amount of *time compression* can be attained;

- A manager can experiment with different alternatives;

- The builder must constantly interact with the manager;

- The model is built from the manager's perspective;

- The simulation model is built for one particular problem;

- They can handle an extremely wide variety of problem types;

- They can include the real complexities of problems;

- They automatically produce many important performance measures;

- They can readily handle relatively unstructured problems.

Disadvantages include:

- An optimal solution cannot be guaranteed;

- Simulation model construction can be a slow and costly process;

- Solutions and inferences from a simulation study are usually not transferable to other problems;

- Simulation is sometimes so easy to explain to managers that analytic methods are often overlooked;

- Simulation software sometimes requires special skills and support.

5.6 Concluding Remarks

Effective negotiation requires a coherent framework linking means to ends. Identifying the fundamental interests and limits of all the parties and assigning values to them is a very important step. Careful negotiation analysis is also important to identify possible barriers to agreement, as well as structural elements that might be optimally rearranged to provide insight and gains during the negotiation process. All these may additionally reveal important moral and ethical issues as well.

A progressive shift from a situational to an institutional view of negotiations may represent a radical change that organizations need to seriously consider in the "information era" in which we live. This will directly impact how negotiators conduct themselves and force radical changes in the way they perceive negotiations. A carefully planned strategy with emphasis in communicating the rationale and benefits of the new approach might be all that is needed. As long as the overhead created by a formal approach to negotiators doesn't overload them, distracts them from their work, or alters their behavior, radically organizational success in that issue is almost certain.

E-negotiations by their very nature lend themselves to such change in mind frames since they free organizational resources related to face-to-face negotiations. In addition, a lot of the formalities that might be required in the form of reporting might be easier to make since everything is more or less in some form of documentation already. In the online world it is a lot easier to provide support to negotiators in the form of case studies and training that the negotiators can customize to their own individual needs. Based on the personal and professional "age" of their workforce, organizations should observe a gain in productivity by institutionalizing negotiations. With more effective and creative negotiators, companies will reap the benefits of closer and more rewarding relationships with suppliers, customers, and their partners.

Negotiation analysis can give valuable insight into the process and, with the use of rigorous academic disciplines from game theory and decision analysis to cognitive and social psychology, can greatly assist a negotiator in preparing and achieving beneficial outcomes. Through formal study and reflection of their own experience and that of others, negotiators can develop their own framework that will allow them to craft innovative negotiation strategies to achieve their goals.

6

Communication

The communication aspect of negotiations involves the exchange of information and offers in ways that convey the intentions of the participants. Communication always involves a sender, a receiver, and a medium through which information is exchanged. It is an open system in the sense that everybody involved is affected by the *environment* which interferes with the exchange process and imposes some sort of "noise" leading to disturbances in the messages. We have seen a special type of noise in previous chapters, the "cultural noise."

Given that communication is actually the implementation phase of negotiations where strategies are transformed into actions, we made a conscious effort to include a heavy section of tips and practical hints in this chapter that are more applied than theoretical. There are a lot of theories out there on how one should translate a strategy into an action plan, but the truth of the matter is that each situation is unique, if not in the details, at least in the place and time that takes place. Regardless all the planning and preparation when the negotiations start, it might be the little details and a lot of common sense that will win the other side over. Social theories anyway are nothing more than averages of situations of high-frequency events and unlike the physical sciences the exceptions are the ones that prove the rule. One should be prepared for both the rule and the exception.

6.1 Communication Tools

In order to get a message across, people generally use their whole body. This is done by using language (oral or print), paralanguage and body language.

6.1.1 LANGUAGE

Language is a system of symbols that represent objects and ideas of the physical and spiritual worlds. It is also an activity and communication framework that creates shared meanings between people. Languages have been evolved by individual groups to address their needs and describe the environment within which they function. The diversity of languages observed (around 6,000 of them) is a direct consequence of the environments (physical and social) that humans occupy on Earth. As a result of this diversity, cultures have developed expressions that, while communicating meaning, defy logic and a common frame of reference: for example, the sentence "The object of this observation is this object" references the word "object" with two different meanings. Other cases include oxymoron expressions, double negatives and positives, as some of the following indicate:

- "act naturally"

- "good grief"

- "nothing better"

- "clearly misunderstood"

- "I don't want anything"

- "I did nothing"

- "yeah, right"

Trying to make a literal interpretation in many languages will lead to confusion.

Language comes in two forms: written and spoken. Spoken language is universally transmitted through a sequence of sounds specific to each culture, while the written form is through specific symbols laid out in a certain direction by specific syntax. In current day negotiations, especially in cross-cultural settings, English is the primary language of communication. Although the advantage of using a common language like English is obvious, there are nevertheless subtle issues that can cause trouble even in English-speaking societies that live apart. To quote an example of differences in interpretation, consider the word "prototype" as used in business. Prototypes in the US are usually considered for evaluation of product designs during development, while in Germany they are used to establish product requirements. This might cause confusion on cross-national teams working on the same projects as they might be pursuing different outcomes.

No matter how strong bilingualism might be in a person, it is only natural that the birth language or the everyday language used in the working environment will be the prevalent one. Using the negotiation language might be an extra effort that will be imposed on the organization and the negotiators. Fluency doesn't mean native, and that means language might be an advantage for some and a disadvantage for others. Extra effort might be needed to compose business-sensitive emails in the negotiation language. This cannot be avoided so one better come to terms with it and also acknowledge that issue on the other side and be extra patient if necessary.

While human beings have developed a plethora of languages, the laying out in written form has generally been expressed in one of two ways:

- Horizontal
  - Left to right as in most Western languages
  - Right to left as in Arabic and Hebrew
- Vertical—always from top to bottom as in Chinese, Japanese and Korean

The impact of these differences can be significant in many ways. Consider the following pictorial description of the function of a washing machine (Figure 6.1). How do you interpret it when looking from left to right and how you would interpret it when looking from right to left? Based on the viewing sequence, the left to right direction that a Westerner uses clearly describes a washing machines as machines that stain clothes instead of cleaning them, while to an Arab it will make perfect sense. Similarly, what button will a right-to-left reader assume is the fast-forward in the QuickTime screenshot of Figure 6.2? What about the information we would present in a browser? Do you put the menus on the left side or the right side according to your audience, or how do you accommodate for top-to-bottom styles? How about when adjusting the browser window? Does the information get adjusted according to the viewer's language?

Figure 6.1   Pictorial Description of the Function of a Washing Machine

Figure 6.2   Button Arrangement of QuickTime Player

All these questions might seem insignificant to people in Western cultures, but are important for other cultures and whether we admit it or not, we need to consider their potential impact on e-negotiations. In that respect, it doesn't hurt to accommodate our content and presentation accordingly, or at least allow the other side to absorb the material presented to them in the most efficient way for them. In any case, we should always be cautious about misunderstandings and go back and forth with clarifications as often as we can afford.

6.1.2 PARALANGUAGE

Paralanguage is the way we say something. It can include tone of voice, volume, and articulation, along with verbal and non-verbal emotional expressions. For example, "Yes" can sound like an agreement or a question depending on the way it is pronounced. Other paralanguage expressions include articulations like "... Hmmm" and "Uh-huh," that, along with tone variations, can indicate a variety of intentions and feelings. More familiar ones include laughing, crying, hissing, whistling, and so on. It is important to know here that paralanguage can be expressed consciously or unconsciously and that both ways say something about the person using it. Emphasizing certain words in a sentence can achieve a conscious alteration of meaning. The sentence "There was nothing we could do" transmits different meaning when we emphasize different parts like:

- "There was **nothing** we could do" to indicate desperation;

- "There was nothing **we** could do" to address helplessness;

- "There was nothing we could **do**" to give an inquisitive/questioning "flavor."

Other intentional physiological responses include:

- Clearing your throat when you want to stall or indicate trouble;

- Yawning to indicate boredom;

- Sighing to indicate relief;

- Cheering sounds to indicate enthusiasm and agreement.

A key factor when using media such as the telephone to conduct negotiations is the tone of voice we are using. It takes very few exchanges to figure out the attitude of participants. Monotone and flat voice with slow speed and low pitch tend to project boredom and a feeling of indifference in the communication. On the other hand, higher-pitched and empathic voice conveys enthusiasm and can positively affect negotiation outcomes. A helpful trick to affect inflections when talking over the phone is to smile while talking. Even though your counterparts won't be able to see that, smiling changes the physiology of your mouth in ways that make your voice fluid.

In e-negotiations, paralanguage expression is a function of the communication mode. In text-only communication, like email, we use font type, size, and decoration to emphasize or distinguish text with special meaning and reference. Another popular form of paralanguage (among young Web surfers primarily) is emoticons like ':)' (smiley face) to convey feelings and impressions and the use of exclamation points and apostrophes to indicate double meaning or titles.

6.1.3 BODY LANGUAGE

Body language is part of nonverbal communication and involves facial expressions, gestures, posture, proximity, touch, and eye contact. In extreme cases, like with deaf people, it can be the only way of communicating so its power and impact shouldn't go unnoticed. Body move when communicating helps alleviate stress and adds meaning to what we say. It's sort of a way for us to "decorate" our speech (like when we play with the font and decoration of our text) by animating aspects of it. Movement becomes unconscious to a great extent and is shaped by our personality traits, our cultural upbringing, and our experience. These unconscious parts of body movement are of interest to negotiators as they might reveal the true intentions and positions of their counterparts. While this might be taught to an extent, one should always be aware of the meanings of body language as it is situational dependent.

Consistent eye contact, for example, might sometimes reflect interest and positive inclination toward the speaker's positions while in other cases might indicate fear of attack from the speaker; so in an attempt to prevent and respond to it we focus our eyes on their eyes. In addition to the confusion with the multiple situational interpretations of body language, one should also be aware of the cultural interpretations of these signals as they might be quite the opposite. In India, for example, head tilting from left to right indicates agreement while in Western societies it is perceived as disagreement.

Some examples of feelings that might be communicated with body language and their associated body moves include:

- Defensiveness—arms folded on chest;

- Anger or antagonism—clutched jaw;

- Impatience—finger tapping;

- Boredom—elbow on desk, supporting head with your hand;

- Frustration—running fingers through hair;

- Doubtfulness—hand over mouth;

- Nervousness—picking fingernails;

- Disbelief—frowning;

- Agreement—nodding.

6.2 Communication Modes

In negotiations, communication modes affect the way information is received and interpreted. The different communication modes are usually analyzed in reference to the dimensions of *richness* and *interactivity*. Media richness is the capacity of the medium to transmit visual and verbal cues, thus providing more clues as to the meaning of the transmitted message; while interactivity is the potential of the medium to allow manipulation by the users and sustain a seamless flow of information between negotiators.

Interactivity can be further subdivided into a temporal dimension and a bandwidth dimension. The first one captures the synchronicity of interactions like taking turns to communicate, while the second has to do with the medium's ability to allow parallel processing of messages from multiple negotiators. All dimensions affect the way information is structured and perceived and the degree of its dependency on the medium for meaningful interpretation. In addition, these dimensions affect the negotiator's ability to decode messages and form a shared sense of understanding (called grounding) and a shared sense of participation in the communication process.

When we negotiate online, we lose the benefit of incoming nonverbal information like eye contact and handshakes that act as warm ups for civilized exchanges. This lack of communication signals impacts the faith and trust negotiators can have about the other party's intentions to honor the agreement, leading everyone to be extra cautious and reserved in their commitments and promises. If you suspect that a lack of trust is hampering the negotiation process, extra care should be taken to rebuild trust between the parties: that means that it might be best to deviate attention to the trust issue instead of the negotiation issue for a while until everybody feels comfortable enough trusting the other party so as to continue negotiating on the target issue. Focusing on each other's reputation might be a good way to rebuild trust and it is quite often used. In addition, the joint creation of ground rules may be a way to further the process and build trust in both the process and the parties.

6.2.1 SYNCHRONOUS AND ASYNCHRONOUS COMMUNICATION MODES

To date, research has targeted on comparing face-to-face negotiations with computer-mediated negotiations without distinguishing between the two communication modes available. We are talking here about synchronous and asynchronous negotiation modes. Also, the focus so far has been on outcomes, ignoring the process as a whole. Scientifically speaking and from the research point of view, the two parameters that have been considered are media efficacy and media richness. The former refers to the information processed per unit of time by the participants, whereas the latter means the measure of emotional and social context that occurs while communicating. These are always addressed in relation to the frequency and importance of each case. It is expected that in less important and trivial situations, high media richness could be counterproductive while critical situations might require immediate feedback and may be affected by variables that need to be communicated (like gender, race, status, and so on).

Synchronous technologies like chat, for example, have the characteristic that the communication takes place in real-time with the only delay imposed by the medium (technology). Asynchronous modes like email, for instance, do not impose the real-time feature and delays in the exchange of messages are expected. A summary of the advantages and disadvantages of the various modes as revealed by research follows:

Online Communication Mode Disadvantages	
Synchronous	*Asynchronous*
• Time pressure and the need for immediate reaction can cause spontaneous and unreflected emotional behavior. • Less time to consider alternatives and to reflect on and analyze the actual situation might result in suboptimal solutions. • Might lead to more competing and offensive behavior. • Information quality and depth is not very rich. • Demands specific communication behavior in terms of communication protocol and process coordination. • More susceptible to mistakes. • Requires parallel processing abilities since there is a lot of information exchanged concurrently.	• Difficult to corner the other side. • It allows the other side to reflect and develop a more efficient strategy against us. • It's not evident who the negotiator is and what kind of support they are getting. • Difficult to deduce the experience status or the depth of situational knowledge of the negotiator. • Requires more structured communication behavior in terms of form and text organization. • Time-consuming richer communication protocol elements (salutations, politeness, and so on) are needed to allow a tying in with previous and upcoming events and give the perception of continuity in time. • Statements can be taken out of context and used in future communications against us. • No ordering of communication exchanges is imposed in terms of time. Earlier emails might appear later.

Online Communication Mode Advantages	
Synchronous	**Asynchronous**
• Allows for more persuasive behavior and less exchange of private information. • Aggressiveness as a planned tactic might impose solutions on the less experienced/ weaker side. • Richer information exchange in terms of signals. • No need for re-integration between past and present—everything takes place in the present. • Time pressure forces negotiators to prepare better. • A lot of information is exchanged concurrently so a better picture can be formed earlier.	• Emerging emotions can be reflected and positively impact behavior. • More quality information might be exchanged since negotiators can devote more time to formulating their responses. • More alternatives might be presented and considered leading to more optimal solutions. • Time allows for simulation and formal analysis of the positions. • Lack of synchronicity might be a convenient and legitimate excuse if strategically used.

6.3 Communication Issues

Communication issues are particularly critical in situations where communication takes place synchronously and negotiators are caught in a dynamic of silencing or anarchy of messages. In such cases, decisions might be made without their input or their input might arrive too late to make a difference. In cases where there is an anarchy of messages, the best practice would be to distance ourselves temporarily to let the spirits die down and allow messages to settle chronologically and order themselves in terms of questions and answers or proposals and counterproposals. Silencing is far more difficult to handle especially in email communications because it is difficult to tell whether it is due to technical issues or part of a tactical move. In such cases, the best approach would be to send "gentle" reminders or enquiries about the status of the negotiation and follow up with other communication modes like placing a telephone call. Copying others might also help create some movement, but it has to be exercised with caution as it might expose our counterparts and trigger a more defensive reaction on their part.

6.3.1 CROSS-CULTURAL COMMUNICATION PROCESS

Effective cross-cultural communication requires that all parties listen carefully and ask questions to remove any ambiguity from the information exchanged and clarify the message conveyed. A critical issue that needs to be considered as we saw in the previous chapter is the proper display of emotions as this might influence negotiation outcomes.

Be aware of the differences in time zones. Some countries also take breaks during working days. In France, for example, it is not a good time to call someone during and after lunch time. Usually people are more focused and have more energy and patience during the earlier hours of their working days than later on. In addition, morning decisions tend to be followed on the same day while decisions made later on in the afternoons might not to be realized the next day. A negotiator must take these issues into consideration and act appropriately.

In addition, it helps to know whether vacations and holidays (including religious ones) are close by as they tend to set peoples' mind frames in vacation mode way ahead of time. This simply means that creativeness will deteriorate the closer we get to breaks from work. In some cases though, one might intentionally leave negotiations for later times especially if a lot of reflection will be required on the part of interested parties. The brain tends to settle during breaks from work and can better process information and come to resolutions. You will observe some times that negotiations take place in retreats where minimization of daily and routine interferences can be controlled.

Another factor that we mentioned in previous chapters that affects negotiations nowadays is the general adoption of English as the communication language. English and its related thought patterns have evolved from the Western-European cultural patterns and characterized by a linear and direct discourse. This is characterized by analytical and systematic problem solving that follows a step-by-step algorithmic kind of approach to solving problems, contrary to other cultures like the Asian one that are more people-oriented and have a more circular and indirect thought pattern and are primarily based on intuition. English, over the centuries, has absorbed many words from other languages (like Greek or Latin, for example) that enhanced its thought patterns to allow digressions from the principle linear discourse, enabling the discussion of several aspects of a problem concurrently.

6.4 Main Communication Mediums for E-negotiations

In all communication modes and mediums, one should capitalize on their advantages and be aware of their limitations. The correct choice and combination of communication modes could be a strategic decision and dependent on the issue at hand. Our focus here will be on e-negotiation modes that are frequently used and will be used in the near future like telephone and teleconference, videoconference and email, while briefly mentioning science fiction style modes like virtual reality, among others.

The basic communication mediums that we present here facilitate and can project some form of social cues (empathy). Their main advantage is that they overcome geographic distance and widely function irrespective of environmental factors (hot or cold, snow, rain, and so on).

General hints that work with all of them include, but are not limited to:

- *active listening and observing*—this is vital for understanding the messages that come across either as language, paralanguage and body language;

- *reflecting or summarizing*—this will help focus on the issues and progress made as it is understood by all parties involved; that common understanding will be the basis for reaching a resolution and moving on to the next steps;

- *asking questions*—this will clarify the content of the messages and eliminate any cultural or situational "noise"; it will reveal a lot about the other side's positions and intentions and allow our messages to go through as we intended.

6.4.1 VOICE- AND VIDEO-BASED

The main communication types we will analyze include teleconference and videoconference. Web-conferencing will also be mentioned as a variety of both of them. General characteristics of all mediums in this category are listed below.

Requirements:

- Access to telephone lines, preferably with conference call capacity;
- For mobile communication, an adequately charged device with good signal reception.

Advantages:

- High availability and ease of access globally;

- Real-time, synchronous communication;
- Immediate, but with reduced negative aspects like intimidation and violence.

Disadvantages:

- Relies on oral communication only; unable to impose print although one can record sessions. If mobiles are to be used, there are battery and reception limitations;
- Technical problems might inhibit communication.

When to use:

- Ideal as an initial ice-breaker;
- Very responsive medium in terms of clarifications and information exchange.

How to use:

- Make sure you have the appropriate phone number and find out if you are calling home or office since this makes a big difference in setting the mood. Home environments are more receptive and less confrontational than business settings. So, based on the issue at hand, one might intentionally choose one or the other. In such cases, make sure you have the home number since in many cultures (like Japanese, for example) they are not listed on business cards. Extreme caution is needed because in some cultures (like French), calling home on a business issue might be considered disrespectful and a violation of privacy. The good thing with today's technology is that it allows you to be sensitive to these issues and take advantage of opportunities as much as possible. If you are uncertain, an SMS stating your intention to call and a request for an appropriate time is much less invasive and will carry you a long way in building a relationship and achieving your goal. SMSs are subtle in the way they act on people. From one aspect, the receiver's, they are alerted to your presence with a minimum disturbance of their life style. From another, you get a clear but not rude feedback as to the other person's intentions. If they respond, you have been acknowledged. If not, then you still brought your issue to attention, but now you also know that the proper way to approach this person would be a more formal one. This information is valuable and has been achieved at minimal cost. Also the fact that you didn't insist will reflect positively on you, given the personality of your counterpart that obviously feels strongly about separating personal and professional life.

— When communicating over the phone, keep in mind that although you might be talking with one person, there could be more than one on the other side and your speaker might be receiving feedback in many ways. Unless you personally know the other person, it is a good practice to assume an audience of more than one. Another good assumption is that the other side is recording the conversation. Although this should require your consent, they might be doing it under the pretense of their policy which is probably stated somewhere in the "small print." It partly depends on how big the stakes are.

i. Teleconference

While the term is widely used for many forms of long-distance communication, we will use the term here as referring to multi-participant voice communication over telephone lines without video. This is usually done by having meeting participants connect through a localized telephone center (usually one of the participants has a call management system) and having an open and simultaneous communication with everybody connected. In addition to the general characteristics of all voice- and video-based mediums listed previously, this communication medium includes the following:

Requirements:

— Availability of compatible equipment (land line, microphone, speakers, and so on) and software;
— High quality/speed telecommunication lines.

Advantages:

— Location independence;
— Minimizes cost because it eliminates the need to travel;
— Requires little scheduling time;
— Flexible in terms of meeting time.

Disadvantages:

- Technical issues might impede connectivity or the quality of signals;
- Ineffective for creating a supportive atmosphere and for complex interpersonal communication.

When to use:

- Ideal for short communications to clarify issues, address concerns, or exchange information;
- When the issues are not critical and can be resolved fast;
- When you know and trust the other person well.

How to use:

- Send meeting-related materials well in advance so that all participants have plenty of time to go through them before the meeting time. This way a lot of time will be saved introducing the material in addition to allowing the participants to come prepared with clarifications and suggestions. The same should also be requested from everybody involved.
- If you are the one who initiates and organizes the meeting, send a request for agenda items when the meeting time is set and submit the meeting agenda a few days ahead of the meeting. Last minute items could be added before the meeting or at the beginning of it, but the main issues should be known to everybody way ahead of the meeting to avoid surprises as much as possible. If, in spite of all efforts, participants come with their own agenda in mind and bring up issues for discussion (intentionally or not) during the meeting that deviate from the original topics, you can politely ask that these issues be addressed in another meeting when everybody will have had the chance to prepare appropriately or at the end of the meeting if there is any time left.

ii. Videoconference

Issues covered in the teleconference section are also valid with videoconference. The main difference here is that in addition to sound, we have simultaneous two-way video transmission. Its primary function is to serve group communication instead of individual as it allows the display of multiple participants. A very popular form of videoconferencing nowadays for individuals with computers and Internet connections is the free service provided by Skype (http://www.skype.com).

Requirements:

- Availability of compatible equipment (cameras, microphone, speakers, and so on) and software;
- High Internet bandwidth connection.

Advantages:

- Approximates face-to-face communication;
- Sets a distance between participants (no violence other than emotional can exist);
- Allows demonstration and sharing of software applications like presentations, whiteboards, and so on.

Disadvantages:

- With the current state of technology, some aspects of communication may be lost or distorted during communication (blurring, signal delays that cause gaps in the conversation, and so on);
- Cost of the required technology (in terms of hardware, software and technical expertise) might be an issue;
- Eye contact is illusionary (actually damaging if you try to apply it) as you can only look at the camera and not your counterpart's eyes;
- Appearance consciousness or otherwise the fact that we are on camera and being recorded might be stressful for some.

When to use:

- Ideal as a supplement to face-to-face negotiations when there are time and location constraints;
- Visual information is an important component of the conversation;

- When travel for meetings is costly;
- Physically impaired individuals (deaf, mute, and so on) need to be part of the discussion;
- Select this mode if you feel conformable speaking in front of a camera.

How to use:

- Arrive earlier to test equipment and connection;
- Use proper encryption and security technology if confidentiality is an issue;
- Check your appearance on screen before the connection. Since we are not all as photogenic as movie stars, if you consider it important you might need to ask for assistance to fix your appearance (make up, clothing, and so on). The screen is like a mirror placed at a certain angle so some parts of your face and body might appear at an angle. The height and angle of the camera is very important so make sure it shows what you want to show. Sometimes you might not want to reveal the material you have in front of you so make sure the camera doesn't capture that or any other props you might want to hide. Position your chair so that you are face-to-face with the camera;
- Use an assistant or a coach behind the camera to provide you with visible cues if necessary;
- When the meeting starts, try not to move a lot as it indicates anxiety and nervousness. On the other hand though, you shouldn't be stiff and rigid either as that is usually an indication of fear;
- Don't be afraid or embarrassed to ask speakers to repeat themselves or give further explanations and clarifications of what they mean;
- Keep some notes as it will indicate you are paying attention and consider what the other side says important enough to be written down and followed up on.

iii. Web-conference

An interesting and popular way to teleconference and videoconference nowadays is doing it online (with Skype being the most popular program). This is primarily done using VoIP technology. With existing software solutions nowadays, teleconference and videoconference participants are allowed during sessions to exchange files, view presentations (like PowerPoint) with pictures and video, and draw and edit concurrently on the same file. In addition, since all the exchange is taking place on the Internet, one can apply the security and encryption options that usually come with the associated software and use hardware protection like firewalls to monitor and control communication signals.

Requirements:

- Ideally, a laptop with webcam and speakers is the best solution as you can have everything in one device in front of you;
- A high Internet bandwidth connection is vital, especially if video is going to be transmitted.

Advantages:

- Can be done from anywhere you are, including home, work, vacation, and so on;
- Almost zero additional cost;
- You can see who is online and available, eliminating the need to preset a meeting time and agenda;
- Allows exchange and manipulation of files on the fly as they are produced;
- Allows multitasking and concurrent execution of other software. You can search the Internet or your files while communicating, for example.

Disadvantages:

- A good quality laptop is usually more expensive than a desktop system;
- The widespread use of technology for informal and non-business related activities might make you unaware of the importance of business etiquette and communication practices. You might be talking to friends and family in your pajamas one moment and the next you might be talking to your negotiation counterpart;
- Synchrony bias might be a problem if the connection is slow or the network overloaded.

When to use:

- When cost is an issue;
- As a quick and easy solution;
- To communicate with persons you already know and have a good informal relationship;
- When either side has the necessary technical capabilities;
- When you need to exchange material and program results while communicating;
- When parties need to access and work on the same document while communicating.

How to use:

- Start the preparations for the conference earlier to test the equipment, the connection, and your physical space;
- Because it might take place in informal settings like your home, you need to be aware of the background image and noises. Light sources (lamps, windows, and so on) should be in front of you or to your side and not behind you;
- Experiment with various settings to see which one is quieter and displays your image clearly. If you don't have time to set up the environment appropriately, switch off the video and just use voice. You can always claim slow connections for that. Ideal backgrounds are monochrome surfaces without too much distraction;
- Do not speak before you establish a connection. A lot of time we start the connection process and we keep about our regular activities until we see the other person on screen. Keep in mind that you usually establish voice connection before video so the other side might be listening to what you say. Although this is insignificant, there are cases where interesting facts can be picked up;
- Make sure you turn off your connection after the end of the meeting. Even when video has stopped make sure voice is also lost. The best way to ensure the other side has stopped receiving signals is to shut down/quit the entire application. Skype, for example, will still be open even when you "x" its window (you need to "right-click" and select "Quit Skype" from its icon on the *Task Bar* to end the program);

- Ensure your online status is what you intended it to be. If you don't want to be visible and interrupted, make sure you select the proper option;
- Use an online ID that uniquely and easily identifies you like *FirstName.LastName* if available;
- Keep a notebook next to you or open up a Word document to keep notes during the negotiation.

iv. Helpful hints for all voice- and video-based communication

Things to remember when conducting voice- and video-based negotiations:

- Make sure you can handle the technology involved or at least that there is someone with you that will handle the details and any problems that might arise;

- Turn off your mobile to avoid annoying distractions and ensure your location is isolated enough from surrounding noises. Ensure that others know you are in a meeting and that you won't be disturbed unnecessarily. Also make sure you don't distract yourself with other activities (like surfing, checking your email, playing games, and so on);

- Make sure you have taken care of bathroom emergencies;

- Ensure there is water around and wet your throat regularly during the meeting;

- Organize the material in front of you so you don't start looking around during the negotiation. This shows you are well prepared and serious about the issue you are negotiating;

- If you intend to record the session, ensure that you have permission to do so from your counterpart. In many cases, make sure you have a notebook in front of you to keep notes of significant negotiation points. It's even better if you have an assistant keeping the meeting minutes;

- Unless there are technical problems and provided that key players are connected, try and start the meeting on time. Delaying always adds to frustration and showcases bad time management skills;

- Unless everybody knows each other, a brief round of introductions is always necessary. You can tell a lot from the way people introduce themselves and the status they want to project. If they emphasize their status, it might be an indication they are not prepared well for the negotiation and they try to intimidate you and put you on the defensive so you can make concessions. With this type of people it might help dragging the negotiations as they will be unable to sustain an in-depth argument;

- Allow latecomers to introduce themselves and brief them on what went on;

- Pending on the degree of familiarity you might have with the other people and their cultural norms, it might be worthwhile at the beginning to allow for some wondering off to chit-chat about general issues (like family news, the environment, and so on);

- Introduce or request the rules of the meeting. It might be that there will be a round of presentations followed up with questions, or speakers could be free to accept interruption and take questions during their speech or at the end of their speech. In any case, it's good to clear the issue from the beginning;

- Identify who will keep the minutes of the meeting and by when they will be circulated for approval;

- If you are keeping the minutes, write them down at your earliest convenience after the meeting is over and send them by email to the participants. If there are any misunderstandings, this will allow each participant to restate their position. Even if you don't get feedback, such a practice serves as a record of acceptance (even if it is passive, like no replies);

- When commenting, avoid sarcasm and irony, even if extreme or ridiculous positions are presented.

6.4.2 TEXT-BASED COMMUNICATION

Negotiating using primarily written messages only recently began to gain its old glory because of the widespread use of Internet and email. In the not so distant past we had become accustomed to exchanging opinions through synchronous communication, either face-to-face or over the telephone. Coming to the online world, a lot of negotiators become frustrated because their familiar expectations of instant access clash with the basic nature of the Internet's asynchronous communication. As a result, text-based (email in most cases) communication often involves anxiety, resulting in distrust for the channel to support the negotiation process. The lack of information regarding the delivery status of our messages creates confusion in interpreting responses. Many times we are not sure if the lack of response is intentional or it is caused by the medium's inability to deliver messages on time.

In spite of their shortcomings, text-based systems are among the fastest, most reliable, and most cost-effective communication systems for alerting and notification. This is the ideal mode of communication during major events as it can reach a wide audience fast and efficiently. In today's e-negotiations, the primary form of text-based communication is email. On occasions one might have to use other forms like Chat, SMS, MMS and bulletin boards, to name a few.

Requirements:

- A computer or mobile with an Internet connection and appropriate software will do the job in most cases;
- Sufficient familiarity with the medium in order to be used effectively. It might be difficult to write a lot in an SMS if you are not fast enough with your fingers;
- Good knowledge and mastery of the negotiation issue is vital since written language is more committed than any other form.

Advantages:

- Can be done from anywhere and reach anyone and anywhere provided, of course, there is network coverage;
- Minimum cost;
- Can be used for bulk message sending. This requires appropriate server technology, but it's quite feasible and relatively cheap

these days. With proper use these servers can target specific devices like mobiles;

- Highly reliable communication system. When voice lines are saturated and cell towers are compromised, text messages can still be delivered because their messages travel on different communication channels;
- Ideal for hearing-impaired individuals;
- Can take advantage of subscription services that deliver screen content of interest to the user;
- Can target location-based delivery. It is easy nowadays to track an individual's position by "monitoring" their mobile reception;
- Allows for reflection and research on the negotiation issue before responding.

Disadvantages:

- A good quality computer (or mobile) can be expensive;
- Limited expressive power;
- Synchrony bias might be an issue;
- It's a definite form of communication as the records can persist forever;
- Mistakes in language or meaning can be damaging.

When to use:

- When cost is an issue;
- In emergency or urgent cases where you need to alert the other side of decisions and events of importance to the negotiation issue, mobile communication is the ideal;
- As follow up to pre-negotiations with other mediums;
- When critical issues (like contracts) need to be explicitly stated in writing.

How to use:

- Negotiation writing aims at getting the other side to do something you want. It's not like writing a novel, a memo, or a report;
- Being clear and upfront will be greatly valued;

- Quantitative information is preferred in print rather than qualitative information and generalizations;
- Keep it short—most reader screens (mobile, Outlook) have limited view panes so displaying all the information on the first screen without forcing the receiver to scroll down will make the message readable and focused;
- Review and rearrange content before sending. Sometimes something important is left at the end where it should be at the beginning, when the receiver has not yet been overwhelmed with information. If you can afford to, have someone else review your message;
- Don't use specific abbreviations that your counterpart might not be familiar with or they could imply something inappropriate for their culture;
- Timing your response can send additional signals that can assist your content.

Email messaging specifics

Email is an asynchronous negotiations mode with all the advantages and disadvantages attached to it. It's a fact of life for any negotiator as the most common form of online communication, and ignoring its potential and pitfalls will only limit a negotiator's ability to conduct business. Transmitting information by email is much different than transmitting it face-to-face, primarily due to the absence of verbal and visual cues. This limits the amount of social cues that can be exchanged so by default negotiators tend to focus more on logical argumentation and the presentation of facts, rather than emotional or personal appeals.

When negotiators try to convey information using a medium with limitations, they adapt to it accordingly. This, in essence, affects the way the information will be interpreted and we might have deviations from the meaning we intended to convey. On the receiving side, email imposes high "understanding costs" because it limits a shared sense of participation and understanding about the communication. Without the clues provided by shared surrounding, nonverbal behavior, tone of voice, or the timing and sequence of the information exchange, negotiators may find it challenging to accurately decode the messages that they receive electronically. In addition, the tendency of email negotiators to "bundle" multiple arguments and issues in one email message can place high demands on the receiver's information processing capabilities.

The absence of contextual cues in text messages focuses negotiators on the actual content of the messages imposing additional requirements for negotiators like:

- *Clarity*—allows information sharing and focus on the precise issues at hand. As a consequence, negotiators focus on the points raised and provide the most effective answers. To avoid unnecessary length, short sentences that summarize content might be ideal. Also remember that text messages can be easily stored and back-traced to retrieve information when needed so avoiding unsure statements and speculation will greatly help avoid confusion. In addition, it forces both sides to be honest and sincere about their representations and commitments.

- *Bundling*—refers to overcrowding your messages with multiple points and arguments. While as we said before this might help identify integrative agreements by encouraging negotiators to present and process issues in parallel, it might also create confusion from information overload.

- *Framing*—refers to the language and wording of a message. With all information passed in the form of text it is important to properly frame the negotiation issues and discussion topics. This starts with the proper wording of the subject domain. It concerns the proper formatting of the message which affects the perceptual frame through which the message content is perceived.

i. Helpful hints

- Don't leave the subject line empty—meaningful titles help message searches and tracking changes. In addition, they guide the reader more specifically to the content of the message and allow them to pay proper attention and prioritize accordingly. Making your counterpart's life easy in that sense will benefit you as it makes you look professional. Another issue you need to consider when selecting titles is to avoid using words that mail filters might pick up as spam. Generally avoid words like "money," "bank," "account," "immediately," "win," names of people or their emails, special characters like "digits 0" (zero), "$," "%," and anything that might have a double meaning. If you don't get a response when you should get one, you might want to consider the possibility that your email was treated as spam and never appeared in the receiver's Inbox.

- Think carefully about who you are CC'ing and BCC'ing as these people might be supervisors or subordinates whom your counterpart might not want to involve at that stage. A general rule of thumb is to keep CC'ing people your counterpart has included or people from your team that you want to involve.

- When referring to someone affected or interested in the negotiation other than your counterpart, you should out of courtesy include that person in the communication.

- Assume there is no privacy and that your email will be read by others not directly involved in the negotiations from both sides. References and positions that you have held in the past might be carried around due to careless (or intentional) use of the "Reply" button that keeps all previous communication with every message.

- Keep in mind that text messages can be stored for all eternity and traces of your "online-youth" will be out there for others to find if they search properly (or illegally in some cases). This can greatly damage your reputation at times you don't expect, even if taken out of context.

- If your email program allows for messages to be sent later than when you press "Send," do set it up for later delivery. That might give you enough time to get back to your message if you change your mind about something you wrote.

- When using text decoration, avoid extremes and stick with traditional fonts (Times New Roman or Arial, size 10 to 12) and styles.

- Avoid wallpapers as they are rather informal and might distract from the content.

- Use color only for highlighting content written into earlier messages.

- Reply within the received text only when you have built strong rapport.

- Avoid using CAPS—it's like shouting your wisdom and can be quite annoying.

- Include links to sources and data. Links have a tendency to trigger curiosity and you increase your chances that the other site will spend more time on your material. If used for purposes of reference, they are an excellent way to support your arguments and "influence" the other side.

ii. Mining for hidden information

In many cases you can reveal a lot by taking advantage of peoples' inexperience with document software like Word. Just make sure that this is not illegal because in some cases the mining of metadata in electronic files constitutes an improper attempt by the file recipients to obtain privileged information that they have no right to see in an effort to gain an unfair advantage over the other side.

- Cut and paste can be revealed in Word by changing the background color to deep blue of someone else's document, provided they used different formatting or text styles. This has the effect of lighting up the paragraphs that were inserted since they preserve their original shading color.

- Look out in general for formatting changes. A lot of times the respondents are secretaries that keep a certain typeset and color. This gives away who is really behind a message or at least you get the picture that your counterpart follows direct orders and uses cut and paste to avoid mistakes.

- Activate the reviewing pane in a document you received to view leftover comments and corrections that might give away clues about the other side's intentions. On the other hand, you can intentionally leave this feature on in your documents to give away "certain" messages that could influence the other party.

iii. Use of visual cues

Be aware that email is displayed by browsers or browser-type software so display can be browser specific. A shared culture in terms of visual elements in emails does not exist yet so widespread adoption and understanding of certain elements is limited. When using visual cues, try to remember that you are not developing a poster or a party invitation and that message writing, although an "art," is not part of the visual arts. Negotiations are considered serious business by most so the image of your message has to reflect this. In addition, you should avoid distractions from the meaning the message carries and the way it should be interpreted. The best way to ensure that your message looks the way you want it to be interpreted is to send it to yourself or a trusted person and get feedback. Elements that affect the appearance of a message include:

- *Font*—make sure you use fonts that will be supported

  - Times New Roman is good in print and on screen;
  - Arial is good for PowerPoint presentations as it increases the visibility of the text;
  - Anything that resembles handwriting needs careful considerations—you don't want to look like you are trying to impress with your tech-skills or your esthetics.

- *Font size*—the most popular ones are "12" and "11". Use multiple sizes rarely—in addition to the effort you have to make to change it that might distract your thought pattern and it shouts out on the receiver side. What you say should be clear enough from what you write.

- *Color*—try and avoid color or at least limit it to one more in addition to black. Use the dark variation of the color you want to use as it will blend nicely while still making a difference. Be careful with using blue as nowadays it is used to display links. It might confuse your less high-tech readers into trying to click to follow a link, only to realize that you either forgot to insert the hyperlink address or they were fools for thinking it was a link.

- *Decorations* (bold, italics, underlining)

- Avoid underlining as it is a leftover of the typewriter era where this was the only way to decorate texts;
- Italics are less invasive than bold, but it is mainly used to indicate terminology or references;
- Bold is reserved for headings, but it can also be used to emphasize critical text that shouldn't be missed or neglected.

- *Bullets* aren't displayed the same by all browsers and can really distort the appearance of your message so you might want to test view your message through other mail clients if it is important enough.

- Things to avoid include:

  - Using paralanguage ("Mmmm," "Huh" — you are not writing a movie script or communicating with your friends);
  - Using emoticons, smileys, icons, or any other special symbol;
  - Changing the background color to anything other than white. Communication should be reminiscent of its print counterpart — that is, on white paper with black letters.

iv. Synchrony bias

A negotiator should try to be unaffected by "synchrony bias." This occurs when one expects their emails will be received and trigger a response immediately. There are two false perceptions here. One that emails will be read as soon as they are sent and one that once they are read they will trigger a response immediately. We tend to forget that most people are not glued to their computer screens "yet" (and according to a general perception will remain so in the future), and that when they do receive and read an email, a lot of people need time to think and prepare their response, especially when the issue they are faced with is a critical one.

In this type of bias, the sender may feel they are being ignored which can be interpreted negatively and result in increased uncertainty. This relates to perceptions of decreased control of the social environment we operate in due to our inability to observe the people involved. Negotiators can use this bias to their advantage and even consider it as a communication strategy in many occasions when they want to cool a heated debate. Technology offers some solution to this in terms of notifying the sender once the receiver has read the email. In addition, another form of communication such as Chat and instant messenger may be considered as an alternative.

To manage the problems created by synchrony bias and prevent a downward spiral of distrust, e-negotiators need to understand and bear in mind the limitations of the medium they are using. This means the need to have alternative ways to check the delivery of their messages and initiate effective follow-up procedures when communication delays are observed. Resending a message claiming uncertainty about the delivery status of previous emails might be a polite way to follow up. As a general rule, never resend a message without positive content. When you don't know what is going on, being polite is better than being aggressive.

Controlling the response time can be a tactical move with a lot of benefits if used properly. The slower pace of email and text message communication allows negotiators to fashion and frame their responses with adequate details to convey the message they want and the information they need or provide. Email provides a searchable thread of communication exchanges so we can hold others accountable to their commitments and the statements made. We can also check our own past communications to ensure that what is being said represents our past commitments and statements. This enables us to verify details instead of giving responses that could later contradict our positions.

HELPFUL HINTS REGARDING SYNCHRONY BIAS:

- Unless there are strategic reasons for the opposite, always respond to an email within 24 hours, even if you only acknowledge receipt of the message confirming that it is under consideration or that it's being processed. This should be followed even if you intend to reject a proposal. One can never know what the future holds so showing professionalism can only add value to a negotiator's image.

- Read a message enough times to ensure there is adequate balance between assertiveness, politeness, and respect. If uncertain, it is always good to have another person you trust have a look at it and give you a second opinion about its content and style.

- "Reply" and "Send" should be done with great hesitation if you want to maximize the potential of the medium. You might want to use the time-delay option we mentioned before.

v. Email security

Email with no security protection has been paralleled to postcards. Anyone can read it. In this sense, standard emails do not meet the requirements of the protection of confidentiality and integrity of the information. An effort to secure email can go a long way to preserving confidentiality. In today's world this can also be achieved at no cost so it would be a good practice based on the sensitivity of each issue to use what technology offers.

Technology-wise, there are solutions like Secure Multipurpose Internet Mail Exchange Protocol (S/MIME) that has strong vendor acceptance and already supports many email products. This protocol makes it possible to authenticate the origin of the email, and to ensure the confidentiality and integrity of its content. In addition, the sender of a message can be informed if their message has been delivered to the recipient or how far it went between communication nodes through S/MIME's ability to offer Message Confirmation Services. This, however, comes at a cost as both sender and receiver need to obtain proper authentication certificates.

Reputable institutions like the Massachusetts Institute of Technology (MIT) have developed their own alternative solutions to address the issue and an example of such a security enhancement is the Pretty Good Privacy (PGP) message-protection software. While it provides the same quality of service as S/MIME, this technology comes free of cost as its part of the open software initiative. On the negative side, PGP is difficult to maintain and needs the expertise of highly trained IT personnel, making its adoption difficult for organizations without the required human experts.

Another technology that has gained in popularity and has been developed to reduce the risk of repudiation and alteration of a message is *digital signatures*. These are cryptographic instruments developed and distributed to previously identified entities by third parties called certification authorities (CA). These can be private (like http://www.verisign.com/) or public organizations that are generally considered impartial and trustworthy enough to provide such services. Digital signatures can authenticate the sender and integrity of a message to the receiver by using a public counterpart of the signature of the sender. It's a kind of key-lock combination that the CA can use to validate a message and ensure its integrity. The technology can also ensure receipt of a message by letting the receiver apply the same process when replying to the message. The delivery time can also be confirmed by embedding in the message a timestamp (date and time) or watermark.

The main issue with digital signatures is the existence of a widely acceptable and trustworthy authority that can guarantee confidentiality and ensure that the technology cannot be tampered with by a sender that will assume a false identity to conduct illegal and unethical acts. Solutions to these issues exist at a technical level and are available for commercial applications. Becoming mainstream in the business world is an issue of commitment by management to invest and continually support widely accepted security practices as they are bound to evolve as technology advances further.

vi. Summary characteristics of email messaging

Requirements:

- Access to a computer or mobile with Internet connection;
- Keyboard skills and computer literacy essential;
- Message management skills are necessary;
- Secure communication protocols for sensitive information.

Advantages:

- Enables long and detailed presentation of proposals;
- Allows the attachment of supporting material (text, images, video, and so on);
- Eliminates emotional tension and negative interpersonal dynamics;
- Allows for more reflection;
- Less invasive than other forms;
- Can express interest and engagement by asking multiple questions in messages;
- Allows for easy storage and access;
- Formal in a sense that whatever is said stays out there for all "eternity'";
- Some East Asian cultures and plenty of people for that matter believe it is respectful and appropriate on occasion to remain silent. The asynchronous mode of email will impose a natural silence;

- Expressive for certain information processing styles like the analytical-rational mode;
- Reduces group differences like gender, age, race, accent, to name a few, thus reducing the impact of stereotyping.

Disadvantages:

- Conveys limited interpersonal information;
- Low typing skills can impede communication—causes frustration and requires time and effort investment;
- Difficult to develop relations and build trust;
- Lack of physical distance prompts negotiators to act tough and choose contentious tactics;
- Raises reliability, security and privacy issues due to the intermediaries involved in transferring the information. Someone can easily intercept and abuse content;
- Limits the expression of intuitive-experiential information processing modes.

When to use:

- Ideal as a supplement to face-to-face negotiations, especially for information and document exchanges;
- When diverse geographic locations are involved that span different time-zones;
- When formal issues need to addressed (including legal ones);
- When personality traits can be an issue for other forms of communication.

Considerations:

- Visual display is browser/software dependent;
- No common culture in terms of visual elements exists;
- Not everyone has the same familiarity with the medium;
- Not everyone is comfortable using it, whether due to their mastery of English or their typing skills;
- It is unnatural in some cultures so they are forced to do it;
- It is an asynchronous mode so you don't know when the other side will receive it;
- There are security concerns;

- It is a good assumption to believe that whatever you say can exist (and haunt you) forever;
- Address as few issues as possible in each email;
- Always review your messages before sending them. If the issue or the point in the negotiation process is critical, take time between reviews to clear your mind. In many cases it is good if you have another pair of eyes look at your message for commenting on your tone and language. When in doubt, neutral language is always better.

ALTERNATIVE MODES

Despite its popularity and power, email might not be the ideal form of text-based negotiation for certain cases. These include situations when a more organized and extended discussion is needed from participants in different locations with different schedules, interests, and perceptions, and in situations where there are connection problems and it is urgent to communicate. The modes we will consider in this category include the Instant Messaging, Short Message Service (SMS), Multimedia Messaging Service (MMS), threaded discussions, and Blogs. The last two modes will be further discussed in later chapters.

i. Instant messaging, SMS and MMS

Instant messaging can be done either online through an Internet connection or wireless through handheld mobile devices with SMS and MMS capabilities.

Advantages:

- Can be used from wherever you are and responses can be instantaneous;
- Safer than chat rooms;
- Less disturbing than phone calls;
- They can be stored and serve as records of what has been discussed;
- SMS and MMS use different communication channels than voice communication, which makes them more reliable and persistent.

Disadvantages:

- Limited amount of information can be exchanged. That makes it difficult to exchange extended argumentation;
- Not good as a persuasive medium;
- Connection and subscription service are a requirement. If there are communication/coverage difficulties, synchrony bias might become an issue;
- There might be synchrony bias if there is no confirmation of delivery;
- If a lot needs to be communicated, one needs to be quite comfortable typing on the device's "keyboard."

When to use:

- Ideal as reminders of daily events;
- For exchange of small amounts of information;
- For confirmation purposes when directions or guidance are required;
- If we need to be physically present at another event.

ii. Threaded discussions

From the point of view of negotiations, we will view threaded discussions as forums (bulletin boards and chat rooms) where negotiators can bring together various parties to exchange positions and evaluate alternatives. Although not as popular as in the past, such forums allow for the presentation of multiple views in a relaxed fashion as participants can take time to research the material presented, reflect on it, and reply at their convenience. Today a lot of the functionality of threaded discussions has been incorporated in the business world as part of knowledge management systems.

Advantages:

- Extremely easy to create and manage;
- No cost is involved since most of them can be developed and run for free;
- It is easily accessible by anyone with Internet access;
- No maintenance in terms of technology is needed since the hosting service covers everything;

- Many people can participate;
- It can be used instead of meeting minutes as it records all message exchanges;
- Its hierarchical structure allows someone to quickly get a feeling of the discussion, especially who is replying to whom;
- In addition to organizing information in strict chronology, it can also sort it hierarchically and topically for easy access;
- Can be used as an alternative to group discussions;
- It can be used as a barometer or even as a laboratory to observe intentions and reactions toward the negotiation issue.

Disadvantages:

- It requires a moderator to prevent inappropriate behavior and monitor responses;
- The imposition of a tree hierarchy tends to fragment discussions within a topic in addition to allowing for deviations from the main topic;
- Participants can carry on personal debates, confronting each other with arguments and counterarguments;
- If the volume of replies is high it might get confusing following the discussion;
- If the discussion has a fast pace, synchrony bias might be a problem as it will mix up the order of the messages. Short replies will appear sooner than long sentences that might carry important information. For example, a simple question might trigger a short response like "I agree" and a long response with explanations as to the opposite. If the latter was to be delivered on time, it might have affected the outcome of the former response;
- It could suffer from groupthink;
- Prolific users may appear as content creators and moderators;
- It can be influenced by the members' familiarity with that style of discussion;
- It requires a group effort to become successful.

What to know:

- The moderator should be experienced enough to know how to guide the discussion and also how and when to end it;

– It requires a group effort to become successful;
– It needs to be followed up with other media like email to summarize the activity and the positions presented.

iii. Blogs

Blogs are diary/journal types of websites where the owner regularly enters commentaries that optionally can include graphics and videos. Being a form of a diary, entries are controlled by the owner of the blog and usually appear in reverse chronological order. Blogs can be personal or corporate.

Advantages:

– Extremely easy to create and manage;
– No cost is involved since most of them can be developed and run for free;
– It is easily accessible by anyone with an Internet connection;
– No maintenance in terms of technology is needed since the hosting service covers everything;
– It helps improve your writing;
– Many people can participate;
– It can be used as meeting minutes as it records all message exchanges;
– Can be used as an alternative to group discussions.

Disadvantages:

– Needs continuous attention and maintenance in the form of updating and renewing its content;
– Needs hardware and software to enable Internet access;
– Not all information can be shared;
– There is no confidentiality as it is a public forum;
– It is an asynchronous mode so there might be time gaps in the solutions and comments presented;
– It might create a sense of competition with replies and counter-replies.

When to use:

- Ideal as a supplement to face-to-face negotiations especially for when many people need to be involved;
- Very good for clarifying specifications;
- Not ideal for day-to-day issues that require immediate attention.

6.5 Final Note

Communication is a vital process in e-negotiations as it is the means by which we exchange offers and counteroffers along with their supporting material. The process is effective and complete when the receiver of the message has understood the meaning the sender intended to convey. It can span distance and time, cross nations and cultures, and use different mediums for message transmission. It can include text, speech and visual representations, and involve expressions of emotion like body language, facial expressions, and paralanguage.

In this chapter we presented the various means of communication for e-negotiations with their advantages and disadvantages in the hope that readers can associate a lot of the material with daily life communications and find practical value in the hints provided. No matter what strategy one plans and adopts in a negotiation, the execution phase can take a life of its own and one might need to improvise and apply all the tricks of the trade available to them. Awareness and knowledge of the communication tools that technology provides along with a dash of common sense might be the best advice one could give to an e-negotiator in dealing with the variety of situations that appear online.

7

Deal or No Deal

In this chapter we bring together all the elements presented in previous chapters to provide a holistic approach to e-negotiations. The evolution in time and the emphasis shifts from one phase to another is what makes each negotiation process dynamic and unique. In an e-negotiation, the environment and people involved are the primary constituents that shape actions and influence the outcome of negotiations. Some people will be more inclined to negotiate due to culture, personality and personal experiences, while others need more exposure and training to acquire the skills to handle negotiations successfully.

Negotiation seen as a process of reaching agreement on matters of mutual interest is essentially the art of persuasion. As such, it can result in one of three distinct outcomes:

- *Integrative agreement*—resulting in the production of increased benefits that are in excess of the sum of the inputs (at least the monetary ones);

- *Distributive agreement*—resulting in the division of the original inputs between the negotiating parties. No innovation takes place here in terms of providing new solutions probably because each party was preoccupied with their own interests;

- *No agreement*—in cross-cultural negotiation settings we see many failures primarily because of the negotiator's inability to consider and adapt to the underlying beliefs of the other party. The best approach in such cases is to recognize the differences, acknowledge their existence to your counterparts, and build on them for constructive win-win agreements. This synergetic approach should be infused in all stages of the negotiation framework, from intelligence to perception to strategy formulation, and finally to communication.

7.1 Negotiation Framework

In this book we followed a problem-solving approach to negotiations, starting with the phases of *intelligence* and *perception,* and followed by *strategy* and *communication.* This is more or less the rational approach to solving any kind of problem in sciences and everyday life (Figure 7.1). When an issue arises and registers in our senses, the first thing we do is to organize the various bits of information and correlate them with related pieces in our memory. Their affinity with our past will help us make sense of what they mean, plan our actions, and finally implement them. Based on the response we get, we repeat the process until we finally reach a satisfactory resolution or walk away. We then move to the next challenge and we go on in life trying to optimize our path. Efficiency and effectiveness shape our learning and guide our future approaches to problem solving and negotiations.

Negotiations are nothing more than challenges we undertake in an effort to resolve an issue that has come to our attention. As we act to solve the problem, we transcend the spiral (Figure 7.2) of *intelligence, perception, strategy,* and *communication* until we reach an agreement or abandon the negotiation. It goes without saying that the length of each phase is not constant. It is obvious that we need to spend more time on the *intelligence* phase at the beginning of the negotiation when we are not familiar with the issue at hand instead of at the end when we will have formulated a clear understanding of the issues and the variables that affect them due to our previous exchanges with our counterparts. *Perception* again is a phase that we would expect to decrease in time as the interaction and information exchange moves on, with our counterpart hopefully gaining a better understanding of the issues and process with time. On the other hand, the *communication* phase and, to a lesser degree, the *strategy*

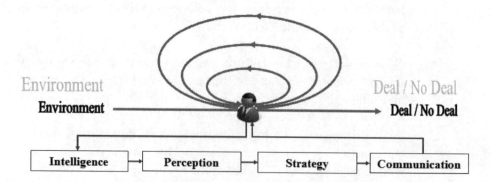

Figure 7.1   Problem-solving Approach—Systems Perspective

phase should be expected to dominate the negotiation as time goes on. Rapid exchanges of information can be experienced in order to clarify issues and reach an agreement.

With certain types of negotiation that are frequently repeated or with familiar cases, we might spend very little time in *intelligence, perception,* and *strategy* and early on go to the *communication* phase where we will spend most of the negotiation time (Figure 7.3). This is a natural and expected move, but we should occasionally reflect on the suitability of our applied strategies even in routine negotiations since exceptions might appear that require additional consideration.

Figure 7.2   Evolution of the Negotiation Phases in Time

Figure 7.3   Negotiations Dominated by the Communications Phase

The transitions between phases can vary in speed and while sometimes it may appear that we jump phases, we do go through them. Even, for example, when we have all the information in advance, it is unlikely that we will formulate a strategy unless we reassure ourselves that the facts are the ones we have and nothing more (meaning we go through to the *intelligence* phase) and that we understand and interpret their meaning correctly (meaning we then pass onto the *perception* phase). Similarly, it is unlikely that we will communicate something without first ensuring it is aligned with our intended strategy: having said that, we should keep in mind that just because we follow such a process, it does not mean that individual elements are rational. Optimization of skills is a completely different issue and has to do with our abilities, our experience, and the situation at hand. As you have probably figured out by now, nothing is really written in stone. Understanding, flexibility, and good judgment will help negotiators choose their approach and strategy specific to the issues they are facing.

7.1.1 INTELLIGENCE AND UNDERSTANDING

Information gathering occurs at all times in negotiations. This is vital if one is to discover aspects and clues that would help redefine the problem and lead to a better solution. Although the information needs at different times in the negotiation will vary, we need to always be aware of and open to elements of information that give away positions, add value to our proposal, and help us improve our strategy.

Negotiations start way ahead of any physical contact with our counterparts. They start with a personal or group need to reach a goal. To satisfy the need, we reach out and start a process of offers and counteroffers until we reach an agreeable settlement or walk away from the deal. This process presumes first of all, that we have identified our need and we have a clear understanding of the various parameters involved that affect it. Subsequently, we have also identified the other party that can satisfy our need. In addition, we have identified something we have and the other party needs so as to motivate them to proceed with the exchange.

When the negotiation process begins, the intelligence phase is conducted by probing behind the positions on the table to reveal the full set of interests at stake. By patiently asking questions, the negotiator can identify the parameters within which the other side is moving and act accordingly. Occasionally, and based on our findings from interacting with the other side and when things get tough, we might go for another full background check to redefine the issue, discover new variables that were initially unnoticed, or redefine the allowable range of existing ones.

Major sources of intelligence during negotiations are the people on the other side of the table. The difficulty many times in e-negotiations is that due to medium limitations, visual cues have to be deduced from text and voice. Even when videoconferencing, one does not have the full picture of what is going on with the other side. By simple reflection we should also be aware of what we project. This can be part of our counterintelligence as we might want to intentionally project different feelings at different times in the negotiation process.

As the shift of the focus is moving from the intelligence phase to the other phases, we rely more and more on our perception of the negotiation process and our focus now moves to understanding the other side's position and promoting our case. The perception phase now requires social awareness to clarify the picture we formed about our counterparts and the negotiation issue, especially due to the reduced social context of e-negotiations. Reduced social awareness in e-negotiations can cause parties to engage more heavily in self-interested behavior when communicating.

Despite the clear advantages of reconciling deeper interests, people have an inherent bias toward focusing on their own interests instead. This hard-wired assumption that interests are incompatible implies one exists at the expense of the other. This means that in many cases enormous value is unknowingly ignored by all parties. Negotiating effectively means more than understanding our own interests and limitations. Since the other side will agree for their own reasons, agreement requires that we also understand and address the other side's issues as a means to resolving ours. Overcoming our natural self-centered tendency is vital if we are to become successful negotiators. Even professional negotiators, especially when in position of power, fail to see or ignore the other side's issues as irrelevant to the negotiation outcome. This immediately undercuts their ability to achieve higher combined gains. One way to avoid this trap is to view the other person as a representative who will have to go back to his boss and try and sell the deal. This will help us support our proposal with strong and convincing arguments the other side will find easier to accept.

As the negotiation cycle progresses, perceptions will begin to solidify. If disagreements and conflict intensify, biases of perception both on our side and the other side should be expected. Behaviors might be perceived as extreme while we might be unaware of the way we are perceived. Leaning toward the idea that the other side is stubborn and extreme might actually lead to the other side becoming like this. Our best defense against such situations is awareness. Additionally, this might be the time to seek consultation from outside parties that have not been involved in the negotiation; they are more detached from the situation so they can be more objective than us and offer a fresh perspective on the issues we are facing.

Perception is also affected by personality traits and logic is not the prevailing power in many negotiations. Consider the well-known case study where you are given $100 and you are asked to split it between you and your counterpart. You start with offering $1 to the other side while you keep $99. The alternative offer is no deal at lot in which case no one wins anything and the $100 amount will be returned to the donor. What do you think it will happen? Logic would suggest that your counterpart accepts this deal as it provides a gain of $1 while the only other alternative leaves no gain at all. In reality, however, it is most certainly sure that most players will focus on what you are making compared to what they are making. The inequality of the split will be perceived as unfair and offending and lead them to reject the offer in an effort to restore "order" (social justice we may say) even though it means leaving them without profit.

Personality traits that can cause problems include aggressiveness, control, passivity, irony and sarcasm, narcissism, and practically most of the dysfunctional spectrum of human behavior. Most of these behaviors can be countered to an extent, past which there is nothing one can do to contemplate their impact. A general rule is to view the negotiation issue as a piece of treasure that needs to be split as equally as possible between the interested parties. In that respect, our attempt will be to minimize the inequalities. As one party is exerting forces to pull the deal toward their end, the other party applies opposite forces to do the same. In addition, we can make sure we understand and monitor key players with the power to sink the deal. Don't lose sight of their interests or their capacity to affect the deal. Some might not be willing to be sacrificed for the benefit of the many and, unless their personal stakes are satisfied, they might be willing to sabotage the process and the outcome.

7.1.2 STRATEGY AND IMPLEMENTATION

While at the beginning we might sit at the negotiation table with an already formulated strategy, it is most likely that we will need to adapt it according to the other side's responses and positions. Recognizing and productively managing the tension between cooperative actions needed to create value, and competitive ones needed to claim it, we can work toward a successful outcome. What will aid our effort is a structured negotiation process accepted by both parties. Every effort should be made to ensure the process is perceived as fair, transparent, and straightforward.

In order to anticipate the other party's moves and better understand their strategy, simulation modeling could be a great alternative. Assuming the intelligence phase has provided adequate data that we interpreted correctly during the perception phase, a good approach would be to simulate the negotiations in role-playing. The best member of our team should play the devil's advocate as we see how our argumentation measures up against it. Given that most human beings and organizations come from the same species (humans that is) and perceive things in similar ways, this will give us valuable insight into the positions we should expect from the other side.

As negotiation progresses, we expect communication to be geared toward more precise language in terms of offers and counteroffers. For successful outcomes, inter-party cooperation will tend to increase and the process will converge toward integrative outcomes. This is a natural consequence of the information exchange process since the parties are becoming more aware of each other's needs and capabilities as time goes by and areas of potential gain emerge.

i. Relationships

Building relationships is a paramount issue in e-negotiations and should never be minimized or neglected. The world might look big, but in certain fields you will be surprised how small it can get. Coming across the same people even by reputation, on opposite sides, or even the same side might be more possible than we think. View your presence in current situations as investments for the future. The best approach would be to acknowledge the other person's interest in building a relationship before engaging in transactions. Keep in mind that relationships can come to the rescue when unforeseen events appear on the horizon. Especially in new ventures and strategic alliances, where goodwill and strongly shared expectations are extremely important, investing in relationships is an important way to reinforce economic contracts.

ii. Affective response mode

Offers and counteroffers involve exchanges of gains primarily in a numerical context. Monetary value and their equivalent benefits pass from one side to the other. The exchange is usually accompanied by persuasive arguments to bolster one's own position. It has been seen that while offer proposals (such as "I propose $55,000") can easily exceed a third of the message exchange, persuasive arguments ("I can't really offer anything more") can easily exceed 50 per cent of the statements being made. Persuasive arguments usually contain affective expressions and evaluation of arguments and dominate face-to-face negotiations. These statements clearly communicate one's feeling about the other's position while carrying no numerical information.

Research has shown that a negotiator's positive affect increases concession making, stimulates creative problem solving, increases joint gains and preferences for cooperation, reduces the use of contentious tactics, and increases the use of cooperative negotiation strategies. Conversely, negative affect has been shown to decrease joint gains, promote the rejection of ultimatum offers, increase the use of competitive strategies, and decrease the desire to engage in future negotiations.

There are many factors affecting a decision to act affectively, and with the right tactic it's possible to have clear ground rules on how to react and what to say. A general strategy that seems to appear frequently is the combination of affective statements with explorative questions and numerical offers or counteroffers (like "This is an impossible deal for me but I could consider an offer of 2 per cent more"). This way you use affective statements to convey emotions while combining it with a numerical offer to acknowledge the other party's concession. The first part asserts your position while the second indicates your willingness to make extra effort to respect your counterpart's interests.

It is generally suggested, at least when negotiating from weak positions, to show dislike in neutral terms that does not come across as accusing the other side for the situation. Usual statements can be "I don't know ....," "I'm not quite sure about this ... maybe if we could ....": these covey unhappiness in a neutral kind of way, inviting the other side to consider them without overloading them emotionally. Furthermore, affective statements disarm the counterpart's anger and annoyance, whether real or part of a strategy. Non-numerical communication modes also invite an intuitive, natural, and pleasure-gain oriented atmosphere that can creatively lead to better solutions. All these should always be in relation to the type of task or situation we face and not applied through all possible negotiation situations.

While some e-negotiation modes (email for example) might suffer from the full expression of affective behavior, in general this type of behavior can also be conveyed appropriately. When properly expressed, this communication style can bring out a greater need for sense making and trigger an intuitive rather than an analytical information processing style. Additionally, in asynchronous communication like emailing we have the added advantage that both sides have plenty of time for reflection and analysis that will allow them to gain the full impact of affective behavior.

iii. Deadlocks

Part of the evil in negotiations is deadlocks. Both sides seem to have barricaded themselves behind their positions, unwilling to make any concessions. The main solution here is the re-evaluation of positions and the development of alternatives. Being creative with alternatives requires first of all to acknowledge their existence and to accept that our solutions so far do not necessarily correspond to the optimal solution that can be found. Brainstorming with our team and even our counterpart might help map alternatives we never thought of or considered before and allow us to accurately evaluate their potential.

Moving from specifics to generalizations, breaking down a problem into constituent elements, weighing them and combining or eliminating them can be very constructive activities. Reconsidering the formal analysis techniques presented in the Strategy chapter might also help in evaluating alternatives.

Redefining the negotiation issues and goal might be required when reaching deadlocks if one is to identify causes instead of symptoms. It might help having an outsider with experience review the situation. While goals are relatively clear for a negotiation, the constraints imposed might be worth reconsidering. If a solution is surrounded by too many constraints, a good approach might be to loosen or eliminate some of them.

Questions to consider and things to remember include:

- What is the problem?

- Whose problem is it?

- Are there acceptable immediate solutions?

- Are there similar case-based solutions that we can use as a reference?

- Our current alternative is not necessarily the best. With this in mind we will be open to challenging our assumptions.

- Asking for help from more experienced professionals is acceptable.

- Compromising our position does not mean we failed.

iv. Walking away

In negotiations, we frequently reach a point where we would prefer to walk away. Surprisingly, this is an option we should have in our mind way before commencement of negotiations. Implementing such a strategy can be very tricky. Make every effort to be convincing enough that you are willing to walk away and that you will walk away if the red line you drew is compromised. When we decide to use this card we better be sure we can afford to follow up on it. It's a good thing to remember that negotiations are not poker games. If they call our bluff and we lose, it will be unlikely that anyone in the future will take us seriously or want to use us as a negotiator. Let the others make that mistake. If our reputation is that of a serious negotiator, our counterparts will consider your intention to walk away as a reality they need to seriously consider in their alternatives.

If we decide to use *walking away* as a strategy, we need to be careful in its implementation. The best approach would be to present it while acknowledging the other side's position with appropriate respect. We can say that our choice is an effort to save both parties time and resources by presenting in advance a limit that, due to the nature of our situation, we cannot cross. This needs to be presented calmly and assertively to convey it as an unfortunate limitation imposed on us.

It is even more difficult in the world of online negotiations to apply such strategy because we can't support it with appropriate facial expressions and body language that most of us use to convey honesty and seriousness. Walking away, if seen coldly, is considered a threat. In that respect, the only thing that can reduce the impact of such a perception is its presentation in "humane" ways that add desperation and a plea to the other side to help us out of this unfortunate situation. It sounds completely insane, but what we are actually saying most of the time is "Please help us gain more from you because we can't give you more without damaging ourselves." This positions the other side in the awkward role of the "abuser" who does not accept our position and thus will be responsible for inflicting damages in the sense of losing gains.

v. e-empathy

Showing e-empathy can be a powerful tool and important skill for negotiating online. Empathy will build trust that can cause actions and intentions to be construed more positively, diminishing at the same time tendencies toward sinister attributions. Negotiators will be more likely to share information with a trusted counterpart, opening the door to argumentation that will lead to more integrative agreements. Showing empathy via communication channels characterized by limited contextual cues and by low interactivity can be quite challenging. We have seen in the Communications chapter some ways to express empathy according to the medium we use. We can always use such practices the way we see fit in negotiations. Questions should focus more on our counterpart's needs toward the end as a display of e-sympathy.

7.2 Negotiation Factors

As we mentioned so far, different environmental factors are going to affect our negotiation approach differently. Since the list of factors can be exhaustive, we will showcase the potential effect of two such factors—the negotiator's age and personality. Age has a very interesting and subtle effect on negotiators as it affects their professional status while personality has the most dramatic impact on negotiations. Both factors impact most negotiation phases so it will help highlight their effects and suggest ways to deal with them.

Age differences might indicate preferences to different communication media and life perspectives and can have a profound impact on the way we act. Younger people that are immersed in the world of the Internet from early on in their lives have preference for online communication and text messaging while older people prefer more immediate and direct media like phone calls. This also translates to the younger population's preference to multitask continually.

Given that "healthy" human beings cannot multitask concurrently and break our intelligence and personality, what eventually happens is time-sharing. Attention is shifted rapidly from one task to another while processing large amounts of information from a variety of sources. Communication takes place in bursts as they move through the negotiation framework and the quality of conversations and interactions is usually less important that quantity and speed.

In addition, different age groups deal with issues differently on a daily basis. If we stereotype cautiously here, we might say that a young person's outlook in life is to gain experience and establish themselves as high achieving and successful professionals. Seeking approval and establishing dominance could be of potential interest to them as they are still in the process of building their image and self-esteem. Eventually at even older stages, the focus moves to maintaining control and a feeling of importance that could lead them to be more controlling as they begin to let go of responsibilities (downsizing) and settle into retirement.

A possible effect of all that in negotiations could be that young negotiators might be more interested in settling the deal and working toward providing and coming up with alternatives while an older person will be more interested in ensuring their parties' gains and ignoring the potential of win-win situations. Having said that, as the negotiations progress, we could observe more flexibility from a younger person than from an older person that at times might even appear as stubborn and controlling. Of course, all the above is always a function of the directions the negotiators received from their superiors and the strategy they follow.

A general hint to remember is that legacy is important for older negotiators and you might need to adapt to their more familiar communication medium (teleconference and videoconference where social queues are picked up easier) as the communication is progressing. If you are the older person in the negotiation don't take it personally and don't alienate your younger counterparts if you appear invisible to them. It might as well be that they multitask as part of their modern lifestyle. Just ensure they got the message right and you are doing the best anyone can do.

Coming to the personality aspects that can influence negotiations, our interests as negotiators lie more on dysfunctional behavior than normal deviations of behavior anyone can express in difficult situations. Given though that the spectrum of human dysfunctions is quite "rich" and based on the assumption that most such cases are unlikely to have ever made it as negotiators, we will just provide some hints on dealing with some of those we could probably encounter.

When facing an aggressive negotiator, hold your ground until their confrontational style loosens up. There is no point in countering the force with an opposite force as this will exhaust your energy. Indicate that you follow their argumentation, but don't give up an inch as the aggressive personality will take this as a sign of weakness and continue with what they think is a successful strategy for them. Typical aggressiveness in negotiators is more of a strategy than a personality trait so you should see their more pragmatic face when the "show" is over. The good thing with e-negotiations is that synchrony bias (even when imposed) might reduce the effect of this behavior.

When facing negotiators that attack you or your positions directly, you are probably on good grounds as your arguments are probably too strong to be attacked directly. A good defense here is to ignore the comments and stick to the issues in a steady and calm way. These negotiators might turn to aggressive behavior if their normal tactic has no effect so everything we mentioned before can be applied here.

When facing negotiators that are passive, we risk getting them to agree to something they can't deliver. In addition, we rarely get the appropriate feedback so our picture of the negotiation issue might not reflect the reality of our situation. The best approach here is to ask questions that trigger responses beyond yes or no and sort of force the other side to open up. Creating a feeling that the other side will not be attacked will engage them in constructive participation. The general rule here is "fear" what you don't see as, in addition to the above problems, it might also be part of a strategy to expose us and our weaknesses.

The behaviors described before are by no means an exhaustive account of all that someone could encounter. Even worse, behaviors are probably going to change as we move along the negotiation framework to smaller and smaller cycles until we eventually converge. If the process is not going very well, one should expect to see more deviations from normal behavior even if that is not part of the typical personality of the negotiators. Time pressure has a way of impacting people, usually bringing out the worst in them. The best practice is probably to be aware of how you act under pressure and, even better, have someone you trust follow up the negotiation and alert you when "Mr. Hyde" instead of "Dr Jekyll" comes out of you.

7.3 Closing the Deal

Hopefully, after a few repeated negotiation cycles, we have a clear view of the problem and understand everyone's positions and stance. This is the stage where all things need to fall in the right place and conclude the process. Getting to this point should be a well thought-out and acted-out process and one should never rush through it to get the results they want. Forcing a process to a conclusion will only increase the likelihood of mistakes that can only inhibit the process and negatively predispose the other side. A good thing to remember is that time and price are usually inversely related. If you want to press for an early resolution, you might need to settle for lower value. In addition, this early pressure might trap the negotiator in a direction from which it will be impossible to backtrack without casualties.

At closing time, effort needs to be made to memorialize the negotiated deal by creating an agreement statement. This can be in the form of a table of what each side concedes to and how both sides will proceed from there on. Even though e-negotiations offer the capability of recording everything, it is a good practice to exchange something at the end in writing. If emails are used in this stage, extra effort needs to be made to clearly state what has been agreed and that each side accepts the terms. This is equal to a valid contract even if no signatures have been exchanged. If on the other hand the negotiations are meant to act as a precursor to signing an actual document, this needs to be clearly stated in the email exchanges.

Closing the deal also means that all parties involved need to go back and sell it to the stakeholders involved. At this point, helping each other build strong arguments as to why the deal got its final shape and that all negative consequences were contemplated is essential for the viability and wide acceptance of the deal. Especially important will be the case of the weakest side that might have made more concessions as they will appear to have lost from the deal. One should be careful though not to indulge in concessions just to please the other side as they might be still negotiating. Selling the deal means that the deal is done and no further manipulation is allowed in the name of any good will.

7.4 Walking Away from the Deal

We have already mentioned in previous chapters how *walking away* can be part of a strategic move. Now we will see what the impact of actually walking away has on us, our counterparts, and the organizations we both represent. Based on the assumption that both sides view the negotiations as an opportunity to gain, they both now are deprived of that opportunity.

There are two reasons why this may happen. First, there was probably no clear understanding of the negotiation issue that led to inaccurate estimations and evaluations by both parties of the potential of the goal they were trying to achieve. There is nothing much a negotiator can do when this has happened other than realize its existence as early as possible and move away from the negotiations to avoid further waste of time and money.

The other reason that negotiations fail although there was realistic potential for gain is "pilot error" or in our case "negotiator error" from either side. Certain signs might give away that the negotiator is not doing well and that it's time to walk away and save time and resources. One reason might be that we are not dealing directly with the decision maker and our communication is not traveling upwards in our counterpart's organization. That might be true even when our counterpart seems to be the actual decision maker.

In e-negotiations this can be true with the older generation of executives that are not familiar with technology and modern forms of communication like email. "Older" decision makers are pretty much alive and kicking and are still part of the executive world, especially in less-developed regions. In such cases, most of the times an intermediary receives your communication, screens the message and presents it to the decision maker. This process might modify our message beyond what we intended since we are in no control of its delivery time and prioritization within the multitude of issues the decision maker is facing. Almost always, these aspects will be decided on by the executive's administrative support staff that will also influence the way our communication will be announced and presented. Don't be surprised if the messenger's agenda is in the way of our message or their perceptions of the importance of a message is different from ours or even their executive's.

Another sign that might indicate a deal without future is when communication is mainly focused on price (unless of course it's a bidding process). These types of exchanges show that the actual interest of the other party is to preserve their interests at any cost. They indicate a limited view of the issue and absolutely no concern or interest for our needs or future cooperation.

Time pressure also is a giveaway sign that the deal might end with you walking away. If you feel pressure from the other side to speed up the negotiation process, then you need to seriously investigate if there is a real time pressure (like in the form of meeting a deadline) or its part of the other side's strategy to rush us in committing to something we might not like. Regardless of the pain involved in walking away, entering into a poor agreement out of fear or because we have been manipulated to do so is far worse. These types of situations are difficult to overcome so it's best to avoid them completely. Remembering our BATNA is also a good way to avoid being short sighted.

7.5 The "Afterlife" Phase

For most people, negotiations end when no deal is achieved or when the deal has been formally and legally accepted and "signed" by all parties involved. This view limits the negotiation as an isolated time period rather than as a human activity that will frequently repeat itself in different settings. As such, we need to make every effort to optimize resources and automate the process as much as possible.

Automating the process has to do with awareness and expectations. This can only be done with proper training and by relying on previous experiences. Training can be done by attending seminars, workshops, courses, reading articles and books, and by observing other negotiators in action. Along with the experience we gain as professionals, all this updating and keeping up will allow us to formulate our own unique approach to negotiations. New experiences and practices will continually mold our practice style and distinguish us as professionals.

One way to preserve the experience of the moment is to imprint it in something that will last. In some cases like email negotiations we are fortunate to already have everything in records. In other cases like videoconferencing and teleconferencing the notes we kept will be valuable. In addition to all that, one should spend a few moments recording (either voice or print) the key moments of the negotiations, the issues raised, and the solutions proposed. This will be a great resource to go back and review and will help us be better prepared for and avoid making mistakes in future negotiations. In essence, by keeping files of each situation we build our own knowledge management system.

A great source of learning is also our counterparts. Observe their style, their body language and what is projected to others; see how they presented their positions and how they argued. If they made us feel uncomfortable or weak, think how this affected your behavior and to what extent it influenced your positions. Running a few "what-if" scenarios might provide valuable insight to what could have been done better and how much you gave in that could have been saved. If you can "fish" your counterpart to give away some of their secrets it will be even better, although unlikely. Professional negotiators know that they might come across you again in the future and that the market is highly competitive so educating someone on their strengths and weaknesses could make you a stronger adversary in future negotiations.

8

Special Topics

8.1 Negotiation Support Systems (NSS)

Technology systems that are designed to support negotiators in their role are classified as Negotiation Support Systems (NSS). These systems were developed and used during the 1980s in the information and communication technologies (ICT) revolution with moderate success due to the social and political implications of the pre-Internet era. As the ability of computer systems to store and access great amounts of information grew, it allowed the development of appropriate models and procedures that processed this information. Supporting negotiation functions and performing simulations allowed for better decision making and the automation of many negotiation processes.

NSS are usually categorized based on their technical characteristics and their methodological approach to negotiations. Their divisions have to do with the way they retrieve, organize, store, and present information and the level of analysis they provide. They can assist in message exchange and meaning extraction to help better explain the positions of the negotiators. Artificial intelligent techniques like Natural Language Processing can help clear collections of messages from noise and analyze their content.

These systems usually try to identify patterns in the language of messages to predict negotiation outcome, even from the early stages of the negotiations.

For an NSS to be acceptable, the system must be perceived to be:

- Useful—meaning the degree to which the users believe that using an NSS will enhance their performance;

- Easy to use—meaning the degree to which the users believe that using a particular NSS would be free of effort.

From the point of view of a negotiator, the most important characteristic of NSS is the role the system will play in the negotiation process and the ease with which the system will be activated (prepared) and used. In that sense, a characterization was proposed that distinguishes them in: (1) preparation and evaluation systems; and (2) process support systems. Following our suggested framework, systems can be categorized based on the negotiation phase they serve or the function they perform.

NSS can help retrieve and organize information (Intelligence phase) and present it in a way that can easily be absorbed by the negotiator (Perception phase). These systems can help reveal patterns and characteristics of the issue and our counterpart that would otherwise require the involvement of other experts. Additionally, they can assist in planning a move by evaluating the utility of alternatives, assessing offers and counteroffers, and suggesting optimal moves. They can be used by one or many parties and allow for the consideration of parties' objectives, constraints, and preferences.

The most popular category of systems today is process systems. They are designed to bring negotiators together and aid their activities. In this category we have the electronic communication media that we saw in the Communications chapter, enhanced with facilitating capabilities to allow for participative decision making and the formulation of agreements.

Although the NSS functionality mentioned above is not an exhaustive one, it does allow for a mapping of the various systems along the suggested framework of this book. In essence, we can say that NSS categorization can be composed of systems that assist in intelligence and perception, systems that assist in strategy evaluation and formulation, and systems that facilitate communication between the participants.

Based on the above discussion, we can summarize the key characteristics/ requirements of NSS as follows:

- Structure and organize the information requirements of the negotiation process;

- Facilitate and organize communication;

- Provide a user-friendly interface;

- Have strong security to ensure confidentiality and privacy;

- Provide support for analytical tools with visual appearance;

- Customizable to communication preference patterns of different languages;

- Enable the exchange of messages and offers.

A further classification that captures the previous characteristics might also be needed to address the specifics of e-negotiation. E-negotiation systems (ENS) can be seen as a subcategory of NSS and specifically refer to software developed and used to support e-negotiations. This is typically done through a browser or client interface that also allows for text, voice, and video communication. A typical such system is the Inspire system (http://interneg.org/inspire) that was also one of the first Web-based negotiation support systems developed to facilitate and support bilateral negotiation. It provides negotiators with a single, standardized case of business negotiations in order to allow for statistically valid analysis.

The negotiation process with an NSS such as Inspire is performed in three phases: pre-negotiation, negotiation, and post-settlement. The pre-negotiation phase closely resembles the intelligence, perception and strategy phase of the framework provided in this book, while negotiation is mainly focused on the tactics and communications. While the pre-negotiation stage assists the user in organizing their material, analyze the case, and select their alternatives, the negotiation phase is primarily used by the system to provide utility values for decision alternatives. The post-settlement phase is used by the system to provide efficient alternatives when the parties achieve an inefficient compromise, in a last attempt to reach an agreement. The software allows for a nice organization of the material and the negotiation process, but efficiency in reaching a resolution is still dependent on the negotiators' creativity and skills. Despite their shortcomings, such systems are valuable because they allow one to focus on the issue instead of wasting time and becoming distracted by procedural issues and the medium used.

One of the difficulties in developing NSS is that user attitudes toward it are difficult to predict due to the widespread location of users within different cultures. This means that a feature might be attractive for one culture, but users from another culture might find it cumbersome and reject it because of different communication patterns, values, and behavioral preferences. For their widespread adoption, there are also institutional issues that need to be overcome like organizational resistance and the legal implications of using such technologies. An additional issue is the huge customization costs that are needed to adapt such tools to the specifics of each organization. This makes their development difficult and costly as an investment so progress is primarily based on academic research.

8.2 Automated Negotiations

Automated forms (also called blind-assisted negotiations or facilitated negotiations) refer to cases where the parties submit proposals in the form of monetary figures (bidding) which are not communicated to the other parties. Software compares the offers and when they are within a given spread, reaches a settlement in the form of an optimum of the best offered and requested value. If the figures are not within the given spread, repeated rounds of offers take place until a settlement is achieved or the time limit has expired. These systems are called dynamic pricing systems and are expected to comprise the majority of the automated negotiation systems in the future.

Automated negotiation is quite successful in that one can find reliable computer systems to conduct negotiation solutions with only monetary transactions, often in the area of insurance disputes. Fees are usually required to use such systems and payment can be on the basis of the settlement amount and the split between the parties or on the basis of time-limited memberships or trust mark fees. The most successful and best known model of automated negotiations is the online auctions popularized by eBay (www.ebay.com). eBay managed to effectively bring the person-to-person trading model to the online marketplace, making the model a huge success. The company allows for reserve price auctions where the seller sets a confidentially reserved price and a minimum price through a deadline. If a buyer matches or exceeds the reserve price they get the item and the auction ends, otherwise the buyer with the best offer is awarded the item, provided it is above the minimum set. If there is no winner, the seller can readjust the settings and resubmit the item for auction. The buyers place their bids through a proxy bidding system that submits their bids incrementally, starting from the top offer in the auction and countering the competitors' offers until it runs out of money or there is no more competition.

Another popular automated e-negotiations mode is the "state-your-price" negotiations model of Priceline (www.priceline.com). While eBay has a successful seller-driven model, Priceline has built a successful buyer-driven model where the buyers set a price for an item they want to buy (reserved with a credit card) and then the system tries to find a seller that is willing to fulfill the request. The service is very popular with airline ticket purchases and has also expanded to hotel reservations, car purchases, and loans. This negotiation model has advantages for both sellers and buyers as it allows sellers to get rid of discounted or promotional products and allows buyer to set prices they can afford.

An interesting and futuristic goal of technology is negotiation models that implement some kind of artificial intelligence for the bidding process. Enhancing models with neural networks, expert systems, fuzzy logic, and case-based reasoning are some of the techniques academics primarily experiment with as part of studying decision support systems (DSS). For interactive negotiations, agent-based modeling dominates the research field and offers some promise for practical implementations. Artificial agents are simple software applications that, like search engine crawlers, search the Web or specific websites (eBay for example) to find items of interest to us. When they locate such items, they report to us and, based on their programming, they might also perform additional functions. The ultimate goal of artificial agents at least for pricing negotiations is for them to act independently and, based on our preferences, surf the web, find deals, negotiate prices, and complete transactions on our behalf. For more interactive types of negotiations it is unlikely that we will see any real-life applications in the near future, at least because of the complexities of translating human interactions into a mathematical algorithm.

Today's automated negotiation models suffer from the shortcomings of any process that cannot deviate from normal behavior. In addition, they cannot guarantee maximum earnings for both sellers and buyers and can also be manipulated by either side. So for a model to be viable and commercially beneficial for the company that offers the service, it has to be constrained and controlled to eliminate opportunistic behavior. Different policies will also have to be set to ensure members' accountability, cover cancellations, and secure transactions.

8.3 Online Dispute Resolution (ODR)

ODR systems have been available for quite some time now, but they have not yet been adopted by businesses to the extent that technology makes them available. Issues of fear and trust in the technology prevented the full adoption of such systems. What we see most of the times is a fusion between traditional and modern approaches instead of fully electronic dispute resolution systems.

Main benefits of ODR for business include time and cost efficiency. Every involvement of a business in dispute resolution costs money since highly paid personnel (like lawyers, executives, and domain experts) will have to be involved and resources (travel and communication being among them) will have to be diverted to take care of the issue. Reducing the overall cost of the endeavor will significantly benefit the business, along with allowing the human resources involved to focus on other important issues of the business. The adoption of ODR eliminates the time zone issues that forced disputants to travel in the past. Nowadays, a Skype conference costs absolutely nothing and has more or less the same effect especially when there is time pressure to resolve an issue. In addition, the use of the asynchronous mode of ODR allows for background checks, the inclusion of experts, and the involvement of critical personnel when needed, and at times that do not conflict with their other obligations and responsibilities.

ODRs can also help in projects where many participants are involved because it enables for fast response and resolution of conflicts between participants that could jeopardize the economics of the endeavors. In addition, the systems can be used for training due to their ability to function as platforms for role-playing in dispute management. The insights gained through such practices and by reviewing past disputes allows ODR systems to also function as knowledge management systems.

Another important advantage of ODRs is their ability to neutralize (due to the absence of physical contact) a hostile atmosphere that might exist or build up in the process between the disputants. While courts have the tendency to blacklist individuals and organizations due to reputation damage, ODR tends to be less intrusive and considered more of a natural part of business, allowing disputants the feeling that if they didn't agree (or one lost over another) now, they might very well happen to do business in the future. This can also be seen in employment disputes since ODRs can help neutralize the conflicts between parties and allow them to reflect between offers and counteroffers.

Apart from the advantages of adopting and using ODRs, one needs to keep in mind the drawbacks of such systems. As with any technology system, ODRs involve implementations of technology that require certain skills and familiarity with it. The perception or inability to make the most out of such systems might lead to fear regarding the quality of the service, leading to the limited adoption and use of such systems. Fee issues can also arise as such systems tend to reduce the need of experts. It is natural to expect a lot of resistance in their adoption, especially in countries that are not technologically advanced and familiar with such tools.

Confidence in the technology is of utmost importance, especially with the many cases of security bridges and online abuse that circulate the news frequently. This can be extended to lack of confidence for the party that initiates or suggests the use of such systems. In this respect, there is also the issue of ownership and control of such systems that might complicate the situation. Neutrality of the technology and its ability to ensure confidentiality is of utmost importance.

As a concluding remark, ODR should not be seen as a competitor of existing systems like face-to-face systems, but rather as an addition to the existing arsenal that provides a more flexible exchange medium for case-based scenarios. Understanding the available opportunities and the barriers of implementing such systems is the best approach for their adoption.

Although beyond the scope of this book, two special cases are worth mentioning:

- **Online mediation**—which is simply the online form of traditional mediation. A third party with no decision power mediates an agreement by acting as a facilitator. The range of disputes that can be handled by mediation is very large and practicing online mediation should be case specific. It becomes difficult, for example, to conduct mediation electronically, especially in emotion disputes and in time-limited situations. Fees are usually computed on an hourly basis.

- **Online arbitration**—which is similar to traditional arbitration, in the sense that a third party chosen by the parties, or nominated by an institution chosen by the parties, renders a decision on the case after having heard the relevant arguments and seen the appropriate evidence. Arbitration traditionally produces awards which have a binding force that is similar to a judgment. Online, non-binding procedures are often proposed and often used.

Online arbitration takes place using both synchronous and asynchronous modes like emails, Web-based communication tools, and videoconferences in both binding and non-binding arbitration. It is highly dependent on the binding character of the outcome, given that binding online awards are usually extremely infrequent compared to the non-binding decisions that might have been rendered. Also, the business depends on the binding character of the decision: the scope of arbitrability is restricted in some arbitration to protect the weaker party while non-binding arbitration does not raise questions of arbitrability. Fees for online arbitration are usually the same as for mediation and in most cases charged on an hourly basis.

8.4 E-diplomacy

One parameter that seems to have been increased nowadays is the number of players in the negotiation games. Creating communities of interest is easy and fast on the Internet. Virtual reality spaces even offer realistic sceneries for someone to wonder and "live." For one thing, now technology controls the way information flows everywhere, making the dissemination of information fast and wide, enabling people to make their own judgments, express their concerns and feelings, and even influence policymakers. This means that the way governments interact is faster and reaches more in almost every part of the world. This requires more accurate and informed responses on the part of negotiators especially in their role as representatives of governments and other establishments.

We shouldn't confuse here the message with the messenger. Although previous technologies like the telegraph, the telephone, the telex, and the fax have affected negotiations and diplomatic practice in their days, they did not have the reach and sophistication of today's and future technologies that are expected to be lightweight, digital, mobile, and highly intelligent. Coming from the post-World War II era when diplomacy was dependent on foreign ministries' agents and their networks, governments and diplomats realize now that there are many more players including non-government players. In a sense, diplomacy reached the masses and allowed experts, non-experts, and interest groups to pursue their individual issues. The playing field increased, and continues to increase exponentially every day, affecting the negotiation rules in ways we haven't seen before and that are difficult to predict.

Among the technology factors that influence e-diplomacy a few worth mentioning include:

- Communication speed;

- The availability of huge amounts of information, free and personalized;

- Easy and affordable access to information technology;

- People's expectations of their influence in policy formulation;

- Non-state actors play a more influential role.

8.4.1 COMMUNICATION SPEED AND INFORMATION ABUNDANCE

Communication speed can bring news fast, but it cannot bring instant comprehension. This means that in cases where the immediacy of information is important, communication speed can be an advantage while in cases where the complexity of an event is high, speed can confuse a decision maker and not provide adequate time to process the information and understand the event. Without understanding, such situations might bring disastrous results. In the case of e-diplomacy, though, one expects that the sooner governments and decision makers know about events, the faster they will evaluate a critical situation and make better informed decisions.

For a diplomat this can be a blessing and a curse at the same time. For one thing, early knowledge about events avoids surprises, but for another, the fast pace of events expects fast responses that cannot necessarily be optimal when they are rushed under pressure. Credibility is at stake since delay can be perceived as weakness either in collecting or in evaluating information and late reactions can be attributed to lack of strength. Speed creates a completely different power game.

In addition, the influence of the information provider changes since nowadays anyone with Internet access can act as a news agency and trigger an avalanche of news feeds and opinions that can influence policymaking. Negotiators have to be aware of these realities and use them to their advantage when they can. Social media sites can be a means for influencing outcomes. Anyone can be a commentator online and either support or condemn positions presented at negotiation tables. Voices can influence other voices to the point of such pressure that negotiators have to take them into consideration. Digital communities have their own logic and outputs can be from well-focused and long-lived to something spontaneous and short-lived.

It is evident that no matter how well trained a negotiator is, the sheer magnitude with which information accumulates is becoming a disadvantage. There will be no time to mine all of the data, evaluate their reliability and relevance, and act accordingly. What is more likely to happen is that negotiators will trust sources they consider credible while paying little attention to less familiar ones. Verification of the accumulated information is becoming more difficult resulting on instinct judgment calls with doubtful outcomes. This reduces the experts' authority because, as we have recently seen with global events, their expertise will be continually challenged by the pressure of information overflow from sources that cannot guarantee reliability of information.

8.4.2 EASE AND EXPECTATIONS INFLUENCE ON POLICY FORMATION

The cost involved in accessing and using new technology drops dramatically every year making it easier for anyone to use technology to interact with others in the world. One can simply consider the $100 initiative where anyone can have a computer with Internet access and contribute by providing information and news 24/7 beyond any national boundaries. The notion of a decision maker under these conditions becomes rather blurred and kind of expanded since influences come from many directions with contributions from any part of the world. In addition, the size of the audience and its expectations has changed. People become accustomed to the information availability; they expect it to be credible and delivered to them anywhere, instantly and at no cost. This opens up people's appetite for more information and leads to greater participation since they can become providers of information and opinions that can form policies and influence events.

The traditional decision making core of ministers, government officials, and policymakers is challenged under the new regime as they become a minority in the information world. People are becoming more demanding to what their leaders think and how they react to the worldly affairs that affect their lives. And the more informed they become, the more likely they are to voice their opinions. The Internet has allowed new networks to form even in real-time, joining people and organizations and allowing them to interact and influence each other. Two-way influential relationships emerge among same-group players and among all players in diplomacy, from citizens to media to government to non-state actors into the development of e-government.

The introduction of the Internet allowed a two-way relationship between citizens and media. The new form of technology allowed citizens that traditionally were the passive receivers of information to become highly active in broadcasting their views into hyperspace. This puts extra pressure on media and challenges their role as experts in aggregation and dissemination of information. This also brings to the foreground issues of credibility and transparency more frequently than in the past. Credibility is essential to trust and it takes time to establish. With almost real-time information delivery, reflection and judgment about its accuracy becomes critical and exerts a constant pressure on the receivers.

In the future, when citizens will be more familiar with the technology and aware of the reliability factor of the information provider, they will seek sources of information outside the traditional media to personally evaluate situations and form their own opinion. Politicians also adapt to today's world and this can be seen by the increase of their personal and policy websites and blogs.

8.4.3 CONCERNS AND ISSUES

The openness and ease of access to information that the Internet provides also has its negatives. For one thing, governments have to guard their online assets and protect the public from unauthorized sources of information that could potentially hurt their citizens by providing erroneous and unreliable information. This is more difficult to achieve than it sounds because it's almost impossible to effectively police hyperspace (take the case of Wikileaks). So what eventually happens is modern governments become very proactive in presenting their cases as early as possible to minimize damages from unreliable sources.

Ruling the Internet is far more difficult and complex than imagined. In the past, centralization was the primary way governments used to control and police states. This is almost impossible to achieve in the virtual world due to the nature of the Internet as a web of interlinked sources, of magnitude that will soon approach the numbers of the actual populations in some states. Opposing forces will be of influence to governments. From one side, reliability of information is vital, imposing control measures on the way information is delivered online, while from another side, freedom of speech is an established right of the people and needs to be respected. What makes it more challenging technically and ethically is the fact that on the Internet citizens are not passive receivers of news from established sources, but they actively seek and choose the sources they will use and trust.

In the case of government and media, we now see that the long-standing symbiotic relationship between them is changing in ways that are difficult to predict. In some cases, we can observe strong dependencies between them as the media face increased competition from local and international players, while in others we see a more hostile relationship as the governments are trying to "narrowcast"/personalize information and services to citizens. Professional bodies like bar associations and chambers of commerce, among others, have always had in their agenda to protect and promote their interests with governments.

In the case of government and non-state actors, the situation is very different since groups in general tend to be more organized than individuals. Non-governmental organizations (NGOs), for one thing, when assisted by technology are much more active in forming opinions and influencing society than in the past. As a result of their participation in the commons these organizations have been able to organize citizens on a global scale and affect the way diplomacy works. NGOs are eager to establish themselves as major players in the formation of policies. In that respect they are strong adopters of the technology and exploiters of its offerings. This naturally challenges the perception of governments that they alone have the right to formulate policy as the elected representatives of the people. In a world, though, where freedom of speech is a principle upon which democracy thrives, it becomes difficult for governments to assert their positions and enforce their policy without the residual influence of technology.

NGOs embraced the Internet and use it to effectively promote their causes. Their websites offer forums for policy debate and sources of policy alternatives.

The reputation of established NGOs attracts governments and public to their online spaces and helps establish and expand electronic communities of various sizes around current issues and affairs. These buildups of networks form expanding, living organisms that distribute processing and decision making. With the use of technology these organizations can organize themselves locally and internationally to act cohesively to influence the public and conduct demonstrations and protests (Greenpeace, against G8, and so on).

In conclusion, the environment is shaped by technology and has redefined the primarily hierarchical nature of diplomacy to a more flat organization of players. The policy space is now shared with newcomers that range from organizations to organized groups to individuals. They all have a voice that grows louder by technology's amplification. One can resemble it with a protest, where instead of a leading person having the speakerphone, we have everybody with a speakerphone. Negotiators and policymakers in the field of diplomacy need to make the leap to the world of e-diplomacy.

8.4.4 FROM DIPLOMACY TO E-DIPLOMACY—THE USE OF TECHNOLOGY

A major challenge for negotiators in the field of diplomacy is the need to respond to fast changing interaction spaces where citizens, non-state actors, and other governments become influential actors. Understanding the Internet requires a different frame of mind and a kind of openness counterintuitive with traditional diplomacy. Far from being familiar with the new technology, it also requires structural and operational changes of the internals of each organization and individual.

Traditional players need to equip themselves with technology in the most efficient and effective way they can. This requires commitment and determination to proceed. There will always be concerns about the type of technology to use, the cost, the security aspects of it, and its legal status, but this is a one way road that every player needs to encompass. The benefits of the Internet are beyond doubt, but an uncontrolled use of this technology is a major threat and concern of governments and policymakers. Because influences are directly affected by what they influence, a loop structure exists that is difficult to predict and control.

There is a lot of uncharted territory ahead for negotiators in the diplomacy field as they develop and become familiar with the use of the Web. While the tendency is that more information benefits democracy, the legal framework under which this dissemination takes place is in its infancy to non-existent in many countries.

The main application area of technology for e-diplomacy nowadays is the provision of information spaces and discussion forums. In e-negotiations this can be used as a pressure point to achieve the desired outcome. This should be done, though, with great care since any information someone posts can be counterattacked with opposing positions from opponents. It's like an infantry battle where both enemies use artillery. If one doesn't use it they are most certainly at a disadvantage. First priority is to ensure that information is readily available online, distributed fast, reaches as wide an audience as possible, and is customized to the needs of each audience. Different content should be delivered to parties based on their interests and their degree of involvement. It makes no sense to send to a wide audience, with a superficial interest on a case, details that do not interest them and will appall them. In such cases, the focus should be on highlights presented in an authoritarian (expert-like) manner. Contrary to that, in cases where there is great expression of interest one should present more detail and allow for a more interactive form of communication and consider feedback as a valuable source of input to the process and issue at hand. Online participation should be used as leverage to assist other forms of negotiations.

8.5 E-ethics

Ethics in practical terms is the set of principles of right and wrong that individuals and organization use to make decisions about their behavior and conduct with respect to others. While certain general principles are universal and transcend time, it is closely related to the social and political issues of each era since they define mainstream behavior. The introduction of changes like technology has a ripple effect that gets stronger with time and shapes the evolution of these rules. For example, while 2,000 years ago it might have been normal to have slaves, today it is considered completely unethical and abusive. Religion as a societal phenomenon is a strong influence on ethical perceptions and practices.

The rapid growth of the Internet and its widespread adoption as an affordable and convenient medium for many human activities like communication, entertainment, education, and business naturally led to great societal changes. The effect is stronger on young people that were raised in the midst of these changes to the extent that this generation has been labeled as the Y Generation. The ease by which young people connect and function online allows them to recognize more the importance and power of knowledge, but deprives them from building the character of generations that created all these revolutions through their labor and inspiration.

While ease of access and interaction of social media helps in the acquisition of knowledge, it carries with it the problems of showing the proper appreciation and respect for traditional social boundaries and ethical behavior. The transcending nature of the Internet that breaks physical barriers makes the multinational dimension of the ethical issues more prevalent. The Internet offers the "illusion" of anonymity since being detected and identified online requires a lot of effort on a global scale. In essence, for the great majority it's like a lawless state of anarchy. Anyone can have an email account and a public profile that is far from their real names and profiles with extreme ease and with no consequences. This misrepresentation is even encouraged many times since you are allowed to have as many email accounts and as many profiles as you want without anyone being able to trace them to you.

In addition to easily having fake identities, our computers through which we access the Internet reside in our homes, so naturally one could think that since everything in my home is mine to do as I please with, the same is true for the computer and anything that appears on its screen. So if a picture from a web page happens to show up on my computer's screen, I can do whatever I want with it as with anything else in my home. The logic sounds so natural that is no wonder that most people fall for it. The action is associated with no real effort so it is natural to assume that no value should be associated with it.

What no one really tells us is that the Internet is more like a library building where we go to borrow books, read them at home, and eventually return them to the library. If one compares the effort involved with the actual physical activity of driving to the library, searching around for what we want, checking it out, driving back home and after we are done, returning it, with the effort of doing the same activity online, it is easy to see how we can get the misconception that the effort differentiable should imply different perspectives and consequently different ethics. The association of ethics to effort/ease is a natural one since our history and personal experiences and observations usually show that great damage requires great effort. The general rule might look like ethics is proportional to effort, ignoring the real analogy that ethics is inversely proportional to damages made. Young people can be more vulnerable to this fallacy due to lack of life experiences and proper education.

In addition to its social implications for the world of online business, unethical behavior is directly related to cost. This comes from damages made to reputation, illegal copy, and distribution of products and services, malicious interventions to their infrastructures and inhibition of their communication and dissemination channels. Almost all big online businesses experience denial of service (DoS) attacks at some time or another that costs them millions of dollars. The attack is so simple to execute that even someone with no real knowledge of its internals can go on the Internet and find scripts that will execute it. All it does is send a signal to the target server to check if it exists. Of course this is what precedes most communication with Web servers with the difference now that while regular customers initiate few such requests, an attacker orchestrates millions of such requests blocking the server from doing anything else other than answering to them.

An activity that, while legal, does cross ethical boundaries is profiling. With the advances in data storage techniques and the cost reduction of its supporting hardware, companies and organizations are able to keep huge amounts of user data like credit card transactions, address details (including emails), subscriptions, state and government records, website traffic, and user interactions with websites, to name a few. This abundance of user data can easily be combined and aggregated to allow reliable profiling of buying patterns online, ideological and political positioning, and general behavior and personality traits of individuals that pose major violations of privacy. Sites like DoubleClick (www.doubleclick.com acquired by Google) and LexisNexis (www.lexisnexis.com) have profiling as their core business activities. Basically, they make money by selling the information they collect to anyone willing to pay for it, while others like Google Analytics (http://www.google.com/analytics/) offer the service for free to add value to their other core business.

The situation with profiling took extreme dimensions with the advent of modern terrorism. Technologies like NORA (non-obvious relationship awareness), which have the blessing of terrorist-fearing governments, incorporate advanced data recording and mining techniques to make associations between users and their preferences and activities. NORA uses multiple sources of information from the Internet, video surveillance, telephone calls, and hit lists to associate individuals with activities and preferences. Based on this information, conclusions can be drawn about users' intentions and actions. The potential for abuse is obvious here and there are many occasions where NORA has been used for purposes other than terrorist activity prevention.

In e-negotiations as in business, ethics goes beyond the simple respect of legal constraints. Making profits within the law is looking at businesses with a very narrow perspective since it focuses on what we shouldn't be doing instead of what we should be doing. Negotiators need to always consider the social pressure under which negotiations might be conducted even when they take place electronically. As long as humans are involved in the equation, environmental pressure will always be an important factor in strategy planning and decision making. Defending our principles is bound to take into consideration economic interests. Any concessions we make are bound to cost us in the sort or the long run. The challenge negotiators will face is where they draw their lines.

Making ethical choices is usually the result of *responsibility* and *accountability*. Responsibility implies acceptance of duties, obligations, and potential cost associated with the decisions we make, while accountability refers to the existence of mechanisms that will determine bridges in accountability and impose sentence to balance damage. The established legal system has the primary responsibility of deciding who is accountable and what to do about that. The concept of responsibility is further extended in the legal field with the concept of *liability* that refers to the legal actions needed to restore damage. The process through which we understand and practice all these concepts is referred to as *due process*.

The concepts mentioned here form the basis for an ethical analysis of technology and e-negotiations. Both are ingredients of the human societies and as such they influence and are influenced by most of what happens in social settings. Societies and individuals progress technology that in return shapes how societies and individuals behave and act creating a feedback loop of actions and reactions. The result is a continuous change of rules and practices that we call *evolution*, at least in the societal sense of the term.

There are no golden rules here as everything is situation dependent. Exercising as much common sense as possible and getting as much consensus as possible is probably the best we can do to keep up with the changes. Following professional codes of conduct, aspiration guidelines, and good practice statements should be a must for e-negotiators. These have been developed by people in the profession in efforts to counter radical and erratic behavior in times of doubt and uncertainty. They represent the cumulative experience of every stakeholder involved including negotiators, clients, public authorities, and the general public.

9

Present and Future Trends

The electronic systems that are available to support negotiations today manage to facilitate the negotiation process by enhancing the capabilities of systems for information storing, processing, and transferring while imposing on communication bandwidth. Transmission of interpersonal cues is reduced so e-negotiations are sometimes referred to as a "cool" medium.

E-negotiations can have clear advantages over face-to-face negotiations. It can be quick, direct, and to the point and due to its impersonal aspect can help distance negotiation issues from personal issues and the personalities involved. Furthermore, when nonverbal cues are removed, potential hostilities are reduced and there is more room for an idea exchange that can solve problems and achieve concession. The depersonalized nature of e-negotiations can eliminate status differences between participants and enables people to communicate on an equal status.

Technology adds more value to young negotiators that lack the extensive networking of more experienced ones. Many of the negotiation practices that negotiators apply in face-to-face negotiations to gain advantage do not translate well in the electronic world. Also, e-negotiations and especially computer-mediated negotiations are a field where young people can have a clear generation advantage due to their exposure to technology from the early stages of their lives. Regardless the age thought it all depends on the negotiator's personality and their experience with the world of 'e' (online world). Regarding information technology, its primary contribution nowadays is to provide the medium for intelligence, simulation, and communication exchanges.

9.1 Technology Innovations

Technology-mediated communication has evolved over the last few decades with the advent of the Internet to a powerhouse where data are transferred at high speeds in sophisticated ways. What we should be able to see in the future is a convergence of the different technologies into small devices that can perform multiple functions. Having computers, TVs, and telephones all in one device that might also be portable exist even now, but in the future it will probably be mainstream. In this section we present a select few just to get a flavor of what exists and what might come.

I. LOCATION-BASED SERVICES

With the popularity of mobile devices gaining ground as the mainstream communication medium, services that provide information specific to a location are becoming very attractive for the mobile user. They offer opportunities for receiving alerts such as notification of sales, traffic jams, ATM locations, restaurants, and people, among others. From the negotiator's perspective, getting information for the specifics of a location on the move might be valuable especially in cases where negotiation issues are still evolving and we need to be updated continually. The way these services work is by collecting location data about the cell tower your WAP mobile is roaming from and identify your position within the influence radius of that tower. Identifying your approximate position within a radius is quite enough to relate it with places of interest to you in your vicinity and inform you about their exact location.

II. SPEECH RECOGNITION

The term is used to refer to recognition systems that convert spoken words to text. Software that performs such functions exists and is packed in most operating systems and their supporting applications so it is freely available for anyone to use. Unfortunately, at present such applications are not error prone in addition to requiring extensive training periods to be able to identify the peculiarities of each speaker's voice. In the future though, as the technology matures, this type of application will gain in popularity, at least among negotiators, as this technology is perfect for keeping minutes and eliminating the need for typing. When enhanced with proper AI software these types of applications will act as a human-computer interface to increase productivity and easy access to the underlying technology.

III. GESTURE-BASED SYSTEMS

It is a fact of life that most of our work is done using our hands. It was only natural then to try and get all this functionality on computer systems in forms other than typing and touching the screen. While in many cases gesture technology will enhance our control (or our feeling of control) and empowerment, it is unlikely that it will gain widespread acceptance for many tasks given its expressiveness limitations. Different systems will need to be devised to address cross-cultural issues and different conventions will have to be adopted to handle various issues. As we mentioned in the Perception chapter, even the simple headshake is puzzling when cultures intermix. Westerners who travel to India experience difficulty in interpreting the Indian horizontal head shake, which to a Westerner is interpreted as disagreement while to an Indian indicates agreement. Similarly, hand-waving gestures of hello, goodbye, and "come here" are performed differently in different cultures. To see a partial list of the range of gestures used across the world, search for "gestures" and "list of gestures" on the Internet.

IV. VIRTUAL AND AUGMENTED REALITY

To a user, the Internet seems to have evolved from a simple 2D interface environment to ambitiously challenge real-life environments and become a *place* in the form of virtual worlds like http://www.secondlife.com. These social networks allow ordinary Internet users to interact as avatars in real-time in shared 3D virtual worlds. People's avatars are visual representations of themselves that are used to immerse them in highly social 3D online worlds. They allow one to move around and interact with others from the safe environment of their computer using facial expressions and body language similar to the ones in the real world. Although initially they were seen as role-playing games (like www.worldofwarcraft.com), they have now grown to become realistic educational and business environments where transactions can take place and business deals conducted.

Virtual worlds allow us to escape reality with its physical and social limitations. We could be in imaginary worlds, wear outrageous clothes, and act as crazy and weird as we want. Apart from that though, they can be used by negotiators as friendly and comfortable gathering places for round-table discussions to explore solutions and exchange ideas.

The downside of using virtual worlds presently is the user's degree of familiarity with the technology and the great amount of preparation it requires. Ensuring everyone has fast Internet connection, the right software and hardware, has registered, and is familiar with the surroundings of the virtual worlds and comfortable navigating and interacting around it can be quite a turnoff at the moment. Keeping the participants (that you don't really see) active and in tune is another major challenge. In the virtual world you have no indication or control of the distractions your participants are facing in their real lives at the moment of the meeting. This is especially difficult if feedback from many is required. If movement and interaction are required in the virtual world (to look at something or someone), additional multitasking is required that will further inhibit the process. Navigating around and typing messages in the virtual world cannot be as efficient as walking and talking in the real worlds. Given that fact, we cannot escape the physical world. Living in two worlds at the same time can only degrade the negotiator's performance and negatively impact the deal.

These are some of the reasons that at the moment only high-tech companies like IBM (http://www.ibm.com/developerworks/opensource/library/os-social-secondlife/index.html) can probably make value out of this technology. Pre-meeting introductory sessions are necessary to overcome some of the difficulties and establish interaction protocols. The overall benefit for negotiations at the moment is that they might provide a fun and engaging environment to brainstorm.

As hardware and communication speeds increase it will be possible to eliminate the movement lag that today's virtual worlds exhibit, and then what we would probably see is a move from the traditional 2D screens that pin us in front of the screen to wearable Internet technologies. This will be the world of augmented reality and the e-negotiator's battlefield. By interfacing virtual computer-generated imagery and projecting it into the real world, we will be able to enhance the physical elements of the real-world environment. This augmentation will enhance people's perception of reality.

Think for a moment that you are in a face-to-face negotiation and, as you look at your counterpart, information is displayed around them about their profile, past performance, and even their physiological signals in real-time. Face and body language can be interpreted and displayed as you negotiate and supporting information about the issues discussed can appear in thin air. Nice you might think, but whatever you can do, the other side will probably also be able to do. It will be like we and the software have merged as one. If that sounds like too much science fiction, just keep in mind that this technology is here and parts of it are already in use by the military. Applicability of such technology is only limited by our brain's ability to handle all this overload of information. Problems with mixing reality with virtual presence are bound to emerge and it is questionable if we are ready to handle such developments.

Due to the critical aspects of negotiations we are definitely going to see the technology being explored to the max to gain competitive advantage. Hopefully though, the implemented and adopted changes will not be faster than our adaptation capabilities. The advantage naturally will be in favor of the young as they will not be hindered by previous experiences and, as always, are by nature more willing to take risks, experiment, and adopt something new.

V. THE IPHONE MODEL

In recent years a new type of technology matured enough to gain considerable market ground and popularity. Network-wise this led to shifting from WWW with its open architecture to a form of semi-closed platforms like the iPhone and iPad that use the Internet for transport. These proprietary types of technologies abandon the Web in favor of consumer comfort and ease. They don't use the traditional protocols and languages, like html, of the Web and they cannot be crawled by search engines like Google. The fact that companies like Apple are making tons of money off of these technologies is a clear indication of their success and the preference consumers show for them.

Challenging the dominance of the browser interface is a major coop for these technologies. They achieved that by exerting tight control over the applications they support for reliable consumer experience while the traditional open WWW can get confusing (Wild West Web, as it's called occasionally). For instance, it's easier, quicker, and more flexible to use an iPad to access Twitter and Google Maps instead of using their Web interface. An added feature is that they do incorporate browsers for those that need to occasionally access the Web traditionally.

From the point of view of the negotiator, having a phone they can carry around and use to receive information from the Web instead of having to go to the Web is quite an advantage. These devices are small enough to easily carry around and at the same time offer necessary applications to use the Internet and communicate from practically anywhere. With the addition in the near future of projection capabilities in them, we might observe the end of the notebook computers. By projection capabilities we not only refer to displays, but also to virtual keyboard and mouse (refer to the online section of the book for more resources on that).

VI. ARTIFICIAL INTELLIGENCE (AI)

Simulating human behavior and interaction is one of the ultimate goals of computer science and a very active field of research nowadays. Efforts to achieve near-human intelligence will mount in the future in an attempt to relinquish most of our automated and repetitive functions to computers. Negotiations (the "e" in this case is implied by default) will be no exception to this trend and while initially AI will function in a supporting role, we can expect to see more of its involvement in automated negotiations in the future.

Any professional negotiator would love to have an "expert" doing intelligence on their behalf, organize and present findings in ways that are easy to read and understand, formalize strategies, and even take care of some initial communications on their behalf. If we let it go one more step and allow AI applications to complete deals as long as they fall within certain parameters, we will have achieved the final step in the evolution of the profession where we actually don't need human negotiators. This, of course, borders with the sphere of science fiction so for the time being we will present some of the AI techniques that might actually add some value to the e-negotiations process. A variation of expert systems already being used in negotiations and legal disputes is *case-based reasoning* (CBR). This is the process by which we approach solutions to new problems based on solutions of similar problems in the past. The US legal system is structured in such a way that judges create case laws and lawyers base their cases on past cases.

One of the most reliable forms of AI today is *expert systems*. This type of technology is quite old actually and has been used extensively. The financial services industry, for example, uses expert systems when they want to decide if someone is eligible for a loan. The methodology is simple. Starting with answers to a preset list of questions, the system will ask further questions and in this way traverse the decision tree of the particular case (see Formal Methods of Decision Analysis in the Strategy Chapter) and eventually reach a leaf with an "Approve" or "Disapprove" decision. The utility of such systems for an e-negotiator should be obvious for organizing alternatives and deciding on the strategy to follow during negotiations. Given that expert systems are based on existing knowledge, their success depends on covering the full range of observable solutions. In that sense, they shouldn't be used for unfamiliar or atypical situations.

Expert systems can further be enhanced with *fuzzy logic*. This technology allows the representation of vague and subjective perceptions and processes to be represented as a continuum with upper and lower limits that makes it easy to process computationally. In negotiations for instance, a ZOPA (see the Strategy chapter) is a kind of fuzzy logic in the sense that acceptable deals are within a range and not at preset values. Human beings marvel at fuzzy logic so implementing it algorithmically allows us to represent things not only as black and white, but also as shades of gray. While we have been extensively using this type of technology in engineering and sciences, we should be able in the future to implement it in negotiations as part of other technologies like the ones presented here.

In an attempt to simulate human intelligence, a major branch of AI moved in the direction to actually simulate neuron behavior and function. Given that neurons are the basic units of our brains that carry and process electrical signals from the senses, an obvious way to replicate some aspects of intelligence would be to simulate these units and, by combining them, achieve some of the functionality of the human brain. This technology is called *neural networks* and has proven ideal in simulating the ability of our brain to draw conclusions and make decisions based on limited information. The fact that we understand each other's writing styles and the fact that we can deduce the elements of a picture even when it's blurred are some of the types of functions our brain performs efficiently. Neural networks are ideal for pattern recognition and as such they can be used to alert a negotiator when certain patterns of behavior of offers and counteroffers appear. Based on that they can alert the negotiator and even recommend follow-up strategies. Similarly to expert systems, this type of technology bases its success on historical data and it's unable to make predictions or discoveries about unusual and unconventional cases.

To make discoveries one needs a technology that can mix the input elements of a problem in unpredictable ways so that out of the ordinary solutions can appear with the potential for some of them to be more useful than the existing ones we have. A type of technology that can achieve that is *genetic algorithms*. Their approach to providing variation is similar to the way human diversity and most life forms are produced by randomly combining parts of the parents'

DNA to create offspring with combined characteristics. Occasionally, the combined traits of the offspring are proven evolutionarily superior to those of the parents, so we end up with more resistive and successful populations. In addition, mutations that take place during reproduction further contribute to diversity that in time can lead to superior species. Applying the same methodology in negotiations we can produce solution alternatives that might be proven superior to our alternatives. The technology, of course, is a type of a heuristic that cannot guarantee optimum solutions within the time constraints of a negotiation, but with an increase in computing power and the improved formulation of negotiation problems it should be able to gain popularity in the future.

The final form of AI technology that we will mention here is *artificial agents*. While we have seen this technology in the special case of automated negotiations in the previous chapter, we want to present them here as the only technology that can actually simulate multiparty negotiations and even moderate such negotiations. While this is especially true for price negotiations, we do expect to see in the future a lot more of it especially in cases where these pieces of software combine with the AI technologies we mentioned before. Independent learning and autonomy will be some of the major capabilities of this technology. In addition, cooperative and collective behavior will raise their intelligence awareness to consciousness levels we usually see in science fiction movies. A major concern will always be the security and control aspect of artificial agents because, given inappropriate commands (like computer viruses, for example), they can act maliciously and damage the negotiation process.

9.2 Beyond Globalization

Before the modern breakthroughs of communications technology everything was localized in the sense that our primary business function was in our physical proximity where we could perform most of our operations. Then came globalization where the work environment broke the physical boundaries of our daily reach and now we are able to conduct business and work with people from all over the world anytime and from anywhere. Two mainsprings made globalization possible. The first was the accelerated growth of technology with innovations in computers and telecommunications and the second was the wave of deregulations and the opening of national and closed economies (like the collapse of the Soviet Union and the Asian meltdown). To the general public though, globalization is primarily attributed to the growth of the Internet. The question now is, what does the future hold? Where could someone go after globalization? The answer can be deduced from the way we focus our perspectives and the forces acting in the business and social environments.

The initial trend of globalization was to perceive the world as a continuum where local trends will be squashed under the pressure of a convergent global culture. Apparently, what this perspective lacks is the fact that globalization is composed of closed local elements that might be quite resistant to change. What we are probably going to see is a balance between globalization and localization forces that might converge in the very distant future. In the near future though, we might see something like the cultural structure of the US where there is a prevalent federal culture within which localized elements live and function (Chinese, Greeks, Jews, Latinos, and so on). From the perspective of an e-negotiator, understanding and acknowledgment of cultural characteristics will always contribute to success. For example, the e-negotiations language might be English, but the way it's used and perceived will be influenced by "local"/cultural elements.

Knowing the world in its entirety will be very important since we will all be influenced by changes that occur in different parts of it. This means that e-negotiators need to have a good grasp of world affairs and reflect on distant events that may underlie and affect situations of interest to them. This is easier said than done because the interplay between global and local, between cultures and subcultures, between states and markets, between pace and space, between urban and rural (to name a few of the opposites) might not be so evident or immediate. These tensions are perceived differently in different communities and parts of the world and cyberspace will reflect these differences in obvious and subtle ways. Being alert and open is probably the best tactic a negotiator can practice to counter all the changes that will take place.

9.3 Reputation Management

Building a profile online is like building a name, while maintaining it is like branding. From the moment we are online we are visible. That exposes us to every threat and damage that is available online. This ranges from the spam email we receive to the influences of every site that tries to get our money, the manipulation of public opinion by lobbies of one size or many, and to every type of malicious software that can penetrate and damage our system.

Although one could outsource this public relations function, we will leave this option for the "celebrities" among us. From the perspective of this book, we will view reputation management in reference to one's presence online. While most references to reputation management online usually refer to damage control and prevention, we will address the issues from the promotion and negotiations point of view.

An easy way to start thinking about reputation management is to go to a search engine and type our name as a keyword. See what comes up or what doesn't come up. It is more than certain there will be others with our name that might even be ranked higher than us. If we are lucky enough they will be irrelevant to our profession so anyone will be able to distinguish them from us. Then we can try our name and profession as keywords and see what comes up. This is more critical than anything else as it is probably the way others will look for us. The purpose of this exercise is to first identify any negative references to our name so we can do something about it, and second to see if our appearance is the way we want to be.

Typing "Harkiolakis," for example, usually pops up as the author of this book along with an archbishop in New Zealand (at least at the time of this writing). Although having a representative of God ranked closely with our name is not such a bad thing, it still dilutes the image we want to project. In addition, references of the author's past research that is irrelevant to e-negotiations will pop up, further diluting the image of the e-negotiator that hopefully the author is trying to project at this stage in his life. If a rare surname can create such confusion, e-negotiators with more common names like Smith should expect to have it worse. The situation gets better when one focuses on social network sites that have a more focused purpose.

To preserve our reputation as e-negotiators our presence online should be serious and as light as possible with content that reflects these qualities. We should avoid the display of "wild life" activities or extreme positions on real-life issues; one needs to also keep in mind that the easiest thing today is for someone to record and post videos on YouTube and other social network sites. So a life of moderation will probably assist the profession of e-negotiations. Cleaning up a mess online is much more difficult that in real life due to the permanence of the medium. The only thing we can do is to dilute the pool of negative impressions by creating a bigger pool of positive impressions. That can be very difficult given that negative impressions are more entertaining and attractive to the human curiosity than positive ones. The rule of the Internet jungle is that the more attention we get (more hits on web pages that include our names), the more visible we become (ranked higher in search engines), so we appear higher in search results which causes more people to see us. So the cycle reinforces itself. Given that ranking has permanence, the only thing we can actually do is create positive responses (websites) that others will view and hopefully, through a similar feedback loop, will raise the ranking of the positives higher than the negatives. This is more difficult than anyone can imagine and has rarely been done successfully.

The best we could do is to build our "islands" of Internet presence where we are in control and protect these territories as much as we can. It is bound that the serious researcher will eventually get to them when seeking the truth so we will get our chance to set things the way we want and present our case the way we intend. These "islands" can be in many forms like our personal website, our blogs, and our profiles and presence on social network sites.

9.3.1 PERSONAL WEBSITES

The first thing in getting a personal website (for professional purposes and not for friends and relatives) is getting a domain name. Searching the Internet we will find many providers of such services (like smallbusiness.yahoo.com and www.godaddy.com). There, we can check the availability of the names that express us and our business. Our first choices should be the traditional ".net," ".com," and ".org" extensions, combined with our name, to give something like www.yourName.net. The ".net" extension is a good extension for negotiators since it suggests networks and networking. If our name is popular enough to have already been chosen by others, we should try combinations of our name with words like "negotiations," "consulting," and similar.

Once we have a domain name we need to choose a Web host where our website will reside. Reliability and support is what we are looking for here. A lot of the businesses that sell domain names also provide Web hosting services so a good choice might be to use these services. It is also likely that they will have combined offers that will make it more economical to get the domain name and hosting from the same provider. The host will take care of all the issues like updating the DNS registries that our domain name is associated with on the servers that will host our website so when browsers look at our URL they will know which server has our web pages.

Having a name to ourselves and a plot to build our online home, we are ready to start designing and building our website. For starters, one should look around and get ideas of how similar websites look and decide on the design and content features we will adopt and the ones we will avoid. If the design and building of the website is too overwhelming and the negotiator is not tech-savvy, it is strongly recommended that they consider outsourcing this activity to a web designer service. Such services are also provided with reasonable fees by the companies that sell domain names and Web hosting so it might not be a bad idea to get everything from the same source. Also, one might consider freely available website templates that cover the most popular options and use them to build a website.

The most important element in a website is the home page. This is our "face" online and the first impressions are going to be formed here. Striving for the best balance between too much and too little is quite a challenge. Optimization of the various elements like video, graphics, images, and text will need a lot of trial and error with much feedback from sources we trust. Another important issue is the speed of downloading our home page through the Internet and the overhead required by browsers to display it. Speed will mainly be affected by the size of the non-textual elements, and overhead is affected by the use of plug-ins and add-ons the browser will need to use to display the page. If a page is developed with Flash and includes animation and video, it will take considerably much more time to download and display than a plain text page with simple graphics. Given that competition is only one "click" away and that viewer patience diminishes on the Web, it is recommended that a serious and simple-looking homepage might be ideal for e-negotiators. Popularity and functionality do not necessarily relate to animated and graphically rich elements. The homepage of Google, for example, is the most popular website in the world with probably the most minimalistic approach to web page design. Suggesting design principles in website technology is outside the scope of this book, but a simple thing to keep in mind is that for every non-text element of a web page, the browser will need to do extra fetching to get it and display it so this back and forth will add to display time. So simplicity and content is much more important, at least from the perspective of the e-negotiator.

Some other critical issues one needs to consider when designing a website is the depth and breadth of the website (Figure 9.1). Websites can be expressed as tree hierarchies of nodes/web pages with the homepage (index.html) at the root, followed by branches and leading to the leaves. Movement is guided by menus that show the options/branches below a node and hyperlinks that point to other web pages in the tree. Hyperlinks are also used to take someone to other websites and web pages. Although much of the success and appeal of a website will be in the homepage, what will follow is equally important at least for the serious visitor that comes to our site for business.

The depth of the site has to do with how many nodes we have to traverse before reaching a leaf of the tree, going from superiors to subordinates. Of course, this varies because branches express different sequences of content. Going too deep will make it difficult to retract in case we want to follow another branch while going too shallow will make it difficult to express complex concepts that build upon others. For the purposes of e-negotiators' websites, an average website depth of 3 to 4 should be enough to get the message across in sufficient detail.

The width of the site has to do with the number of nodes that extend at the same level under a superior node. This also varies as each node can have many subordinates, but, in general, providing too many options can be very tiring to the eye and confusing. A minimum of 3 and a maximum of 14 should be the limit of the number of subordinates as anything else will make it look unnatural or difficult for the human eye to traverse. A general principle for the average human mind is that it can comfortably handle 3 to 7 items at a time. Logic and common sense should guide the design and structure of a website more than what theory or experiments suggest.

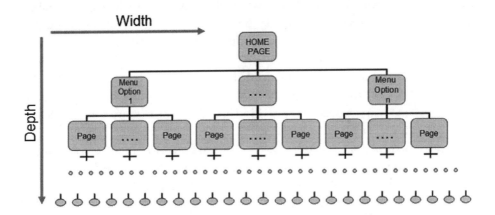

Figure 9.1   Typical Website Structure

A brief summary of some useful tips include (more on the book's website):

- *Comfort is important.* Reading-page dimensions should ideally fit the length of a typical screen display (like a 15-inch screen). Avoid long text that forces the user to use the scroll bar to read the rest of the text. Ensure that your page resizes with browser window resizing to avoid the need for cumbersome horizontal scrolling. For long sections you might want to consider having a link to a PDF file that the users can download and read at their convenience. In such cases, users are used to scrolling down and it will be natural for them to do so with such documents. The visual appearance of the text is also a key ingredient of comfort, so anything that deviates from the familiar looks of print material (books, newspapers, and so on) is not going to contribute positively. Keeping the font size between 10 and 12 for anything other than titles is recommended along with popular fonts like Arial as they allow comfortable reading even at low screen resolutions.

- *Appropriate content is king.* Your target is your present and potential customers, not your competitors, so customize content for them. Including your negotiation philosophy, your achievements and customer testimonials help a lot. Case studies are also good to showcase your style and achievement because they help your potential clients identify with your existing clients. Another element that also helps when there is not much history behind your name is to include popular case study analysis, tutorials, guidelines, and tips, and provide resources that could be of help to potential clients (like legal aspects of negotiations). Providing introductory and advanced material should be an option for the visitors to view. Too sophisticated presentations are good to gain the respect of the competition, but can project you as too academic for the average customer. It's best to support your case with links to other pages for demanding visitors rather than put everything in one long page. The main concept should be clear and simple and provide links for more. If you are familiar with creating podcasts (radio type presentations), you might want to consider developing some for further analysis of what you present. When developed in the form of tutorials, customers can download them and listen to them at their convenience.

- *Update frequently.* Adding new content and removing the old regularly shows that you are active and serious in having your website as a supporting element of your job. The website is going to be visited a lot when you are negotiating as part of the other side's intelligence on you. Certain messages can be passed to the other side through your web pages so if that is what you plan, make sure references and leads exist even on the homepage that will guide the visitors to what you want. With every update, make sure you back up everything. Even if the service you bought provides such services, it is always a good idea to back up everything somewhere locally. Something that many people do with their personal websites (usually small in size) is to have mirror images of their website locally where they make updates and changes. When they are done they upload the whole site on the Internet over the old one.

- *Interactivity adds to visitor engagement and retention.* It is a natural consequence of providing a sense of control even if that is in the form of feedback. Although a lot of that can be done through other means like social network sides and emails, your website provides a unique advantage—full control. You say what you want to say without anyone censoring your material.

- *Respect privacy and copyrights.* Of primary importance nowadays is respecting the privacy of website visitors especially when they provide personal information like mail and email addresses, credit card information, and personal views and preferences. Having your visitor provide all these details in exchange for services you provide to them has to be done in a transparent way and with their full consent. We are not referring here to security issues that are of major concern as much as to the terms of use of a website and the way privileged and personal information is treated. Notifying the user of such issues when they perform transactions on your website is essential. While it is understandable that alerting the user shouldn't be at the expense of the experience and the service provided, it is nevertheless imperative that at least we follow the mainstream practices. Having links at the bottom of our homepage that redirect to our privacy policy and terms of use should suffice. Looking at similar links of well-known websites and drafting similar policies should work just fine also.

If you plan to use logos (like, say, your customers') you need to have a written (email at least) confirmation that they are allowing you to do so. The same applies to customer testimonials, images, and graphics that you didn't develop or buy. Giving proper credit also adds credibility to your website as it shows you are professional and well connected.

When quoting emails make sure you include them as pictures and not as text. If you have to, use text type in forms understandable by humans and not web crawlers. Examples of such approaches are "name @ domain" (a crawler will consider spaces as separating different words), "name at domain," and so on.

i. Promotion and maintenance

Being in cyberspace means nothing if no one knows we exist. Same as in real life, one needs to interact with others, be visible, and socialize if a difference is going to be made. Joining communities online is something we will discuss later on. Here we focus on what can be done to attract others to our online "world." In order to do that, we have to rethink how we found others as this is the most probable way for others to find us. Provided someone knows a few things about us like our name and profession, the first thing they will do is type our details in a search engine and hope that we will surface in the first or second screen load of hits. We are mentioning here the first couple of screen lists simply because most people, instead of looking at the endless list of hits that might have been produced, will probably start modifying their query terms instead to see if they can get what they want faster and within the first screen of hits.

The method that Google uses to decide the order by which results will appear for a search query is called *PageRank*. In essence, it is an algorithm that numerically weighs various elements of a web page to decide their importance within the existing set of web pages. While the internals of the algorithm are proprietary and secret, it is certain that for each of our web pages it ranks, it does consider keywords we inserted in the corresponding *meta* tag field of the html file of a web page, the title and URL of a web page, references to our web page from other web pages, and, of course, the terms in the text of a web page, placing more weight on specially formatted text like paragraph titles. Our efforts to increase our ranking for certain keywords therefore should focus on all these elements.

Some hints to increase the ranking and relevance of our websites include:

- URL page names should reflect the content of a web page. Avoid names like "page134.htm" and prefer names like "e-negotiations_presentation.html," for example. This will also make it easier to maintain the website as we can deduce content from the name. If you include non-textual elements like pictures, graphics, and video, make sure also that their names in the html file indicate content. Don't use names like "picture1.jpg" unless you don't want them to be found: names like "e-negotiations_strategy_graph.jpg," although cumbersome, are easier for web engines to crawl and file.

- The *meta* tag in the html file should be properly filled with meaningful keywords that reflect the content of each web page. This is probably one of the most significant elements for web page ranking.

- Ensure your website URL is mentioned in other websites like blogs, social network sites, and emails. Include it when providing feedback and in general whenever you interact online.

- Use meaningful paragraph titles in the text with bigger and decorated font (the headings < h1 > tags in html) because search engines place higher value on them.

- Avoid nonsense or silly stuff, even in insignificant areas of your website. You wouldn't like to appear at the wrong places. When in doubt, try a portion of your text as queries in search engines and see what comes up.

Having done all that, the next thing we should do is inform the world about our content. Although search engines will be updated at some time with the changes we are making, it is far better to alert them ourselves. On the Internet there are plenty of services that will do that for us (in exchange for a little bit of our privacy of course, like our email address), but we can get the same effect more or less if we do it ourselves. Given that most search engines check each other, submitting our URL to the top ones like Google (http://www.google.com/addurl/?continue=/addurl) and Bing (http://www.bing.com/webmaster/SubmitSitePage.aspx) should be enough.

The next step in informing the world about our changes is more personal and involves direct marketing through social networks, blogs, and emails. A brief announcement in any online forum we participate in should be enough to attract attention. Just make sure it's not something that imposes on others and is treated as spam. Only when we have something that could add value to the members of our networks should we announce it. This is even more important when we invite people by email to visit our website. It's like inviting someone to your home so it better be something worth seeing there.

ii. RSS feeds

A less invasive and more sophisticated way to promote a website is by using RSS (Really Simple Syndication) feeds. This is an XML-based form of communication used by websites and blogs to distribute news headlines and other content on the Web. It is a subscription service that websites provide for anyone interested in their content and can be tracked and personalized to the needs of the user. Although similar to email subscription, RSS feeds are less invasive, they preserve privacy and can be aggregated in user homepages provided by most service providers like Google, Yahoo and MSN (usually formatted like http://my.provider.com). By subscribing to RSS feeds, users can customize the frequency and type of news they want to receive.

From the technology point of view, RSS are essentially XML-formatted documents with their own tags. More resources on RSS feeds are available on the book's website, but the typical outline of an RSS document will look like:

```
<rss version="2.0">

<channel>

<title> some title/title>

<link> http://www.somename.com/</link>

<description> .... </description>

<item>

...... some news
```

```
</item>

</channel>

</rss>
```

iii. Web analytics

As with most interactive activities, we need feedback to evaluate the impact of what we are doing online and a measurement of the success of our promotion initiatives. *Web analytics* is the process by which we collect measurements and reports on our website usage. This goes beyond measuring Web traffic, to include analysis of all activities taking place on our websites. Devising and observing performance indicators of our website (and for intelligence purposes, someone else's website) is a valuable process for obtaining insight about the popularity and functionality of web pages: this information compared with other sources, like email response rates and print marketing, can augment the information collected and provide a more accurate picture of the website performance.

For most websites, a free service like Google Analytics (http://www.google.com/analytics/index.html) should be just fine. Google Analytics will give enough insight into a website's traffic for effective marketing decisions to be made. Some of the information collected includes page views, visitor profiles including geographic origin, pages viewed and time spent on them, recurrence of visitors, reference links they followed to get to your website, and whether they used a search engine or through a direct link/reference to our site from another site. You can also set alerts where Google Analytics will email you a report on events of your choice (like new visitors, geographic origin, and so on) as frequently as you choose. Finally, the service allows you to monitor your site's performance by setting goals to follow like URL destinations, time on site, and pages viewed.

9.3.2 PERSONAL BLOGS AND WIKIS

One of the most popular activities on the Internet is building and maintaining online journals. These are short public speech sessions where we present to the world audience. Blogs are a type of online journal that we can update in real time as frequently as we want. They are under the control of the owner/author and other people are allowed to view and comment. Wikis, on the other hand, are blogs that can be updated by many people. A popular form of wiki is Wikipedia (www.wikipedia.com).

A key characteristic of blogs is the timeline. Everything follows a chronological order like a real-life discussion, with the main difference being that the medium is online writing. A variant of *blogging* is *micro-blogging* which resembles real-life telephone conversations that are meant to be permanent and disposable. Its value could be debatable for e-negotiators since all this functionality is also included in regular blogs. Of real value though are blogs where a negotiator can present positions and take advantage of the collective intelligence and feedback of anyone involved or interested in the negotiation issue at hand.

Creating a blog or a wiki differs from creating a website. Blogs and wikis tend to be more current than websites, and need to attract a relevant audience fast. That requires a more engaging design and appearance with frequently updated content to attract recurrent and active participants. To that end, choosing proper titles, tagging, categorizing, and promoting take time and continuous effort. On the other hand, if successful, the rewards can more than outweigh the investment. Apart from the apparent value to the negotiator, blogs can also function as e-commerce sites with advertisements and promotional material that can provide additional monetary value and revenues. One should be very careful though not to dilute the content with these extras and distract the visitor from the actual purpose of the blog. Professional *blogging* themes are usually conferences, tradeshows, and round-tables where the issues you are involved in are the main or part of the discussion theme. Case studies and practical tips on negotiations issues could be attractive to present while triggering useful debates.

Summary characteristics of blogs and wikis

Advantages:

- Provide controlled (and hopefully better) information about a negotiation issue;

- Assist in building better relationships with clients as they can interact directly with a real person that provides personalized responses;

- In controlled environments, like corporate intranets, they can be a great source of knowledge sharing;

- Provide feedback and awareness to the negotiator about what is perceived by others;

- Good for building reputation and showcasing the negotiator's talent and expertise.

Disadvantages:

- Many times it's difficult to say something in a way that is interesting and clear;

- It can be created by anyone including non-experts. This dilutes the market for competent professionals who additionally have very little time to blog;

- Building a blog can be quite easy, creating the deception that this is all it takes. Blogs need more time and effort to maintain than build and this type of dedication and investment is not anticipated by many. As a result, if not properly maintained this can have a rather damaging effect on the negotiator's reputation. A way out might be to remove the blog once it has served its purpose. Bad impressions stay longer so it's better not to be out there if you are not going to look good;

- The views expressed and their influence on the participants might not be what the negotiator intended. Extreme positions can easily be expressed even in ways that might not be appropriate so one has to be very careful and clear about their expectations when building a blog.

Rules When Blogging:

- Use English as the most popular and "universal" language online;

- Think well of what you want to say before writing. As with everything else on the Web, a record of what you say is bound to perpetuate in time and get back to you unexpectedly;

- Structure your writing to convey the message you want in a way similar to print publications that everyone is familiar with;

- Always presume your readers are intelligent so avoid oversimplifications and obvious statements. The quality of the readers is more important than the quantity;

- Most people are informed so extended explanations are not necessary. What we can do to ensure everyone follows at the same pace is add links for additional and background information for those that want to explore more or become familiar with the discussion subject;

- Link your source and references to the material you present. Especially if you are using specialized terminology with a not-so-familiar audience, make sure you provide links to further information and explanations;

- Watch out for intellectual property violations especially when using pictures and video. When you want to include proprietary content, you need to acquire the appropriate permission from the owners. Alternatively you can provide the link to the resource for visitors to follow;

- Acknowledge all the help you get for setting up each post. Courtesy is a virtue that will help in promoting your site as content providers might link to your blog;

- Promote the blog on various occasions and in forums either online or offline. The purpose of the blog is to attract and engage the appropriate public. This is not going to happen by itself. People need to be guided by invitations or reference links on other sites.

Most of the characteristics of blogs are also included in wikis. The purpose of wikis though is different in the sense that wikis can be edited by many so they represent consensus more than different opinions and positions. Many times wikis can have an associated discussion page, but their primary purpose is to function like an encyclopedia of existing knowledge. For that reason, they are embedded with many links to other resources that support claims and expand the areas covered. Building a wiki has more permanence to it and intends to serve as reference to a current state of matter. When news and issues are concerned, wikis need continuous updating by many to stay current. Authority and expertise of the authors is of great importance so attracting proper writers and building reputation is important and difficult at the same time. Experts might be more willing to participate in wikis as their permanence and status as reference sources can add more to reputation than blogs.

Nowadays there are many free tools and services (an Internet search will provide many of them) that allow someone to easily build and maintain blogs and wikis. Ease of use and low cost though come at the expense of control and security. The providers of those services have complete control of the material presented under their domains so no real guarantee exists that whatever we have online today will continue to exist tomorrow. Backing up the content to our own storage mediums is the responsibility of the owner and should be done regularly. Nothing can compete with having our own domain, website, and hosting hardware. When cost and lack of technical expertise is an issue, a blog or a wiki are good solutions.

9.3.3 SOCIAL NETWORKS

The increased popularity of the Internet as a gathering place saw immediately the formation of networks of people with common interests or functions. Social networking sites allow us to connect with people we know and people with similar personal and professional interests to ours. They function as an update service for news and announcements that members post to inform their peers in their networks and interact on whatever is of interest to them. Along with their networking capabilities, social networks are a cheap and efficient medium for promotions and public relations. As you add contacts to your network or join other networks, you have the ability to see what networks others are joining and expand your sphere of influence and networking resources. Updates are transmitted automatically to members of a group and allow for commenting and participation in discussions. Their format is extremely easy to follow and manage for anyone with basic computer skills.

For e-negotiators, apart from serving as public relations mediums, social networks allow experimentation by pitching a story through the network and create pressure on the counterpart's side. Corporations nowadays are very keen on building and maintaining active social network sites. Any involvement they observe in their networks and any issues relating to them on other networks are of great importance to them. Engaging in social network activities can be an important element of strategy in negotiations and should not be overlooked by e-negotiators. This is especially true for government sites that rely on public opinion to formulate policy.

An issue that is raised many times with social networks is privacy. Breaches can be the result of faulty implementation, loose policies, and malicious attempts. All these usually result in identity thefts and retrieval of emails and personal information that can be used to expedite members. After resolving these issues, social networking sites offer an added advantage to those concerned with privacy as they function like "closed" networks and as such they belong to the dark Web concerning search engines. Crawling social network sites by traditional search engines like Google and Bing is usually only allowed for certain sections that members tag as public.

A non-exhaustive (more on the book's website) select list of some popular social networks include:

- LinkedIn (www.linkedin.com) is a social and career networking community that allows users to connect with other professionals in their field, find jobs, post announcements, start discussions, and network with employees, consultants and business partners. The e-negotiations group (http://www.linkedin.com/groups?most Popular=&gid=3373713), for example, was built as a follow up to the print edition of this book in order to serve as a resource for negotiators that perform all or part of their jobs online. LinkedIn in that sense serves as a credibility builder for marketing the book as it shows the world some aspects of the book and also brings together people that the book has reached.

One of the most attractive features of LinkedIn is the character limit it imposes on posted text. This enforces quality in favor of quantity in addition to making messages less disturbing, straight to the point, and easy to read. In this way, a profile becomes like an abbreviated résumé that simplifies reading for similar-minded professionals. It can also be easily saved as a PDF by others. When profiling your counterparts, a first look at LinkedIn will give you clues about whom you are dealing with. Even their absence from such networks has something to say about them. Building a profile is extremely easy while maintenance requires minimum effort. The same applies when building a group.

LinkedIn is probably the ideal social networking site for the professional e-negotiator. One can build a profile that will be viewed by other professionals in the field and help promote oneself as a professional. In addition, it also serves as a benchmarking tool since we can see how others with similar skills present themselves. It can also be a safe place to find qualified answers to questions we might have as it allows us to search the Question and Answer sections for previously asked questions.

When building a LinkedIn profile one needs to ensure that all elements reflect their professional qualification and status. Especially when building the summary section, keyword optimization should be considered as this section will be indexed by search engines like Google. In addition to professional identifications like "negotiation," "online," and "winning," including buzz words like "reciprocity," "tipping point," and whatever seems popular in the field, will greatly increase the chance of being found. When promoting, in general there are two strategies one can follow. The first is to become a LION (LinkedIn Open Networker), where anyone can connect to us, and the other is to be an "Ambassador," where others need to get our approval before connecting with us. The second option is by far the most appropriate for e-negotiators because it's less disturbing and we can ensure that members add to our credibility. The saying, "show me your friends and I'll tell you who you are" better expresses our point here.

- Twitter (www.twitter.com) is a social network that allows users to set up a profile and post continuous updates about what they are doing at any given moment, either by logging onto the Twitter.com site or sending a text message via phone or instant messaging. What sets it apart from other social networking sites is the limit of up to 140 characters of text of each message (*tweet* is the proper lingo) you send. As such, it's a great tool to use to update friends and relatives on what you are doing each moment—sort of like sending group SMSs. This led a lot of people to believe that "tweeting" is just a waste of time. Before agreeing with that view one needs to consider the purpose of using it. Twitter is not as personalized and not as invasive as SMS—the users choose to receive tweets while with SMS that is not an option. Tweets in that respect are something someone chooses to receive and from that perspective they are supposedly welcomed.

It allows negotiators to be connected to networks of professionals who share their views and keep in touch with what has been said about them, their organizations, their products and brands, and anything else that relates to their professional life. It can provide a steady stream of ideas, content, and resources about their area of expertise and in general one can tap into the knowledge of the many. The question of what to do or say in Twitter so that the whole endeavor is not just a waste of time has a lot to do with what we are doing or plan to do in the future. This varies according to our needs and the strategy we want to follow. From the negotiations point of view, showing up just when the negotiation issue arises and trying to build some activity will easily be identified as a marketing effort to sell than an effort to contribute. Professionals value constructive participation that can lead to gains and it's unlikely they will fall for an advertiser's trick to gain attention and increase sales.

To gain the potential advantages of Twitter one needs to be there and interact. In other words, you have be an active part of the community. This is what adds value to social networks and establishes them as successful mediums of communication. In essence, Twitter is like *micro-blogs* with a corporate look that someone else maintains. The more we put into them, the more we get. The return on investment that one can have is probably difficult to evaluate, but making a decent effort will definitely be worth it; if nothing else, to look you are not left behind.

- Facebook (www.facebook.com) is the most popular social networking site at the time of this writing. It allows someone to connect with people, organizations, and unions, and be part of personal and public networks. It's the basic form of connecting with someone as "friends," sending messages, and building a profile for our self or our business. It gained a lot of popularity because of its simple format and its capability to include multimedia (pictures and video). That allowed members to join networks organized by school, workplace, and activities of interest, and share each other's news, experiences, and views. Its appeal grew even more with younger generations as it allows anyone from age 13 and above to freely become a member. It is, after all, a site that was founded by college students. An extreme example that shows the influence of social networks in our lives is the fact that even courts (Australia: http://legalblogwatch.typepad.com/legal_blog_watch/2008/12/ court-papers-served-by-facebook.html, New Zealand: http:// legalblogwatch.typepad.com/legal_blog_watch/2009/05/courtoks-service-of-summons-on-facebook.html at the moment of this writing) serve notifications and processes to defendants on Facebook.

A key Facebook characteristic that contributes greatly to its growth and popularity, even between businesses, is that control of participation is in the user's hands. This means we don't receive promotional material from groups we are not members of and that we can't be reached by members we don't like. To connect with someone we either have to be invited by email or allowed to join by the sites/people we want to connect with. This opt-in feature is unlike traditional methods that advertisers and marketers use to "invade" our lives.

For e-negotiators, the most important issue in social networks is promotion in order to attract and maintain an audience appropriate to their field and interests. Value grows with numbers and "exclusiveness." Having a lot of followers with irrelevant interests and orientations (referring to business here) is like having a crowd instead of a group. The network can also serve as a source of revenue as everything that we mentioned on blogs and wikis applies here too.

Given the ability of social networks to cover different aspects of our lives, what is suggested for professional negotiators that join general interest networks like Facebook is to have different profiles/accounts for their personal and professional lives. Another option that can be very useful and save a lot of time is to have your accounts in various social networks interlinked so one can reference the other. This way duplication of effort will be minimized while preserving the image and presence of the negotiator.

9.4 Keeping "Fit"

One thing about the future is certain and that is its uncertainty. We can only speculate about it and make projections based on what we know about the present and the past that led to it. Based on these projections we prepare as best as we can to handle the unknown. For an e-negotiator, the future is closely tied with the progress we make in keeping up with technology. That is mostly a curse because technology changes faster than anything and in unpredictable ways in the long term at least. The time we need to keep up with world affairs that could potentially affect our clients and the new trends and evolutions in the profession could very well amount to a big proportion of our time and effort nowadays. Staying alert requires consumption of news feeds at unprecedented rates today compared to the past. Joining news sources online and offline like newspapers and professional and academic journals, and participating in conferences, workshops, and seminars should be part of our normal life.

While online sources can be located easily enough by anyone with basic "surfing" skills, the offline sources will have to be located and attended by each negotiator in accordance with their interests, their clients, and their job functions. An Internet search can provide a list of many associations and interest groups one can join in addition to professional and academic journals in the field. Most of these journals have alert services that inform us of new issues and their content so one can only buy the content that interests them without costly subscriptions. A visit to Amazon.com or other online bookstores once or twice a year to search for new books on a subject should also take care of any new developments that might appear in print.

A good option might be to join RSS feeds of associations, publishers, and online forums in our areas of interest. RSS feeds as we saw before makes the process of monitoring content updates more efficient. By subscribing to RSS feeds one can get the news on topics of interest as soon as they become available on the Web, thus allowing them to always be updated and hopefully ahead of the game. E-negotiators should register for RSS feeds of major newspapers and magazines and a number of blogs that are relevant to their clients. This will help them figure out the most current trends and issues along with their driving forces and people involved. Also, online news services like Yahoo! News (http://news.yahoo.com/) provide such services that can easily be customized to our interests.

While acquiring new knowledge and enhancing our expertise is of great value, preserving our wit and gaining insight about our professional performance and practices is also important. Reflection on job performance is often neglected and occasionally confused with other aspects of our life like our personality and behavior. Updating and training on dealing successfully with job issues is something that should not be neglected. In this category, the services of a professional like an executive coach might be considered as it can help us reflect, enhance our insight, and develop our professional and leadership skills. If a mentor is not around to assist in that, an Internet search will provide many alternatives to choose from. One just needs to remember that while using coaches and mentors can improve performance, these support mechanisms are not solution providers. They rather act as reflectors of our thinking and decision and action styles to allow us to become more aware of ourselves and the situations we are facing, eventually leading us to better decisions and actions.

9.5 Quality of Life

As technology grows in power and invades many aspects of our life, so does the negative social cost of it mount accordingly. Many of these negative consequences are in the health domain and express themselves as unhealthy physical and mental behavior. Physical symptoms from using technology can range from health diseases to pure addictions that, unless properly treated, can really damage one's constitution and performance.

The most important threat to an e-negotiator's physical health today seems to be the *repetitive stress injury* (RSI). This occurs when using the computer a lot, as certain muscle groups work toward repetitive actions. Excessive use of the keyboard and mouse causes the most common RSI—the *carpal tunnel syndrome* (CTS), in which the median nerve that crosses the wrist's bone structure is pressed. This is expressed in pain and our inability to use the keyboard or mouse. The way to deal with RSI is to position ourselves as naturally as possible (our elbows need to be at a 90 degrees angle) and to relax the hand muscles regularly. Using an ergonomic keyboard and mouse will greatly help along with proper monitor stands and footrests. Using muscle relaxing exercises is also a must. The basic idea is to simply contract your muscles in the opposite direction from what they are used to when using the keyboard and mouse. Searching the Internet will provide a lot of practice material in accordance with everybody's preferences.

In addition to RSI, other occupational illnesses caused by computers include back, neck, and leg pains. A frequent one is the *computer vision syndrome* that refers to any eye strain and associated headaches, along with blurred vision and dry and irritated eyes related to computer screen use. Taking breaks from the screen is the only solution to that. For the tech savvy there is even software (like http://themech.net/eyesrelax/) that will pop up regularly to remind us to take a break and suggest exercises to perform.

Computers not only affect our physical health, but they also affect our mental state with impact on our psychological and social behavior. The term used for these types of illnesses is *technostress*. Symptoms include fatigue, impatience, aggravation, and hostility, to mention a few. Depression and personality disorders don't follow far behind. The cause is the absence of human contact and the fact that our expectations are influenced by our activities. Working with machines that perform certain tasks with speed and accuracy and are attentive to our needs with no emotions becomes so familiar that it transfers to our expectations of humans and organizations in real life. This means that if addicted, we become impatient with others and expect them to perform as fast and efficient as computers. In other words, our reality becomes quite distorted with subsequent negative consequences for us and our real-life environment.

Socially, in the future computers might be a major cause of alienation, taking the role that television used to play in the past. Maintaining a balance between work and family is a major challenge for e-negotiators. When the two lifestyles merge in time and place, proper adjustments need to be made to avoid confusion and have one deprive from the other. Separating work from pleasure online is just a "click" away so it can become very tempting to deviate from normal work and mix the two. Either way, the impact of "living" online can be very threatening and damaging to close social relationships, especially with family and friends. Weakening the institutions of family and organization can have an unprecedented impact on society.

9.5.1 ERGONOMICS FOR E-NEGOTIATORS

E-negotiators have the advantage of working from almost anywhere with an Internet connection. This is related to certain issues that, environmentally speaking, need to be met in order for our job to be rewarding and successful. A habitat environment that takes care of the primary physical needs of any worker is a basic condition for our survival. Being productive while preserving a balanced life is the ultimate goal. The challenge here is to optimize the various physical "spheres" around our working position in time.

The most obvious environmental element for e-negotiators is their tool of trade—the workstation. We will focus here on the computer or, to be more precise, nowadays, the portable computer (laptop or notebook). Portable computers come in the form of laptops that in essence replace entire desktop PCs while offering a mobile platform. They are fully featured computers with full feature keyboards, widescreens, and all the applications found in workstations. If the e-negotiator needs to run heavy applications this is probably the best choice they can make. Notebooks on the other hand are stripped down versions of laptops optimized for maximum portability. In that sense they are lighter than laptops, have smaller screens, and minimal graphics subsystems. If the e-negotiator moves a lot and doesn't need heavy applications to perform their work, this is the ideal system to have. Usually this is the solution for the majority of e-negotiators since their primary software needs are Internet and office applications (Microsoft Office). If the work done is from a more or less standard location like home or corporate office, a useful enhancement might be the addition of a second monitor. This is extremely useful when we need to view multiple sources of data while typing at the same time. Having a document open on one of the monitors and Internet on the second monitor can be very efficient when researching and communicating in real time. In idle time one of the monitors can be used for meditation, relaxation, and inspiration by displaying whatever helps us in that direction.

Given that nowadays there are computers anywhere we go, an even better solution for maximizing portability is to carry most of your stuff on a USB stick and use the computers at the places we go. Options range from having a complete operating system like stripped down versions of Linux (http://www.pendrivelinux.com/universal-usb-installer-easy-as-1-2-3/ and http://www.linuxliveusb.com/) to a collection of our most valuable applications like Internet browser, office suite, Skype, and antivirus (http://portableapps.com/news/2009-03-02_-_suite_1.5). In cases where big files exceed the available memory on USBs, synchronizing your files with Internet services that keep backups of them (https://www.sugarsync.com/ or http://www.live.com) will solve the problem and allow you to access them from anywhere with an Internet connection. Another alternative to moving around and having the computational power of our workstation is to actually log on to our computer from anywhere in the world using services like www.LogMeIn.com

Moving away from our primary tool of trade we first encounter the work environment. This can range from a desk in our library to a lounge chair on the beach. Negotiating on a stool is bound to affect anyone and not in the most productive and efficient way. Comfortable positioning with minimum distractions should be the ideal. By distraction here we don't mean that nothing should allow our mind to drift or gaze occasionally at the beautiful beach in front of us. These are relaxing subconscious distractions that help us clear our mind and settle our thoughts. We are more particularly referring to distractions from family and people around us that are not related to the negotiation process. "Isolation," at least for continuous stretches of time, is very important for e-negotiations as it is for most other productive mental activity.

9.6 Conclusions

In the future we are likely to see online negotiation systems especially in online dispute resolution that will reflect both the diversity of cultures and the unique sociopolitical structures of each region around the globe. These will be customized to address issues related to business, peace building, and conflict transformation using technologies available in each region.

As the digital divide between developed and underdeveloped nations shrinks, we should see more and more the transition from traditional negotiations to e-negotiations gaining ground. The global culture that the Internet imposes, and the richness of the Web as a medium that encompasses more and more of our senses, will reduce the need for face-to-face negotiations. That said, and as technology becomes a leverage of the rich on the poor, one might not be surprised to see instances of social discrimination and marginalization in efforts to undermine negotiations in fragile social and political environments. Hopefully, when this happens technology will be able to transform conflict by strengthening existing capacities and social networks to facilitate wider and more effective use of the communication mediums.

For sure, what we will observe in the near future is the emergence of hybrid systems where devices will be small, mobile, intelligent, and able to adapt to each user's needs to create non-invading experiences that will complement our conduct and presence in negotiations. Future systems will engage people rather than overwhelm them with sophisticated systems that bear little or no relation to our daily lives. In simple terms, technology will become second nature and disappear from our conscious life.

From the presentations in this book it should be obvious that bargaining power and strategy formulation are a manifestation of complex situational factors as filtered through our perceptions. Negotiations require a whole range of talents, from strategic vision and creativity to persuasiveness and self-awareness. In the world of e-negotiations, certain skills carry more weight than others due to the nature of the communication mediums we use. It takes time and practice to become aware of the interplay of the various parameters in a negotiation process and requires someone to be alert and informed about trends, practices, and future directions.

Our professional tendencies and practice choices tend to unify themselves over time into categories of preferences that we mostly use in negotiations.

It's a kind of mainstreaming we perform as we get older which we tend to call experience. Regarding technology, we get used to certain ways that work for us in the long run and we forget to update and modernize ourselves because the old ways still work. These habits sort of become like an old car that only we can drive because we know exactly how it behaves and what to do to make it work. Instead of fixing the car we prefer to accommodate its idiosyncrasies because we are familiar with them.

A personal suggestion to balance the need for the new with the familiarity and comfort of the old would be that if our current performance with the tools we have more than covers our work needs in a comfortable way, then don't change it. If we feel that we take too long to conduct our business and it's tiring to us, we might want to consider investing time in updating ourselves with tools that will increase our efficiency and productivity.

Learning and being familiar with current and future trends requires patience as there will be a learning curve with new technologies and formats. Keeping track of the evolution of the profession by joining civic or professional organizations, online groups, and blogs will greatly assist e-negotiators in their endeavors. If we can't be one step ahead of the competition, at least we need to make an effort to walk in synchrony. At the same time, we need to be aware of the isolation factor that work might impose on us. Sitting in front of a screen can distance one from the real life around them. Computers can become very addictive to people with no other interests and, especially nowadays that work and home tend to merge, one needs to establish and maintain good boundaries in order to perform well in both.

Bibliography

Aaron, M.C. 1995. "The value of decision-analysis in mediation practice.". *Negotiation Journal* 11(2), 123–33.

Abadir, S. and Halkias, D. 2012. "Teaching negotiation skills to foster social innovation.". *International Journal of Social Entrepreneurship and Innovation* 2(2), 234–42.

Adair, W., Okumura, T., and Brett, J. 2001. "Negotiation behavior when cultures collide.". *Journal of Applied Psychology* 86, 372–85.

Adair, W.L. and Brett, J.M. 2005. "The negotiation dance: Time, culture, and behavioral sequences in negotiation.". *Organization Science* 16, 33–51.

Adler, N.J. and Graham, J.L. 1989. "Cross-cultural interaction: The international comparison fallacy?". *Journal of International Business Studies* 20(3), 515–37.

Allred, K.G., Mallozzi, J.S., Matsui, F., et al. 1997. "The influence of anger and compassion on negotiation performance.". *Organizational Behavior and Human Decision Processes* 70(3), 175–87.

Angur, M.G., Lofti, V., et al. 1996. "A hybrid conjoint measurement and bi-criteria model for a two group negotiation problem.". *Socio-Economic Planning Sciences* 30(3), 195–206.

Arunachalam, V. and Dilla, W.N. 1995. "Judgment accuracy and outcomes in negotiations: A causal modeling analysis of decision-aiding effects.". *Organizational Behavior and Human Decision Processes* 61, 289–304.

Barry, B. 1999. "The tactical use of emotion in negotiation." In *Research in Negotiation in Organizations* Vol. 7, eds R.J. Bies and R.J. Lewicki. Stamford, CT: JAI Press, 93–121.

Barry, B., Fulmer, I.S. and Goates, N. 2006. "Bargaining with feeling: emotionality in and around negotiation." In *Negotiation Theory and Research*, ed. L.L. Thompson. New York: Psychosocial Press, 99–127.

Bartlett, C. and Goshal, S. 1991. *Managing Across Borders*. Boston: Harvard Business School Press.

Bazerman, M.H., Curhan, J.R. and Moore, D.A. 2001. "The death and rebirth of the social psychology of negotiation." In *Blackwell Handbook of Social*

Psychology: Interpersonal Processes, eds G.J.O. Fletcher and M.S. Clark. Oxford, England: Blackwell Publishers, 196–228.

Bazerman, M.H., Curhan, J.R., Moore, D.A., et al. 2000. "Negotiation.". *Annual Review of Psychology* 51, 279–314.

Berry, M. and Linoff, G. 1997. *Data Mining Techniques for Marketing: Sales and Customer Support.* New York: Wiley.

Blount, S. and Larrick, R.P. 2000. "Framing the game: Examining frame choice in bargaining.". *Organizational Behavior and Human Decision Processes* 81, 43–71.

Boyd, D. 2004. Friendster and publicly articulated social networking. *Conference on Human Factors and Computing Systems*, April 24–29.

Brett, J.M. 2001. *Negotiating Globally: How to Negotiate Deals, Resolve Disputes, and Make Decisions Across Cultural Boundaries.* San Francisco: Jossey-Bass.

Carnevale, P.J. and Probst, T.M. 1997. "Conflict on the Internet." In *Culture of the Internet*, ed. S. Kiesler. Mahwah, NJ: Erlbaum, 233–55.

Carnevale, P.J. and Pruitt, D. 1992. "Negotiation and mediation.". *Annual Review of Psychology* 43, 531–82.

Cohen, R. 1991. *Negotiating Across Cultures. Communication Obstacles on International Diplomacy.* Washington, DC: United States Institute of Peace Press.

Conlon, D.E. and Hunt, S. 2002. "Dealing with feeling: The influence of outcome representations on negotiation.". *International Journal of Conflict Management* 13, 38–58.

Croson, R. and Glick, S. 2001. "Reputations in Negotiations." In *Wharton on Making Decisions*, eds S. Hoch and H. Kunreuther. New York: Wiley, 177–86.

DePaulo, B.M., Lindsay, J.J., Malone, B.E., et al. 2003. "Cues to deception.". *Psychological Bulletin* 129(1), 74–118.

Drolet, A.L. and Morris, M.W. 2000. "Rapport in conflict resolution: Accounting for how face-to-face contact fosters mutual cooperation in mixed-motive conflicts.". *Journal of Experimental Social Psychology* 36, 26–50.

Dutton, W.H. 1999. *Society on the Line: Information Politics in the Digital Age.* Oxford, England: Oxford University Press.

Ebner, N. 2007. *Trust-building in e-negotiation. Computer-mediated Relationship and Trust: Managerial and Organizational Effects.* Hershey, PA: Idea Group.

Eid, M. and Diener, E. 2001. "Norms for experiencing emotions in different cultures: Inter- and intra-national differences.". *Journal of Personality and Social Psychology* 81, 869–85.

Elfenbein, H.A. and Ambady, N. 2002. "On the universality and cultural specificity of emotion recognition: A meta-analysis.". *Psychological Bulletin* 128, 203–35.

Elfenbein, H.A. and Nalini, A. 2003. "When familiarity breeds accuracy: Cultural exposure and facial emotion recognition.". *Journal of Personality and Social Psychology* 85, 276–90.

Eliasberg, J. and Gauvin, S., et al. 1992. "An Experimental Study of Alternative Preparation Aids for International Negotiations.". *Group Decision and Negotiation* 1, 243–67.

Falcao, H. 2010. *Value Negotiation: How to Finally Get the Win-Win Right*. New York, NY: Pearson Education.

Faure, G.O. and Rubin, J.Z. 1993. *Culture and Negotiation. The Resolution of Water Disputes*. Newbury Park, CA: SAGE.

FCO. (2004). Foreign and Commonwealth Office, *e-diplomacy: The FCO Information and Communication Technology Strategy*, London: FCO, January. Available at: www.fco.gov.uk

Fisher, R., Ury, W. and Patton, B. 1991. *Getting to YES: Negotiating Agreement Without Giving In*. (2nd edn). New York: Penguin Books.

Forgas, J.P. 1998. "On feeling good and getting your way: mood effects on negotiator cognition and bargaining strategies.". *Journal of Personality and Social Psychology* 74(3), 565–77.

Fortgang, R.S., Lax, D.A. and Sebenius, J.K. 2003. "Negotiating the spirit of the deal.". *Harvard Business Review* 81(2), 66–76.

Friedman, R.A. and Currall, S.C. 2001. Email escalation: Dispute exacerbating elements of electronic communication. Paper presented at the annual meeting of the *International Association for Conflict Management*, Salt Lake City.

Friedman, R., Anderson, C., Brett, J., et al. 2004. "The positive and negative effects of anger on dispute resolution: evidence from electronically mediated disputes.". *Journal of Applied Psychology* 89(2), 369–76.

Galinsky, A.D., Mussweiler, T. and Medvec, V.H. 2002. "Disconnecting outcomes and evaluations in negotiations: The role of negotiator focus.". *Journal of Personality and Social Psychology* 83, 1131–40.

Gelfand, M.J. and Dyer, N. 2000. "A cultural perspective on negotiation: Progress, pitfalls, and prospects.". *Applied Psychology: An International Review* 49, 62–9.

Gelfand, M.J. and Christakopoulou, S. 1999. "Culture and negotiator cognition: Judgment accuracy and negotiation processes in individualistic and collectivitistic cultures.". *Organizational Behavior and Human Decision Processes* 79, 248–69.

Gelfand, M.J., Higgins, M., Nishii, L.H., et al. 2002. "Culture and egocentric perceptions of fairness in conflict and negotiation.". *Journal of Applied Psychology* 87, 833–45.

Gelfand, M.J., Nishii, L.H., Holcombe, K.M., et al. 2001. "Cultural influences on cognitive representations of conflict: Interpretations of conflict episodes in the United States and Japan.". *Journal of Applied Psychology* 86, 1059–74.

Gelfand, M.J. and Realo, A. 1999. "Individualism-collectivism and accountability in intergroup negotiations.". *Journal of Applied Psychology* 84, 721–36.

Goates, N., Barry, B. and Friedman, R.A. 2003. Good Karma: How individuals construct schemas of reputation in negotiation contexts. Paper presented at the *16th Annual Conference of the International Association for Conflict Management*. Melbourne, Australia.

Graham, J.L., Mintu, A.T. and Rodgers, W. 1994. "Explorations of negotiation behaviors in ten foreign cultures using a model developed in the United States.". *Management Science* 40, 70–95.

Graham, J.L. and Mintu-Wimsat, A. 1997. "Culture's influence on business negotiations in four countries.". *Group Decision and Negotiation* 6, 483–502.

Griffith, T.L. and Northcraft, G.B. 1994. "Distinguishing between the forest and the trees: Media, features, and methodology in electronic communication research.". *Organization Science* 5, 272–85.

Gross, R. and Acquisti, A. 2005. Privacy and information revelation in online social networks. *Proceedings of the ACM CCS Workshop on Privacy in the Electronic Society* (WPES '05).

Harasim, L.M. 1993. "Networlds: Networks as a social space." In *Global Networks: Computers and International Communication*, ed. L.M. Harasim. Cambridge, MA: MIT Press, 15–34.

Harkiolakis, N. 2007. "Six-dimensional approach to online privacy. *Int.*". *Journal of Technology Transfer and Commercialization* 6(1), 56–63.

Harkiolakis, N., Halkias, D. and Stamoulis, D. 2006. Barriers to the Introduction of Technology in Small Family Business Enterprises in Greece. *International Congress of Applied Psychology (ICAP)*, Athens University, Athens, Greece, July 11.

Hofstede, G. 1980. *Culture's Consequences: International Differences in Work-related Values*. Beverly Hills, CA: Sage.

Hofstede, G. 1989. *Cultural Predictors of Negotiation Styles. Process of International Negotiations*. F. Mautner-Markhof. Boulder, CO: Westview Press, 193–201.

Hofstede, G. 1991. *Cultures and Organizations: Software of the Mind, Intercultural Cooperation and its Importance for Survival*. New York, NY: McGraw-Hill.

Hong, Y., Benet-Martinez, V., Chiu, C.-Y., et al. 2003. "Boundaries of cultural influence: Construct activation as a mechanism for cultural differences in social perception.". *Journal of Cross-Cultural Psychology* 34, 453–64.

Hordijk, L. 1991. "Use of the RAINS Model in acid rain negotiation in Europe.". *Environmental Science & Technology* 25(4), 596–603.

Jagatic, T., et al. 2007. "Social phishing". *Communications of the ACM* 10(5), 94–100.

Jessup, L.M. and Tansik, D.A. 1991. "Decision making in an automated environment: The effects of anonymity and proximity with a group decision support system.". *Decision Sciences* 22, 266–79.

Katsh, E. and Rifkin, J. 2001. *Online Dispute Resolution: Resolving Conflicts in Cyberspace*. San Francisco: Jossey Bass.

Kersten, G.E., Koszegi, S.T. and Vetchera, R. 2002. The effects of culture in anonymous negotiations: Experiment in four countries. *Proceedings of the 35th Hawaii International Conference on Systems*.

Kersten, G.E. and Noronha, S.J. 1997. Supporting International Negotiations with a WWW-based System. *Interim Report 97–49*, IIASA, Austria.

Kopelman, S. and Rosette, A.S. 2008. "Cultural variation in response to strategic display of emotions in negotiations.". *Group Decision and Negotiation* 17, 65–77.

Kray, L.J., Thompson, L. and Galinsky, A. 2001. "Battle of the sexes: Gender stereotype confirmation and reactance in negotiations.". *Journal of Personality and Social Psychology* 80, 942–58.

Kurtzberg, T. and Medvec, V.H. 1999. "Can we negotiate and still be friends?". *Negotiation Journal* 15, 355–61.

Kwon, S. and Weingart, L.R. 2004. "Unilateral concessions from the other party: Concession behavior, attributions, and negotiation judgments.". *Journal of Applied Psychology* 89, 263–78.

Lai, H., Lin, W.J. and Lin, J.Y. 2008. What happen to cross-cultural dyadic e-negotiation? *Proceedings of the 41st Hawaii International Conference on Systems Sciences*, IEEE, 1530–1605.

Lewis, R.D. 2005. *When Cultures Collide: Leading, Teamworking and Managing Across the Globe* 3rd edn London, UK: Nicholas Brealey Publishing.

McGinn, K. L., & Croson, R. (2004). What do communication media mean for negotiators? A question of social awareness. In M. J. Gelfand, & J. M. Brett (Eds.), The handbook of negotiation and culture (pp. 334–349): Stanford University Press.

Mannix, E.A., Tinsley, C.H. and Bazerman, M. 1995. "Negotiating over time: Impediments to integrative solutions.". *Organizational Behavior and Human Decision Processes* 62, 241–51.

McGinn, K.L. 2006. "Relationships and negotiations in context." In *Negotiation Theory and Research*, ed. L.L. Thompson. New York: Psychosocial Press, 129–144.

Mestdagh, S. and Buelens, M. 2003. Thinking back on where we're going: A methodological assessment of five decades of research in negotiation behavior. *16th Annual IACM Conference*, Melbourne, Australia.

Morris, M.W., Larrick, R.P. and Su, S.K. 1999. "Misperceiving negotiation counterparts: When situationally determined bargaining behaviors are attributed to personality traits.". *Journal of Personality and Social Psychology* 77, 52–67.

Nadler, J. and Shestowsky, D. 2006. "Negotiation, information technology and the problem of the faceless other." In *Negotiation Theory and Research*, ed. L.L. Thompson. New York: Psychology Press, 145–172.

Naquin, C.E. and Paulson, G.D. 2003. "Online bargaining and interpersonal trust.". *Journal of Applied Psychology* 88, 113–20.

Nash, J. 1953. "Two-person cooperative games.". *Econometrica: Journal of the Econometric Society* 21, 128–40.

Neale, M.A. and Northcraft, G.B. 1986. "Experts, amateurs, and refrigerators: Comparing expert and amateur negotiators in a novel task.". *Organizational Behavior and Human Decision Processes* 38, 305–17.

Novemsky, N. and Schweitzer, M. (2004). "What makes negotiators happy? The differential effects of internal and external social comparisons on negotiator satisfaction.". *Organizational Behavior and Human Decision Processes* 95(2), 186–197.

Ocker, R.J. and Yaverbaum, G.J. 1999. Asynchronous Computer-mediated Communication versus Face–to-face Collaboration: Results on Student Learning, Quality and Satisfaction. *Group Decision and Negotiations* 5(8), 427–40.

Potter, E.H. 2002. *Cyber-diplomacy: Managing Foreign Policy in the Twenty First Century*. Montreal, Kingston: McGill-Queens University Press.

Rangaswamy, A. and Shell, G.R. 1997. "Using computers to realize joint gains in negotiations: Toward an 'electronic bargaining table'.". *Management Science* 43(8), 1147–63.

Rubin, J.Z. and Sander, F.E. 1991. "Culture, Negotiation, and the Eye of the Beholder.". *Negotiation Journal* 3(7), 249–54.

Sinaceur, M. and Tiedens, L.Z. 2006. "Get mad and get more than even: When and why anger expression is effective in negotiations.". *Journal of Experimental Social Psychology* 42, 314–22.

Snyder, C.R. and Higgins, R.L. 1997. "Reality negotiation: Governing one's self and being governed by others.". *Review of General Psychology* 1, 336–50.

Tannen, D. 1995. "The Power of Talk: Who Gets Heard and Why.". *Harvard Business Review* 5(73), 138–48.

Thompson, L., Medvec, V.H., Seiden, V., et al. 2001. "Poker face, smiley face and rant 'n' rave: myths and realities about emotion in negotiation." In *Group Processes*, eds M. Hogg and S. Tindale. Malden, MA: Blackwell, 139–63.

Thompson, L., Nadler, J. and Kim, P.H. 1999. "Some like it hot: The case for the emotional negotiator." In *Shared Cognition in Organizations: The Management of Knowledge*, eds L.L. Thompson, J.M. Levin, and D.M. Messick. Mahwah, NJ: Erlbaum, 139–61.

Tinsley, C.H. 2001. "How we get to yes: Predicting the constellation of strategies used across cultures to negotiate conflict.". *Journal of Applied Psychology* 86, 583–93.

Tinsley, C.H., Curhan, J.J. and Kwak, R.S. 1999. "Adopting a dual lens approach for examining the dilemma of differences in international business negotiations.". *International Negotiation* 4, 1–18.

Tinsley, C.H. and Pillutla, M.M. 1998. "Negotiating in the United States and Hong Kong.". *Journal of International Business Studies* 29, 711–28.

Tyler, C.M. and Raines, S.S. 2006. The Human Face of On-Line Dispute Resolution, *Conflict Resolution Quarterly* 23(3), Wiley InderScience.

Ulijn, J.M. and Campbell, C. 1999. "Technical Innovations in Communication: How to Relate Technology to Business by a Culturally Reliable Human Interface." *Proceedings of the 1999 IEEE International Professional Communication Conference*, ed. Terrance J. Malkinson. Piscataway, NJ: IEEE Professional Communication Society, 109–20.

Ulijn, J.M. and Kumar, R. 1999. "Technical communication in a multicultural world: How to make it an asset in managing international business, lessons from Europe and Asia for the 21st century." In *Managing Global Discourse: Essays on International Scientific and Technical Communication*, eds P.J. Hager and H.J. Scheiber. New York, NY: Wiley, 319–48.

Van Kleef, G.A., De Dreu, C.K.W. and Manstead, A.S.R. 2004. "The interpersonal effects of emotions in negotiations: A motivated information processing approach.". *Journal of Personality and Social Psychology* 87(4), 510–28.

Walther, J.B. 1995. "Relational aspects of computer-mediated communication: Experimental observations over time.". *Organization Science* 6(2), 186–203.

Walther, J.B. 1996. "Computer-Mediated Communication: Impersonal, Interpersonal and Hyperpersonal Interaction.". *Communication Research* 23(1), 3–43.

Weisband, S. and Atwater, L. 1999. "Evaluating self and others in electronic and face-to-face groups.". *Journal of Applied Psychology* 84, 632–39.

Wheeler, M. 2002. Negotiation Analysis: An Introduction, *Harvard Business School*, June 13.

White, J.B., Tynan, R., Galinsky, A.D., et al. 2004. "Face threat sensitivity in negotiation: Roadblock to agreement and joint gain.". *Organizational Behavior and Human Decision Processes* 94, 102–24.

Index